WOMEN
CLIMBING

200 YEARS OF ACHIEVEMENT

To Etsu, Emma and Tamsin

Mlle Henriette d'Angeville on the summit of Mont Blanc in 1838. *(Alpine Club Library Collection)*

WOMEN
CLIMBING

200 YEARS OF ACHIEVEMENT

BILL BIRKETT & BILL PEASCOD

The Mountaineers · Seattle
A & C Black · London

First published 1989 by
A & C Black (Publishers) Ltd.
35 Bedford Row, London WC1R 4JH

First published in the United States of America
in 1990 by The Mountaineers
306-2nd Ave. W.
Seattle WA 98119

ISBN 0-89886-240-X

Photoset by Rowland Phototypesetting Ltd,
Bury St Edmunds, Suffolk
Printed and bound in Great Britain by
BAS Printers Ltd, Over Wallop, Hampshire.

Acknowledgements
The author and publisher would like to
thank the many individuals and staff
from institutions and other publishers who have
helped with or contributed to this book
in some way.

Contents

Right Miriam O'Brien (married name Underhill) amongst the Chamonix Aiguilles.
(Alpine Club Library collection)

Preface

Bill and I sat in the Glenridding Hotel at Patterdale in the English Lake District, and as we ate our large breakfast we looked out across green fields to Ullswater lake, twinkling blue in the sunshine. We talked of the little crag we were intending to visit: Sheffield Pike, only small, but steep, clean and attractive-looking. I had suggested we climb it and had pointed it out to Bill the previous evening from the hotel window, remarking that no climbs had yet been made on the rock. Typically, he was immediately enthusiastic to climb it.

I informed him that my father (Jim Birkett) had mentioned it to me, and that he was surprised that no routes had yet been climbed there. Bill nodded and talked about those early climbing years in the 1940s when both he and my father were climbing. He highlighted something which I thought I had never experienced. He said,

'You know, your dad and myself were the first climbers from a working class background to make an impact on the climbing scene in Britain. If you were working class, at that time you were looked down upon or felt to be subservient to the establishment. Although I longed to be part of the climbing fraternity, I was ashamed to be a coal miner; when I mixed with other climbers I used to hide the fact, attempt to put on a cultured accent and keep my coal-blackened fingernails out of sight. I know it's a feeling you can hardly conceive in this day and age, but it was there. The answer, for your dad and myself, was to climb harder and better than anyone else. Climb so hard they had to sit up and notice us.'

Our conversation turned to this and that, and then significantly we both remarked on the performance of a young French woman on the British Mountaineering Council's French Ladies' meet, held in Britain in 1980.

'What was her name?'

'Catherine Destivelle.'

'She led some hard, extreme climbs.'

I guess both our minds' eyes went instantly to a photograph of an attractive girl in some climbing magazine; and the equation was the same for both of us. Nothing said, we both felt, without due consideration: how can a woman, a mere girl, so obviously feminine, climb that hard?! In the light of subsequent experience and knowledge I know this attitude to be plainly ridiculous, born of ignorance; I cannot defend it, but equally I could not truthfully now deny it.

I suppose it was an automatic reaction after years of social conditioning. Bill had just returned to Britain after spending 30 years, essentially non-climbing years, in Australia, and I had never, in my small circle of hard rock climbers, known any woman to climb at anywhere near our standard of difficulty!

We thought for a while; then Bill said,

'Look mate, why shouldn't women climb hard?' After further discussion, ruminating over qualities of natural balance and technique, toughness in a difficult situation, and resolute determination – all qualities we knew women to possess from (sometimes hard) personal experience – we both concluded,

'Why shouldn't women climb equally as hard as us, as men?'

We both realised, of course, that we (unspokenly) had just applied the same blind prejudice to women that Bill had so devastatingly experienced as a 'working class' climber in Britain in the 1940s. The idea grabbed us. We wanted to know more, to look at the real facts, and we wondered if women had actually done much climbing!

Leaving our table for the morning sunshine, we walked to Steel Pike to complete our new climbs.

But the idea stayed with us and fascinated us, and we began comparing notes. We quickly exposed our naivety, and the idea to collate our notes and write the book came simultaneously. We buzzed with excitement. It became our passion. The more we discovered and the more we wrote, the greater our enthusiasm for the project became; retrospectively, this time spent together writing or locked in conversation, constantly refuelled by Etsu Peascod (both in vitals and grammar), was very precious – no, more than this, it was priceless.

This adventure for us was new and unknown: the response we did not ever dare imagine, or perhaps we did! When we actually started talking, writing and climbing with the many people who helped us, we were overwhelmed by their generous response. The co-operation was always very positive and very sincere. The truth is that the times spent preparing this book were thoroughly enjoyable. From all over the world we have met, and often climbed, with the most incredible personalities.

I travelled to Japan to talk with Junko Tabei, in whose presence I felt thoroughly humbled; it was all made possible by the amazing translatory powers of Etsu Peascod. Bill and I travelled to Switzerland and met Loulou Boulaz and Yvette Vaucher, and Bill returned again to complete the research. East and West met beside a Lakeland log fire when Wanda Rutkiewicz and Molly Higgins joined us all – myself, Bill, Etsu and Emma Peascod – at Melbecks. That was an amazing meeting. Gwen Moffat talked with Bill and myself for an evening, and we enjoyed a night of great hilarity. Catherine Destivelle and her boyfriend showed me their tremendous prowess on the Fontainebleau boulders, and enabled me to sample the high delights of French cuisine; they were perfect hosts. Jill Lawrence and Louise Shepherd, who worked so hard and so meaningfully, answered our seemingly inadequate questions, while Alison Hargreaves climbed brilliantly for my cameras.

For Bill and me it was a privilege to meet and climb with such wonderful people, and we literally enjoyed every minute of it. But selfishly, perhaps, the greatest joy of all for me was to be lucky enough to climb, work with and know Bill Peascod. Our friendship was, I think, the greatest gift anyone could ever wish for in life. We were simply dotting the i's and crossing the t's, with the hard work done, when Bill died suddenly, climbing with Don Whillans and myself on the Great Slab of Clogwyn du'r Arddu in Snowdonia. For Bill it was the perfect climber's death: he knew and suffered nothing. Perfectly poised, having climbed the crux in the beautifully nimble Peascod style, his heart simply stopped working.

So I stand alone, on the rocks, to be counted. I am sure any mistakes are all mine.

Bill Birkett

Introduction

This is the story of women in climbing and mountaineering, ranging from the first female ascent of Mont Blanc (Europe's highest mountain) in 1808 to the incredible achievements of today's rock climbing superstars. The story is related by selecting an important figure from each area of significant development and concentrating on her individually. There is much background information, and we have presented a complete, if brief, picture of the whole.

Each person chosen has a very remarkable and fascinating contribution to make. Most of the material gathered here is original, and is either taken directly from the selected women and their contemporaries, or from the closest possible source; we have attempted to leave no stone unturned, nothing unsaid.

Climbing – taking on and conquering the challenge of the cold, high mountains and the smooth, vertical walls of rock – is much more than a sport, as you will discover. It is a way of life: an expression of thought and action, a personal statement, something in your blood. Good climbers are dedicated to their sport, and will react equally and appositely to adversity in order to follow their chosen route, and all the women featured here are (or were) climbers of the highest standard.

It is not an easy way of life: the risks are immense, but the rewards are even greater, and let us not imagine that the women in this book chose to climb for any reason other than because *they wanted to* – the strongest possible reason of all. Herein lies another feature of their stories, that of personal courage and self-expression.

Yet behind all this, the thread that links them inexorably together is freedom. It is a freedom which has not been easily won, and which often has been conditional on contemporary social pressures. On many occasions the physical and mental difficulties of the climbing itself have proved secondary to the prejudices and problems imposed by society. This claim is reflected by the hard facts.

In 1786 Mont Blanc was climbed by Dr Michel-Gabriel Paccard and Jacques Balmat from Chamonix, and it was not until 22 years later, in 1808, that Marie Paradis became the first woman to reach the highest point in Europe. Her reason for tackling the climb was one of good sense and sound practicality: she thought success on the mountain would reflect on her little tea shop at its foot. She was right, of course.

The first 'real' woman mountaineer was Lucy Walker, who dedicated her life to the mountains. Her first route was climbed in 1858 and her last in 1879, a span of some 21 years of Alpine achievement. She climbed consistently with her favourite guide (Melchior Anderegg), and was always accompanied by a third party.

Her contemporaries became yet more radical, and some dared to wear trousers on the hills. One even remarked to a certain male climber after making an ascent of an Alpine peak: 'You said no woman could manage it'. He replied, 'I said no lady!'

The American, Miriam O'Brien, trod very firmly on male egos by climbing the hardest Alpine routes of her day, and as she put it, 'not only guideless but manless'[1]. This really did shake the establishment; it had no answer, save that women should not climb that hard – they had no right!

Nea Morin's involvement with the mountains stretched for over 30 years, from the 1920s to the 1950s. Her early passion was to climb *en cordée féminine* but, for her, climbing progressed naturally into a family affair. This great activity of climbing and her rapport with the mountains was to be shared with those she loved.

When in the 1930s the race was on to climb the largest and most challenging Alpine faces in Europe – the north faces of the Matterhorn, the Grandes Jorasses and the Eiger, names that cannot fail to impress, that send a shiver, both of excitement and fear, down every climber's spine – standing there shoulder to shoulder with the best Alpinists of the day was the Swiss woman Loulou Boulaz. She was there, as you will read, purely on merit.

The Second World War, most obviously, shaped the future of the modern civilised world and profoundly affected the thoughts of the individual. Gwen Moffat was a product of these rapidly changing times, an individual who decided to abandon conventionality. To her, freedom to climb was the most important idealism of all. Ultimately, she won widespread respect, becoming Britain's first fully qualified woman rock climbing and mountaineering guide, and writing one of Britain's classic mountaineering autobiographies.

Himalayan climbing is popularly considered to be the ultimate form of mountaineering. Claude Kogan, in the 1950s, provided a wave of achievement that caught women's interest in the high peaks on a grand scale. Many say her greatest moment came in 1955, not on the mountains but when she became 'the first woman ever to lift up her voice in the sanctuaries of the Alpine Club.'[2] High on the Himalayan giant of Cho Oyu, Claude paid the ultimate price; she was swept to her death by an avalanche which left absolutely no trace.

Another Swiss climber, Yvette Vaucher, noted for her great endurance on the most frightening and difficult climbs in the Alps, could well have been the first woman to gain the summit of Everest. But it was not to be. This honour fell to the diminutive Japanese, Junko Tabei. Against all the obstacles put in her way by a society which strictly regards the woman's place to be in the home, she spent three years (during which time she gave birth to a daughter) organising an all-women expedition to the highest mountain in the world. At the age of 36 she stood on its summit.

The American Molly Higgins, a member of the tragic 1974 international expedition to the Russian High Pamirs, on which eight Soviet women lost their lives, took on the rock climbing challenge of Yosemite. In doing so, she added a new dimension to women's climbing. Significantly, her philosophies pointed the way for the modern rock athletes of today.

Certainly, the most accomplished woman mountaineer of modern times, and undoubtedly one of the world's most distinguished mountaineers of either sex, is the incredible Wanda Rutkiewicz. Against extreme adversity she has a tremendous record of success and endeavour. The fight for equality and freedom is her way of life.

Catherine Destivelle, Jill Lawrence and Louise Shepherd are all excellent free rock climbers cast in the modern mould. But each has something very individual to say in the wide context of this story. Catherine, a brilliant climber, is naturally gifted. Hers is the joy of floating up holdless-looking walls of rock with no apparent effort. Jill centred her attention on leading one of Britain's E5 (see appendix) climbs and was the first woman to do so. She represents the changing attitudes and shifting horizons of British women climbers.

There could be no more fitting conclusion to this book than the story of Australian Louise Shepherd. Honest-speaking, forceful and utterly dedicated, she is an international rock climber of world-wide repute. She climbs at the highest levels of performance, both repeating existing climbs and pioneering new routes.

This book journeys through vast changes of thought, achievement and attitude, as exemplified by Louise who declares, quite openly, that women will not only one day climb equally as hard as men, but that they will, indeed, climb harder.

In any brief book such as this, it is impossible to do justice to all of the many fine climbers and mountaineering personalities who have trod the rocky stage. Even to attempt to do so in any depth would have led us towards a tome of unmanageable proportions – and worse, one that could never have been finished because of the new stars who are constantly rising. However, we feel we have related a fascinating history, and I can only hope you derive as much pleasure in reading it as we did in researching and writing it. (Bill Peascod was responsible for chapters 1 to 7 and Bill Birkett wrote chapters 8 to 13.)

Bill Birkett

References

[1]Miriam Underhill, *Give Me The Hills* (Methuen, 1956), p. 62/[2]Cecily Williams, *Women On The Rope* (George Allen & Unwin, 1973), p. 165

1

Lucy Walker and the early years

Climbing in the nineteenth century

The exploration of the high Alps had until the early nineteenth century been undertaken at a very slow pace. Between 1800 and 1840 a few significant first ascents were made: the list includes the Gross Glockner (1800), Ortler (1804), Jungfrau (1811), Finsteraarhorn (1812), Tödi (1824), Mont Pelvoux (1830), the lower summit of Piz Palu (1835) and Central Aiguille d'Arves (1839). After 1840 the pace of exploration took a significant turn, and reached its hottest in 1865 (when over 40 hitherto unclimbed Alpine peaks were ascended, including the most notorious of them all, the Matterhorn).

The urge to climb mountains is not easy to explain. Ronald Clark asks, 'How did it happen? What were the circumstances of the age which made the rise of mountaineering nearly inevitable . . . ?[1]' That they went to the mountains for scientific reasons, for conquest, because it was fashionable to do so, to salve their consciences finding something in the mountain world that might redress the balance of the factory world, is clearly enough part of the story, and Clark puts forward all of these as contributing to the urge. However, as he rightly points out,

> to climb, continuously, season after season, to think of mountains and mountaineering so that the subject becomes half of one's life . . . means that the attraction must have some deeper and less material reason behind it than these motivations.

Those who gravitated to climbing did so in the wake of the great, historic adventure seekers. And although most did not climb for notoriety, many of them left vivid records of their trials and success (and many a gleam of light steals from below an upright antiquarian bushel – to the delight and relief of present day mountaineering historians).

Mountaineering was not a pursuit that automatically received public acclaim, and the tongue that 'clacked' in respect of some climber's well-publicised feat was equally ready to 'cluck' should any harm fall to him or her, or worse still, to their companions.

The earliest climbers met with a good deal of criticism and acrimony, particularly from the general public on the occasion of some highly dramatised disaster (such as that which followed the first ascent of the Matterhorn), when the survivors of an accident were severely castigated for putting into jeopardy the lives of those bent upon their rescue.

Ruskin[2] was one of those who took exception to the developing sport – even though he later joined the Alpine Club.

> You have made race courses of the cathedrals of the earth,

he admonished:

> The Alps themselves, which your own poets used to love so reverently, you look upon as soaped poles in a bear garden, which you set yourselves to climb and slide down again with shrieks of delight.

Mont Blanc

On the 8th August 1786 two climbers, Jacques Balmat, 'a bold young Chamonix guide', and Michel-Gabriel Paccard, 'the village doctor'[3] trod the summit of Mont Blanc. The fact that a substantial financial reward had been offered by the distinguished Genevese scientist, H. B. de Saussure, to the person or persons who could make the first ascent of Europe's highest mountain may, or may not, have been a considerable inducement.

Marie Paradis

Twenty-two years after the first ascent by the two men, Mont Blanc was climbed by an 18-year-old woman from Chamonix. Her name was Marie Paradis and, unfortunately, we know little about her. She has been variously described as owning tea rooms in Les Pèlerins[4] and as a Chamonix maid servant[5].

It seems that she was encouraged in her venture to climb the mountain by her Chamonix friends, one of whom was Jacques Balmat, then 46 years of age, who with Marie and several of his brothers made a second ascent of the peak. It would appear that Marie found the going quite difficult and tiring, and she is said to have implored her friends to dispose of her by throwing her into a crevasse. However, she *did* make it to the summit, albeit exhausted by the effort, and one cannot but admire the pluck of the young woman. As Coolidge says when speaking of Balmat[6]:

> The glaciers were still regarded with awe, and it required enormous courage to venture one's life in these trackless deserts of ice, seamed everywhere with yawning chasms, ready to engulf the unwary visitor.

The circumstances would have changed very little by 1808, and any ascent at that time must still be regarded as a very bold venture. It seems that the publicity accorded her feat did indeed (as her friends had suggested it might) have quite a favourable influence on her tea room business!

Henriette d'Angeville

The next ascent of the mountain by a woman was a much more organised and notorious affair. It was that of Mlle Henriette d'Angeville, in 1838. There was nothing romantic about her, according to Clare Eliane Engel. She was, Engel informs us[7],

> A spinster who loved Mont Blanc because she had nothing else to love. She had a clear, bold, haughty, precise mind; she succeeded in her climb by sheer will-power and became one of the lionesses of the season, a position she enjoyed, having a morbid passion for self advertisement.

Possibly Mlle d'Angeville may have been 'madly jealous' of George Sand's 'glamorous reputation' or of the 'man's apparel which she paraded in Chamonix'[8] in 1836, and if this were so, it is difficult to hide a feeling of admiration for the dramatic way in which Mlle d'Angeville proceeded to restore the balance of public recognition.

She set off for Mont Blanc with a vast entourage and an incredible quantity of comestibles including wines, brandy, a cask of *vin ordinaire*, legs of mutton, tongues, dozens of fowls and much more. Nor did her dress leave anything to chance: her wardrobe included a checked climbing suit, trousers (emulating

George Sand?), a long coat, several hats and a feather boa. She gave explicit instructions to the guides as to what to do with her remains in the event of her demise, and kept a detailed record of her imagined heart failure and miraculous recovery on reaching the summit.

One feels impelled to give Mlle d'Angeville full marks for dramatic effect, and it is easy to accept that after her ascent of the mountain she did become, to her delight, the toast of society.

Lucy Walker

The Alpine Club was formed in Britain in 1857. Its first members were drawn from the professions in the middle or upper-middle classes. There were no miners or plumbers, nor were there any women!

From the very beginning, therefore, climbing – certainly of the organised, establishment variety – was a male-oriented preserve.[9]

On the first published list of members of the Alpine Club are the names of Francis Walker and his son Horace, members of a well-established business family from Liverpool, and both very fine mountaineers. Frank had traversed the Theodule pass between Zermatt and Aosta at the age of 20, in 1826 when climbing was in its infancy. He was also, in 1865, at 59, with Horace on the first ascent of the Brenva ridge on Mont Blanc. He continued to climb until a short time before his death in 1872.

Horace, says Coolidge[10], was born in 1838 and began his Alpine career in 1854, at the age of 16. His best climbs, however, were made after 1865, when, as well as the Brenva ridge, he climbed to the highest point of the Grandes Jorasses (Pointe Walker, which he reached with his guides in 1868, and which is also the terminal point of the huge Walker Spur: see page 52).

However, prior to these great climbs, another event occurred which was to have profound significance as far as women's interest in mountaineering was concerned. In the season of 1858 Frank was accompanied by his daughter Lucy, who made her first tentative forays into Alpine activities. True (as has been indicated), she was not the first woman to cross a high Alpine pass or reach a summit, but she was to become the most consistent, the *first* really dedicated woman climber. Her climbing career spanned twenty years – at a time that was not the easiest for mountaineers generally, and for women in particular.

Lucy Walker and Melchior Anderegg

Although she had doubtless been to the Alps on prior occasions with the family group, her list of excursions began in 1858 with the crossings of the Theodule (Papa's early pass) and Monte Moro. The following year the family were staying at the Schwarenbach Inn in the Bernese Oberland, and Lucy acquainted Papa with her desire to climb the nearby Altels.

Melchior Anderegg, she was told by her father, would be the best guide to take her on the ascent. The successful expedition they made to the summit of the Altels was the beginning of a long and very splendid relationship between Lucy and Melchior. Of course Lucy was not permitted to climb with Melchior alone: Papa or Horace or both were usually in the party. The thought of two people of the opposite sex alone on a mountain at night, or even strolling on a glacier, was more than nineteenth-century moralists could absorb.

Miss Lucy Walker, president of the Ladies' Alpine Club 1913/15 and first true lady Alpinist. *(Alpine Club Library collection)*

Of the 90 or so climbs that Lucy made with Melchior, many stand out. They included in 1862 The Monte Rosa (Dufourspitze), the second-highest peak in Europe, and the Finsteraarhorn in the same year. In 1864 the season included the Eiger, Rimpfischorn and Balmhorn (the latter being a first ascent), also with the family and Melchior.

In the next few years came the Jungfrau, Weisshorn, Dom des Mischabels and the Mönch. In 1870 the Aiguille Verte, by the Whymper Couloir, was the best climb; yet it was the following year that made the greatest impact so far on climbing history and the public at large.

Lucy Walker and Melchior Anderegg. *(Alpine Club Library collection)*

The Matterhorn

The period 1854 to 1865 has been called[11] the 'Golden Years of Alpine Mountaineering'. It was a time of great activity, camaraderie and excitement that culminated in the ascent of the Matterhorn. The years that immediately followed this event were markedly different.

Coolidge brings the scene to life. Coming into Alpine climbing just a few days after *the* accident (the Matterhorn) he recollected vividly[12],

> the sort of palsy that fell upon the good cause after that frightful catastrophe of July 14th 1865 [when, on the descent from the summit, four climbers fell to their deaths; the rope broke between Peter Taugwalder and Lord Francis Douglas], particularly amongst English climbers.
>
> Early in July 1868 the present writer [Coolidge] met in the Gleckstein cave on the Wetterhorn, Mr. Julius Elliott [who was killed next year on the Schreckhorn]. In the course of conversation Mr. Elliott revealed, almost under the seal of confession, his

Back row, left to right: ?, Melchior Anderegg, A. W. Moore; front row, left to right: Frank Walker, Lucy Walker. *(Alpine Club Library collection)*

strong desire to attempt shortly the Matterhorn from the Swiss side. This feat he achieved a fortnight later. It was the first complete ascent on that side since the accident. It caused a very great sensation as it proved that the expedition was not so absolutely certain to end fatally.

Fully knowing the mountain's reputation (and the palsy), in 1871 Lucy elected to make an attempt upon it, and in so doing sowed the seeds of legend. On the 20th July, six years to the month – if not exactly to the day – after its first ascent, Lucy, accompanied by Frank Walker and Fred Gardiner with Melchior and (according to Whymper[13]) four other guides, climbed the Matterhorn by the Hörnli (that is, Whymper's) route. This was the nineteenth ascent of the mountain, the tenth by the Zermatt side, and the first by a woman. (Despite the commotion Coolidge had made about the first and second ascents, he does not mention Lucy's success in his book.)

In the newspaper world she became an overnight sensation, despite the fact that she had been an experienced mountaineer for years.

Punch published a poem in her honour: it is not likely to make the *Oxford Book of English Verse*, but it was ultimately recorded in the *Alpine Club Journal*[14]:

A climbing girl

A lady has clomb to the Matterhorn's summit,
  Which almost like a monument points to the sky;
Steep not very much less than the string of a plummet
  Suspended, which nothing can scale but a fly.

This lady has likewise ascended the Weisshorn,
  And, what's a great deal more, descended it too,
Feet foremost; which, seeing it might be named Icehorn,
  So slippery 'tis, no small thing to do.

No glacier can baffle, no precipice balk her,
  No peak rise above her, however sublime.
Give three times three cheers for intrepid Miss Walker.
  I say, my boys, doesn't she know how to climb!

1858 to 1879

Lucy climbed seriously from 1858 to 1879. Throughout these years she missed only two seasons: 1872 when Papa died, and 1874 when brother Horace was climbing with Moore, Grove and Gardiner in the Caucasus.

Her material needs on the mountain were taken care of by Mrs Walker and her helper Kate Barrett who, while the climbers were on the peaks, moved from base to base to meet the party, repairing clothing and administering to their requirements.

Although as far back as Mlle Angeville's ascent of Mont Blanc trousers had been worn on the mountains by women, there was a general acceptance by the women of the mid-nineteenth century that they should not be seen to be so clothed. Some hid climbing breeches beneath their skirts; the latter were then removed when the climb was reached. Lucy Walker always climbed in a print dress. There were rumours that on the Matterhorn ascent she actually adopted the more daring wardrobe – but one doubts this!

Despite her connections, Lucy did not escape the petty nastiness of lesser beings. Of her it was said[15],

> In those far-off mid Victorian days, when it was even considered 'fast' for a young lady to ride in a hansom [cab], Miss Walker's wonderful feats did not pass without a certain amount of criticism which her keen sense of humour made her appreciate as much as anyone else.

There was one particular summit which she did not climb, and she was quite prepared to give her reasons for not doing so. Apparently another female climber had made the ascent, and afterwards had remarked to a certain male climber, 'You said no woman could manage it'. The reply came: 'I said no *lady*!'[16]

Meta Brevoort

For decades Lucy's attitude and success served as an inspiration to scores of female climbers. Meta Brevoort, matriarchal aunt of that indefatigable Alpine chronicler, Coolidge, fell under her spell – and went on to achieve an impressive list of ascents, usually with her nephew and Christian Almer, not to mention their dog Tschingel, who climbed with them for ten seasons. Wonderful Meta, large of form and spirit: she who danced a quadrille and sang the then banned *Marseillaise* on the top of Mont Blanc; who just missed being the first woman on top of the Matterhorn; and who, after an exciting ascent in the Oberland, wrote an article called 'A Day and a Night on the Bietschorn'[17] and submitted it to the *Alpine Club Journal* under her nephew's name (knowing it would never be accepted under that of Meta Brevoort). She died after a short illness in 1876.

The Pigeon sisters

From Meta Brevoort to the end of the century, Alpine history is coloured with a number of outstanding women climbers. Two of these were the remarkable Pigeon sisters, Anna and Ellen. In September 1869 the pair, together with a guide and porter, crossed the Sesia Joch between Zermatt and Alagna. It had only been crossed once before, some seven years earlier by two members of the Alpine Club. It had been described at the time as '"a most daring exploit", possibly a tour de force which should never be repeated'[18].

Because of the severity of the climbing, certain members of the Alpine Club were more than a little sceptical of the Pigeons' efforts, and the latter were required to provide notes of the expedition before the Club was finally convinced that the passage had been made. The facts seem to indicate that, due to the guide's lack of knowledge of the area, they missed the easier pass they intended to cross, and walked onto the Sesia Joch instead. The guide and the porter spent so much time searching out the way that it became quite late. The sun began to set as they finally found a way down the glacier. The porter proved to be utterly incompetent, so whilst the guide worked out the descent, one of the sisters acted as sheet-anchor to the party and brought up the rear throughout the whole of the nine-hour descent. They had spent 18 hours on the mountain before they reached safety. Despite the undoubted courage, tenacity and ability of the sisters, Ellen in 1892 wrote with some sadness to Coolidge: 'In days gone by many members of the Alpine Club would not speak to us'.[19]

Other early climbers

It would be improper to journey through these golden and silver years without at least making passing references to several other quite remarkable climbers, for example Isabella Straton and Emmeline Lewis-Lloyd. They could not see any earthly reason why mountaineering should be reserved for men, and set out to prove their point in the most indisputable of ways: by doing the climbs themselves.

Isabella, who was quite wealthy, made the first winter ascent of Mont Blanc as well as summer ascents of numerous other plum peaks with her guide Jean Charlet. Snapping her fingers at the conventions of the day, she married Jean and settled down in Chamonix, where their two sons took to climbing at an early age and carried the Charlet name forwards to the twentieth century.

On to the scene in the 1880s came two women climbers who were to make notable contributions to mountaineering: Katy Richardson and Elizabeth Hawkins-Whitshed (who was to marry Aubrey Le Blond).

Katy Richardson

Katy began climbing when she was 16, and in 11 years made well over 100 major ascents, including the first traverse of the East Ridge and Ice Ridge to the Dôme du Goûter, the complete traverse of the five points, north to south, of the Grands Charmoz, the first traverse of the Petit to the Grand Dru, several peaks in the Dauphiné, the first traverse of the Zinalrothorn and most of the (by then) established classic peaks.

Elizabeth Le Blond

Elizabeth Le Blond, who had married at 18, became, with her husband, immersed in the social set that surrounded the Prince of Wales. A breakdown in health, and widowhood at the age of 21, found her turning to the mountains for solace and enjoyment (much to the disgust of certain members of her family). It was amongst the hills that she discarded 'the shackles of conventionality'[20] and went on to make some notable winter first ascents around Chamonix and in the Engadine, as well as summer-time ascents of the major peaks.

Lily Bristow and Mary Petherick

It would be remiss of us to end this period of mountaineering history without a reference to a great male climber and two of his protégés: A. F. (Fred) Mummery, his wife Mary, and their friend, Lily Bristow. Mummery married Mary Petherick in 1883 and slid out of the mountaineering limelight for a short time. Little is known of Fred's and Mary's mountain activities for three years after the marriage date. The first indication we are given of Mary's involvement with climbing is in 1887. In this year, with her husband and Alexander Burgener, Mary climbed the Jungfrau, Zinal Rothorn, Drieckhorn and the Taschorn, making the first ascent of the Teufelsgrat (the Devil's Ridge) in the process. The climb created a great stir in the ranks of mountaineers of the day. A 28-hour expedition, hard ice, rotten rock, a lost ice axe, and two injured guides embraced all the ingredients of a mountain epic.

Little was heard of Mary after this ascent; even Mummery himself, apart from a visit to the Caucasus in 1888, seemed to quieten down somewhat until his visit to the Alps in 1892. As well as by his brother-in-law, W. J. Petherick, he was accompanied on this occasion by Lily Bristow. In Chamonix they were joined by a group of British climbers, some of whom were to leave a trail of success over many Alpine summits and British crags. It included W. C. Slingsby, J. N. Collie and Geoffrey Hastings, together with Ellis Carr, Godfrey Solly, C. H. Pasteur and his two sisters.

With Carr, Collie, Petherick, Pasteur, one of the sisters and Mummery – but without guides – Lilly traversed the Aiguille des Charmoz, making an auspicious beginning to her mountain career. But it was the next two seasons that were to see her climbing talents rewarded. In 1893, Mummery, Bristow, Collie, Slingsby and Hastings again met at Chamonix. In that year she climbed the Grépon, the second traverse (guideless), the Petit Dru, and later the Zinal Rothorn and the Matterhorn. On the Dru, Lily led much of the way; the Zinal Rothorn and the Matterhorn by the Italian ridge were also guideless ascents.

It was in respect of these ascents by Lily that Mummery resurrected the following [21]:

It has frequently been noticed that all mountains appear doomed to pass through the three stages: An inaccessible peak – The most difficult ascent in the Alps – An easy day for a lady.

Male attitudes

Attitudes towards dress, men, and social niceties were fairly heavy crosses for these early women climbers to bear, and although the sensibilities of the times may have been quite prepared (but not always) to allow *men* to 'dice with death', they were not prepared to make the same concessions to women. Antagonism was shown to them by men *and* women – friends and relatives as well as the public at large – whose only exposure to mountain climbing, it is fair to say, would be the lurid reports that followed some accident.

The woman's place was in the home, the conventions went, bearing children and feeding her man (his stomach as well as his ego – and smoothing out every wrinkle in his path that could lead to the slightest likelihood of him taking a tumble from his exalted pedestal, it might be added!).

The commonly-held belief of the day was that women ought not to be seen dressed like men in rough clothing and climbing mountains – and as for wearing trousers or breeches or sleeping the night on a mountain with a *man* . . . the mind boggled at such indelicacies.

It is true that the public at large had not been silent in its criticism of male climbers, but it did at least, in time, credit their activities with the 'dignity of danger'. Women were not so fortunate, particularly in regard to the attitude of male mountaineers.

Whymper (of Matterhorn fame) and Coolidge were not in the foremost ranks of those who saw fit to sing the praises of women climbers. For example, Anna and Ellen Pigeon, who made the first female traverse of the Matterhorn, up the Breuil side and down the Zermatt, were given short shrift by Whymper so far as their gender was concerned. They were simply recorded as 'E. and A. Pigeon',[22] although much was made of the bad weather and the necessity of a night passed on the open mountainside.

In his appendix to *Scrambles amongst the Alps*,[23] in the section on the Subsequent History of the Matterhorn, Whymper writes of Felicite, the daughter of J. B. Carrel, without actually mentioning her by name.

Apparently three Maquignazes – Caesar Carrel, J. B. Carrel 'and a daughter of the last named!' – set off to make the fourth ascent of the mountain (the third from the Italian side). Having left Breuil at 5 a.m. the *previous* day, they reached the shoulder of the final peak some time after 7 a.m. on the 13th September 1867. After passing 'the cleft which had stopped Bennen [seven years before] they clambered up the comparatively easy rocks on the other side until they arrived at the base of the last precipice. . . . They (young women and all) were then about 350 feet [107 m] from the summit!' Whymper continues:

J. J. and J. P. Maquignaz alone ascended (from here); the others had had enough and returned. It should be observed that ropes had been fixed, by J. A. Carrel and others, over *all* the difficult parts of the mountain as high as the Shoulder, *before* the ascent of these persons (sic) . . . The young woman declared that the ascent (as far as she went) was a trifle, or used words to that effect; if she had tried to get to the same height before 1862, she would probably have been of a different opinion.

Male ego appears to have taken a distinct thrashing from young Felicite's flippancy. But Whymper got his own back: he does not list her in his appendix E,

'Ascents of the Matterhorn'. The names of the five men are given with the remark, 'Only the first two named ascended to the summit'.[24] However, posterity, thank goodness, has handled her more kindly: the point she reached is now known as Col Felicite.

The Ladies' Alpine Club

The Ladies' Alpine Club, women's reply to the Alpine Club, was formed in Britain in 1907, largely as a result of the efforts of Elizabeth Le Blond, who became its first President. This was followed in the next year by the formation of the Ladies' Scottish Climbing Club. These clubs became the focal points towards which the women climbers of the day turned. As one would expect at this time, these clubs were aimed at mountaineering activities rather than 'rock gymnastics', although many of their members were very fine rock climbers as well as mountaineers. It is not generally known, for instance, that Mrs C. W. Nettleton, who traversed the Monte Rosa in 1900, climbed the Cinque Torre and the Kleine Zinne in 1901; did the Blaitière and the Grépon traverse in 1903 (she leading); and had also led an ascent of the notorious Kern Knotts Crack in the English Lake District in 1897, with O. G. Jones as second (it is said) – a year after Jones had made its first ascent. She was 23 years old at the time.

Lucy Walker, who still continued to visit the Alps long after her harder climbing days had ended, devoted over 50 years of her life to the mountains. Throughout her latter days she was regarded with awe – a legend and inspiration to many women climbers. At its formation she joined the Ladies' Alpine Club, and in 1913 became the Club's President. She died in her eighty-first year, just after completing her term of office in 1916. She had been greatly loved and was deeply missed.

Coolidge wrote of her[25]:

> She was a very remarkable woman to have climbed so steadily and so long! My Aunt [Miss Brevoort] would certainly never have started if Miss Walker had not set the example.

However, perhaps the last word should be left to that great mountaineer, Charles Pilkington[26]:

> Her love of the mountains remained undiminished and year after year she returned to scenes of her early triumphs . . . In the early years of this second period, 1880 to 1912, the same temperament and qualities which had carried her to the top of the Matterhorn remained undiminished and with her life-long friend and guide Melchior Anderegg, she made many long and tiring journeys, which were the anxiety and wonder of other members of the party . . .
>
> Her energies were immense . . .
>
> Travelling in her company was always enlightened by her great vivacity, her pithy remarks and her interesting reminiscences of former travels, while her memory shed an old-world and fascinating interest on the peaks and valleys. . . These recollections seldom had reference to her climbing exploits, unless there was some quaint occurrence or troublesome experience to adorn the tale. Rather would she tell you, when looking at some trimly tweed-clad maiden how in her early days she climbed in a white print dress, of the difficulty of managing it on mountains, and of restoring it as nearly as possible to its original shape and colour on her return to civilisation. . .
>
> She will always remain to all who knew her a gracious memory, surrounded by all the best traditions of Alpine climbing and mountain travel.

Mrs Aubrey Le Blond (circa 1910), first president of the Ladies' Alpine Club. *(Alpine Club Library collection)*

Chronological list of events

1786   First ascent of Mont Blanc.
1808   First female ascent of Mont Blanc, by Marie Paradis.
1836   Lucy Walker born.
1838   Ascent of Mont Blanc by Henriette d'Angeville.
1857   Alpine Club formed.
1858   Lucy's first excursions of the Alps: Theodule and Monte Moro.
1859   Lucy met Melchior Andregg: Ascent of Altels.
1862   Monte Rosa and Finsteraarhorn.
1864   Eiger, Rimpfischorn and Balmhorn.
1867   Ascent of the Col Felicite on the Matterhorn, by Felicite Carrel.
1868   First ascent of the Matterhorn.
1869   Crossing of the Sesia Joch by the Pigeon sisters.
1870   Aiguille Verte.
1871   First women's ascent of the Matterhorn, by Lucy Walker.
1887   First ascent of the Teufelsgrat, by Mary Petherick.
1892   Traverse of Aiguille des Charmoz, by Lily Bristow.

1893 Lily climbed the Grépon, Petit Dru, Zinal Rothorn and Matterhorn.
1907 Ladies' Alpine Club formed: Lucy Walker became founder member.
1913 Lucy became President of Ladies' Alpine Club.
1916 Lucy completed presidency of L.A.C. Died aged 81.

Lucy Walker's climbs

Year	Month	Day	Peak
1858	July		Theodule
			Monte Moro
1859	July		Titlis
			Oberaarjoch
		8, 9	Strahleck
		15	Tschingel Pass
		18	Altels
1860	July	7, 8	Jungfrau (almost)
		13	Weissthor
		16	Adler Pass
		(?)	Strahlhorn
		21	Mont Vélan
		25	Col du Géant, 1861 (?)
		28	Col d'Hérens
1862	July	1	Gauli Pass
		8	Oberaarhorn
		9	Finsteraarhorn (with Horace W.)
		12	Alphubel Pass
		15	Monte Rosa
		19	Triftjoch
		23	Aiguille du Goûter
		25, 26	Mont Blanc
1863	July	16, 17	Zumstein Spitze
1864	July	1	Grivola (almost)
		4, 5	Grand Combin
		7	Col du Sonadon
		8	Col de La Reuse de L'Arolla
		9	Col de Valpelline
		12	Rimpfischhorn
		15, 16	Aletschhorn
		21	Balmhorn (1st ascent)
		25	Eiger
1865	June	23	Sustenhorn
		23	Sustenlimmi
		27, 28	Jungfrau
	July	4, 5	Moming Pass
		8	Breithorn
		10, 11	Grivola
1866	June	23	Mönchjoch
		27, 28	Wetterhorn
	July	6	Ewigschneefeld (? Horn)
		9	Weisshorn
		13, 14	Dom
		17	Biesjoch

Year	Month	Day	Peak
1867	August	13, 14	Mönch
		13, 14	Mönchjoch
		19, 20	Schreckhorn
		26, 27	Blümlisalp
1868	June	26	Mont Pourri (attempt)
	July	2	Col du Géant
		8	Col du Tour
		12	Pigne d'Arolla
		13	Col de Valcournera
		14	Theodul
		20	Lyskamm
		23, 24	Gross Viescherhorn
		25	Mönchjoch
1869	June	28, 29	Dachstein
	July	9	Watzmann
		16	Hintereis Pass
		18, 19	Ortler Spitze
		23, 24	Piz Bernina
1870	June	24	Uri Rothstock
		27, 28	Trift Pass (Triftlimmi)
		29, 30	Lauteraarjoch
	July	6	Jungfraujoch
		9	Beichgrat
		10, 11	Baltschiederhorn
		19, 20	Aiguille Verte
		23	Buet
1871	June	24	Diablerets
	July	1	Wetterlücke
		5	Monte Leone
		8	Castor
		8	Felikjoch
		10	Schwarzthor
		13	Weissthor
		15	Balfrin
		17, 18	Weisshorn (attempt)
		20, 21	Matterhorn
1872			*Father died*
1873	June	20	Titlis
		23	Wendenjoch
	July	3, 4	Jungfrau from Wengern Alp
		9, 10	Täschhorn
		11	Weissthor
		14	Monte Moro
		17, 18	Weisshorn
		19	Riffelhorn
		22	Col Durand
		26	Rothhorn (attempt)
1874			*Did not visit Alps: brother Horace in Caucasus with Moore, Grove and Gardiner*
1875	July	7	Wildstrubel
		14, 15	Allalinhorn
1876	September	3	Col de Seilon
		10	Passo d'Antrona
1887	June	28	Galenstock
	July	5	Weissthor
		12	Mischabelhorn (Dom)

Year	Month	Day	Peak
1887	July	12	Alphubelhorn
1878	(?)		
1879	June	20	Col de Collon
		26, 27	Monte Viso
	July	2	Col du Mont Corvé
		5	Theodul
		12	Nord End (attempt)
		22	Mondelli Pass
		24	Basodino

References

[1]Ronald Clark, *The Victorian Mountaineers* (Batsford, 1953), p. 17/[2]John Ruskin, *Sesame and Lilies* (1865)/[3]W. A. B. Coolidge, *The Alps in Nature and History* (Methuen, 1908), p. 211/[4]Claire Elliane Engel, *Mountaineering In the Alps* (George Allen & Unwin, 1971), p. 63/[5]Arnold Lunn, *A Century of Mountaineering* (T. Fisher Unwin, 1906), p. 72/[6]W. A. B. Coolidge, *The Alps in Nature and History*, p. 211/[7]Claire Elliane Engel, *Mountaineering In The Alps*, p. 63/[8]loc. sit./[9]A. L. Mumm, *The Alpine Club Register 1857–1863* (Edward Arnold, 1923)/[10]W. A. B. Coolidge, *The Alps in Nature and History*, p. 242/[11]Ronald Clark, *The Victorian Mountaineers*, p. 57/[12]W. A. B. Coolidge, *The Alps in Nature and History*, pp. 239 and 240/[13]Edward Whymper, *The Ascent of The Matterhorn* (John Murray, 1880), Appendix/[14]Frederick Gardiner, 'In Memoriam Miss Lucy Walker' (*Alpine Club Journal*, volume 31, number 214, February 1917), p. 98/[15]loc. sit./[16]Sir Claud Schuster, *Men, Women and Mountains* (Ivor Nicholson and Watson, 1931), p. 61/[17 and 18] W. A. B. Coolidge, 'A Day and a Night on the Bietschorn' (*Alpine Club Journal*, volume 6, August 1872–May 1974)/[19]Ronald Clark, *The Victorian Mountaineers*, p. 175/[20]Aubrey Le Blond, *Day In, Day Out* (The Bodley Head Ltd, 1928), p. 90/[21]A. F. Mummery, *My Climbs in The Alps and Caucasus* (T. Fisher Unwin), p. 160/[22]Edward Whymper, *The Ascent of The Matterhorn*, Appendix/[23]Edward Whymper, *Scrambles Amongst The Alps* (John Murray, 1893), Appendix E/[24]loc. sit./[25]Since Bill Peascod's death, Bill Birkett has been unable to trace this reference./[26]Charles Pilkington, 'In Memoriam' (*Alpine Club Journal*, volume 31, number 214, February 1917–October 1917), p. 101

2

Miriam O'Brien – an American on the Aiguilles

After the First World War

With the end of the First World War came a time of questioning. Women, in particular, were not prepared to revert to a pre-1914 kind of servitude. It is true that men and boys died or were maimed in the front lines, but they did not hold an exclusive right to suffer for their particular king or country. Shells from long-range guns or bombs from a night sky did not differentiate between men, women and children.

In politics and in society women demanded to be heard. It was not all women, of course (there were many lonely voices), but there were sufficient numbers to make it clear that change was not only necessary, but imminent.

The War had tempered women's metal: its name was Independence. Of course, there are numerous examples of women who displayed the same spirit long before 1914. In the mountains the Pigeon sisters, Isabella Straton and Emmeline Lewis-Lloyd, Katy Richardson and Mary Paillon rank high amongst those climbers of the nineteenth century who were determined to do it their way, even though, in the event, they co-opted (as did most male climbers) professional male guides to assist them in their projects.

It was in the immediate post-war years, 1919 and 1920, that the emancipated female mountaineer began to emerge. No longer was she to be found ducking into the background because some pompous member of the Alpine Club was holding forth in the sitting room of her hotel. Guideless climbing had been accepted for some time, despite the controversies that had raged in the male camp. The war had simply proved conclusively that that which, by their determination, Lucy Walker, the Pigeon sisters and Lily Bristow had shown to be possible was now an incontrovertible fact. Women could stand up to punishment; they had faced up to and overcome the tribulations of wartime in their own ways; they were quite capable of taking on the challenge of the mountains – and they were equally determined to think for themselves on mountaineering as well as many other matters. One such thinker was Emily Kelly.

Emily 'Pat' Kelly and the Pinnacle Club

Emily 'Pat' Kelly was primarily a rock climber. She was the wife of Harry Kelly, the distinguished pioneer of many notable rock climbs in the English Lake District between the two world wars. Pat was not only a graceful climber, but also a determined leader who loved to participate in that area of the sport which may still tend to raise the odd eyebrow: solo climbing. Solo climbing means precisely what it says. The climber is alone – dispensing with the usual safeguards of rope and fixed or applied 'protection points' (pegs (pitons) hammered into the rock, or

Emily 'Pat' Kelly who was instrumental in founding The Pinnacle Club in 1921. She was primarily a rock climber and is seen here on the Scoop of Castle Naize (a British gritstone outcrop). *(Sid Cross collection)*

slings and snaplinks hung over spikes, or the artificial metal 'chock-stones' much used nowadays) and the support of other rope members. Solo climbing is regarded by many as the purest form of climbing. To climb solo one has to be both competent and sure of one's competence. Pat Kelly was such a climber.

The Pinnacle Club was formed in 1921, its birth largely due to the far sightedness of Pat Kelly, who was its first Honorary Secretary. Mrs Winthrop Young was its first President. This Club, says Cecily Williams,[1] was 'the first rock climbing club founded by women for women.' In no sense, Cecily Williams assures us, was this a feminist gesture.

But it is equally interesting to read what Pat herself had to say.[2]

> The Pinnacle Club was born in the Spring, is a healthy child, and growing well, and looking back we wonder how it happened. Perhaps we got tired of being taken in hand by men climbers, kind and helpful though they might be, perhaps we sympathised with the would-be climbing woman who had no man friend to take her in tow; what would then become of her latent climbing powers, if she were never to be able to exercise them, except by favour? As in other walks of life, women wanted to find their own feet: it was very splendid for some women to be always able to borrow crutches in the shape of a man's help, and a man's rope, but it is even better to find we have feet of our own *and can climb some things as well as a man climber*. There need be no question now of who shall lead when two climbers marry; they can take it in turns.

This last comment, possibly said a little playfully, proved to be most prophetic. In 1920 we were on the edge of the great development of the 'husband–wife' climbing team.

Possibly the most important aspect of the formation of the Pinnacle Club was its stress on *rock climbing* as a basic requirement for entry to the club – a modest requirement, to be sure, but nevertheless a quite significant one:[3]

> The qualifications for Full Membership shall be proved ability to lead an ordinary climb of moderate difficulty.

The Pinnacle Club has continued to grow. Pat Kelly would have been proud of it; tragically, she died just a year after the Club's formation, following a fall on Tryfan.

Other inter-war climbers

Dorothy Pilley

Dorothy Pilley (later married to I. A. Richards) was probably the best known of British women climbers between the two World Wars – although even the turmoil of the second of them did not halt her mountain activities. These were curtailed in 1958 in a much more mundane, but none the less effective, way – by a drunken driver piling up his car in the track of Dorothy's. Her hips and hip joint were badly damaged in the crash that followed.

Climbing Days,[4] Dorothy's autobiography, tells her story in rich detail. The 'Great Year', 1928, culminated with the first ascent, with her husband and Joseph and Antoine Georges, of the north ridge of the Dent Blanche. With her husband she continued many years of exploration in the U.S.A. and other parts of the world.

Dorothy Thompson

On the scene in the mid-'20s arrived a small, lightly-built young woman, a person of most retiring nature and remarkable tenacity; someone who, like many of today's fine climbers, hid a considerable climbing ability behind a shy exterior. Her name was Dorothy 'Tommy' Thompson. It was Dorothy Pilley who introduced her in 1922 to Joseph Georges, and just as a great mountaineering relationship had developed between Lucy Walker and Melchior Anderegg 60 years previously, so did this meeting between Tommy and Joseph Georges lead to some remarkable climbing achievements.

Tommy's little-known book, *Climbing with Joseph Georges*,[5] published shortly after her death in 1961, tells affectionately of her love of the Alps and the splendid climbs she did there. She was the first woman to climb the Brouillard Ridge. Much to her surprise, Joseph Georges only told her this when they reached the summit:[6] 'Do you know, Mlle, that you have made climbing history today as the first woman to climb the Brouillard Arête – the first woman to climb one of the Val Veni ridges?'. Her story of this episode is a delight. There is one particularly appealing part where, in passing through seracs – 'discoloured peaks of melting, dirty, hideous, unhealthy looking snow' – J.G. says tactfully, '"It would give me much pleasure if you were to put on crampons!"'[7]

She was also the first British woman to climb the Brenva ridge to the Col Brenva; the party had to descend by the same route because of bad weather. The same team also traversed the Aiguille Bionnassay and made the first descent of the Peuteret Ridge (this took 34 hours).

In the mid-'30s she turned to ski-mountaineering, an activity which kept her absorbed into her fifties.

The hey-day of the all-women team, Alpinism *sans-homme* or *la cordée féminine*, was still to come. In 1900 Elizabeth Le Blond and Lady Evelyn McDonnell had dispensed with the services of guides and other male support to climb Piz Palu, a feat that was, as Dorothy Pilley says,[8] 'hushed up and regarded as somewhat improper'. It was after 1920 that women made their first real impact through manless ascents.

In 1928 the Grépon was led by a woman. Dorothy Pilley wrote,[9]

> The Alpine Journal wavered between incredulity and stern disapproval, announcing the first woman's lead of the Grépon with a hesitating 'it is reported' and declaring that 'Few ladies, even in these days, are capable of mountaineering unaccompanied.'

The cause of this Alpine eyebrow-lift was an American climber of the most outstanding ability. Her name was Miriam O'Brien. She began to blaze a trail through the annals of post-World War I climbing that earned her the reputation of being 'undoubtedly the greatest lady climber that America has produced'. So wrote Arnold Lunn in *A Century of Mountaineering*[10] in 1957.

Miriam's early life

Miriam O'Brien (whose greatest love as a child was climbing trees), was six years of age when taken by her parents into the wilds of New Hampshire in the U.S.A., to the foothills of the White Mountains. It was her first contact with the wilderness. The memory of that trip never left Miriam.[11]

> I got there my first taste of the wild, uncrowded places of the earth and even at six years old I liked it. For years afterwards I cherished those impressions.

The European Tour

Miriam O'Brien came from comfortably-off Bostonian-Irish stock. As befitted the daughter of a solid Boston newspaperman, Miriam, when 16, was taken by her mother on the European Tour.

They arrived in the spring of 1914. By July they had reached Chamonix. On one of the days they ascended on foot the 1,525 metre (5,000 ft) track up to the Brevent, a splendid viewpoint to the north of the Chamonix valley. From here, across the valley, the Mont Blanc massif spread before them. She was entranced. It never entered her head that one day she would make mountaineering history on the jagged ridges that radiated from Mont Blanc's summit.

A month later, when war arrived, they were in Switzerland where because of the disruption of transport services that normally would have got them back to America, they decided to make the best of things and visit Zermatt whilst problems were being resolved.

The first sight of the Matterhorn left her speechless – as it has done to so many. They walked up to the Gornergrat for a better view of: Monte Rosa, the

Matterhorn, Dent Blanche, Obergabelhorn, Rothorn, the Weisshorn. The seeds planted in the soils of the White Mountains were germinating, unknowingly, amongst these magnificent peaks of the European Alps.

The early 1920s

It was six years later, in 1920, before she saw them again.

> It would be gratifying to report that we started in at once on serious climbing, but far from it,

she wrote.[12] And indeed the season yielded ascents of only moderate ambition.

The 1921 season fared little better. The turning point came in 1924. The season appeared to carry all the marks of a repeat performance: simple, unambitious ascents offering no great challenge to climbers far less fit than she was. The best of these climbs was the Pointe de Zinal.

On the balcony of the Schönbühl Hut Miriam fell into conversation with a tall, lightly-built mountaineer in his mid-thirties. It was George Ingle Finch, the controversial inclusion in the 1922 Everest team, whose fitness for the attempt was suspect but who, in the end, confounded his critics by reaching, with J. G. Bruce, the highest point on the mountain at the time: 27,306 ft (8,320 metres). 'Don't waste time on trivial climbs,' he advised her. 'You could do the Matterhorn!' It was a turning point in her career. Two days later she traversed the Wellenkuppe and the Obergabelhorn. Quite suddenly, after some years of indifferent Alpine activity, she became a mountaineer.

In the early 1920s Miriam joined the Appalachian Mountain Club, and it was with members of this group that she developed what was to be her great love – rock climbing – on the numerous routes on the New Hampshire cliffs.

It was predictable, therefore, that her first big season in the Alps, in 1926 when she was 28 years of age, should be in predominantly rock climbing areas: the Dolomites of Northern Italy and the Aiguilles of Chamonix on Mont Blanc.

In the Dolomites

In 1926 her skills nurtured in her beloved New Hampshire blossomed and glowed splendidly in the remarkable peaks around Cortina in Northern Italy. These peaks of the Eastern Dolomites are a staggering panorama of huge buttresses, inaccessible-seeming summits and breath-takingly steep faces of cream- and orange-coloured rock, and to a non-climber they appear to be utterly unassailable. To Miriam O'Brien they were intoxicating. It was climbing, she said,[13] that was a good deal longer than any she had done before – and a good deal steeper.

The exposure (that is the feeling of being out in space with nothing but fresh air underneath you) all seemed so startling that she even lost her sense of the perpendicular. She wondered why, on one climb, her guide was moving slowly although the climbing appeared to be quite easy. When he began to pull the rucksacks up on a rope, the rope and sacks swung away from the wall showing it to be overhanging. But it was remarkable, she stated, 'how fast one can get used to exposure, and even acquire a taste for it. To my mind, it spiced up the climbs enormously and without adding an element of danger.'[14]

Miriam made one significant comment which is worthy of recording in full:[15]

This Dolomite climbing hardly needed any spicing up at all, being the best fun I'd met in my life! In common with many women, I felt that these Dolomites were made just to suit me with their small but excellent toe- and finger-holds, and pitches where a delicate sense of balance was the key, rather than brute force. While it helps, of course, to have tough muscles, the prize fighter would not necessarily make a fine Dolomite climber. *But the ballet dancer might.*

The Dimai family

Miriam's guides during the early Dolomite years were members of the long-established Dimai family: Antonio, the father, and his two sons Angelo and Giuseppe. To Miriam, Angelo Dimai of Cortina was the most beautiful rock climber she had ever met – one so graceful that when he climbed he seemed to float up the rocks with no effort. For years she studied his technique and analysed his style with a view to emulating his skills. 'If I am not a prettier rock climber than I am, it is not for lack of trying under a perfect example,' she was to say later.[16]

After numerous dazzling ascents with this remarkable team, she returned to Cortina again the following year. Her group numbered half a dozen or so, and their meeting with their guides was a happy occasion. It was here that Antonio Dimai took her to one side and, barely concealing his excitement, whispered to her not to go with the others next day.

> The exciting news turned out to be that Angelo had a new climb for me on the Torre Grande, the first route that any climber had succeeded in working out up its precipitous south wall, the hardest route so far made anywhere on that tower, and one of the most difficult in the whole Dolomite region . . . I was to make the first tourist ascent [it had only been climbed for the first time a week before by Angelo with Giuseppe and Arturo Gaspari] and he (Angelo) would like to call it the Via Miriam.[17]

It is clear that Miriam was both excited and flattered by the obvious regard the Dimais had for her and her ability. They had put off several other requests by others for the first tourist ascent. Angelo had told all of them that this honour had to go to Signorina Miriam. But it was difficult to keep the wolves at bay. They must get on and do the climb. So, with little more than one practice climb to toughen them up, Miriam with her friend Margaret Helburn, Angelo Dimai, Antonio Dimai and Angela Dibona climbed the Via Miriam. The day was 7th July 1927. It was an ascent of which she was justifiably proud. (The guide-book[18] still describes it as 'a fine classic route' and gives it a Grade V grading of difficulty.)

The Aiguilles of Chamonix

For all her delight in climbing the steep, exposed Dolomite walls, the Aiguilles of Chamonix were Miriam's greatest love in the Alps.

Mont Blanc, as every mountaineer knows, is a complex massif of rock, ice and snow. Its ascent by the snowy hump of the Dôme du Goûter, on past the high Vallot Hut and up the Bosses Ridge to the summit, is regarded by many as nothing more than a long laborious snow plod of no great technical difficulty, although the weather and the altitude may cause one to rethink that assessment.

The massive peaks, ridges, walls, spurs, couloirs and glaciers which support and buttress this highest point in Europe are another matter – and comprise,

Miriam O'Brien (married name Underhill) amongst the Chamonix Aiguilles. *(Alpine Club Library collection)*

arguably, the most varied and exciting climbing complex on the Continent. The very names of these features conjure up dreams for the mountaineer: names such as the Mer de Glace, the Grandes Jorasses with its magnificent northern wall, Mont Dolent, Mont Maudit, the Brenva Face and its Brouillard, Peutery and Innominate Ridges. All these and more have fed the eyes, hearts and minds of climbers for many decades.

The climbing history of the Aiguilles

The greatest excitement was to be found in the later years of the nineteenth century in the conquest of those fantastic needles of red granite which bordered the basin of the Mer de Glace glacier. They are known collectively as the Chamonix Aiguilles, after the small town that lies in the valley of the River Arve to the north of Mont Blanc. The summits of all the major Aiguilles had been reached, usually by the easiest route, by 1882. These climbs were invariably classics of their kind: generally the ascent, in the first instance, of some steep couloir to a gap (or brèche) between two peaks, and then a continuation along a narrow ridge of superb granite to the right or left to gain the summit.

The Chamonix Aiguilles were particularly the preserve of British climbers. Virtually all the major Aiguilles (ascended between 1864 and 1882) were done by British parties (which usually meant, of course, that one or more Britons were in the party and the actual leading of the team up the climb was done by a local guide! It was a convention at the time that the person who paid the guide got the credit for the ascent).

The most coveted of the Aiguilles were in the area known as the Grands Charmoz. Walt Unsworth wrote:[19]

> They had all been attempted, naturally enough, and none more often than that pinnacled ridge which forms such an obvious challenge – the Aiguille des Grands Charmoz. So long as the Charmoz remained unclimbed, no true mountaineer could even look out of his bedroom window at Chamonix without feeling a sense of defiance on the part of the mountains.

The Charmoz is seen 'like a savage granite stickleback'[20] serrating the skyline, with the summit of the Grands Charmoz proper standing up as a ridge of huge shattered spikes. From the highest of these teeth the ridge falls sharply into a gap, a brèche, before rising steeply again to another, larger and higher, separate summit. This latter is known as the Grépon, and the gap between them, the Charmoz-Grépon Brèche, which, on the western side of this great ridge, is at the top of the Charmoz-Grépon Couloir. It is a pronounced break in the western wall of the face which overlooks the small, though steep, Nantillons Glacier. On the eastern side of the superb Charmoz-Grépon skyline the rock falls away in a stupendous wall of red granite for something like 760 m (2,500 ft), then steep ice and rock for another 610 m (2,000 ft) to the Mer de Glace glacier.

In July 1880 A. F. Mummery with his great guides Burgener and Venetz climbed the Charmoz at their first attempt.

The following year, 1881, Mummery with Burgener and Venetz returned to Chamonix. The Grépon, probably at this time the most desired ascent in the area, was their objective. Mummery had reached the conclusion that the Grépon could best be climbed from the Mer de Glace side up the great wall of red granite. A determined attempt which failed convinced him he was wrong, and they returned to the Nantillons side and climbed to the top of the Charmoz-Grépon Couloir.

Looking up the Mer de Glace with the imposing Mer de Glace face of the Grépon on the right. At one time it was regarded as the hardest route in the Alps. It was climbed guideless and manless by Miriam O'Brien and Alice Damesme in 1929. *(Bill Birkett)*

It is now history that Venetz made the ascent of a crack which later became known as 'the Mummery Crack' and thus pioneered a route to the summit of the Grépon that acquired a reputation of great ferocity – and became the best known crack pitch in the Alps.

Mummery's earlier objective, the Mer de Glace face of the Grépon, was indeed a much harder route than he imagined. It was climbed exactly 30 years later in 1911 by another fine British mountaineer, Geoffrey Winthrop Young, and two companions, the party being led by Josef Knubel and Henri Brocherel – the former one of the greatest guides of all time.

This then was the earliest ascent of the Mer de Glace face of the Grépon. Sixteen years later its reputation was still very high.

The Grépon

Miriam was back in Chamonix in 1927, and her first objective was a delicate subsidiary pinnacle soaring into the sky from a wall of rock adjacent to the southern end of the Grépon and to the left of the Mer de Glace face as one examines it from this glacier.

At the time her guide was Alfred Couttet, a rock climber of outstanding ability. With Alfred she had already made three attempts on the needle-like spire in 1926, only to be repulsed on each occasion. Now, in early August, a year later, they left the Montenvers Hotel just after two in the morning, equipped for a possible forced bivouac and accompanied by Georges Cachat who was to act as porter.

Their route skirted under the Mer de Glace walls of the Grépon and passed the Red Tower of Winthrop Young's route on that climb. Then, crossing the couloir at the left end of the face, they climbed up on to the broad slabs below the Aiguille de Roc, as it had been named. This time they climbed swiftly, urged on by the promise of bad weather in the distance. The final spire, split by a thin crack, was the crux of the climb, but Alfred managed to lasso a rounded knob of rock away to the left near the far edge of the summit spire. After a pendulum from the knob and a haul up on the rope he was over the difficulty and the summit was theirs. The others followed and, just nine hours after leaving the Montenvers, they found themselves with the first ascent of the Aiguille de Roc to their credit.

However, there was no time for relaxation. Underneath them were well over 600 m (2,000 ft) of steep rock. Above them hung a storm-filled sky. They were now racing against the weather and were hoping desperately to get off the steeper, upper section of the slabs before it broke. But their luck did not hold. Miriam wrote:[21]

> We hurried as I have rarely hurried. To save time we roped down frequently, as fast as three people could, but even so we did not reach our goal before the storm broke.

They were lashed by rain, hail and snow. At one point they were in a fierce electrical storm. The rocks began to glaze with ice. The situation was becoming increasingly serious. When the storm came the guide/client relationship was abandoned. Georges pushed on downwards, and Alfred descended as 'last man'. It was Miriam's job, in the middle, to safeguard the others as best she could and to ensure that the ropes to both of them travelled as smoothly as the elements would allow.

> For hours I handled those twisting, kinking ropes, cold, wet and icy and in general I kept them in order pretty well. For Alfred did not omit comment on my lapses.[22]

Hour after hour they forced their way down, with the climbing gradually becoming easier. At one point she had hallucinations and thought she could see three people climbing not 46 m (50 yards) away in the same direction. She asked Alfred where they had come from – but neither Alfred nor Georges could see anyone.

Finally, the ordeal was over. On the glacier they took off the ropes. The knot on her waist line was so tight and hard-frozen that Alfred did not hesitate, but simply cut the rope from around her waist.

Just after 8 p.m. they reached the hotel. They had been climbing for 18 hours. Their friends congratulated them enthusiastically on their successful ascent, but she noted wryly,[23] *that* part of it was comparatively forgotten. For the last nine hours it was not getting *up* that had mattered, it was getting *down*.

A week after this first ascent, Miriam and Alfred accompanied by her friend, Margaret Helburn, and the best known Chamonix guide of the day, Armand Charlet, climbed the Grépon by its Mer de Glace face: the route of Knubel, Winthrop Young, etc. Miriam and her party thus made history again. It was the first female ascent of the most formidable climb of its day in the Mont Blanc region.

Leading on the Grépon

Success after success followed this wonderful season. In 1928 with husband-to-be Robert Underhill, Armand Charlet and Georges Cachat, Miriam did the first complete traverse of all five points of Les Aiguilles du Diable. All the points had been climbed separately – sometimes two of them in one trip – but never the whole sequence in one expedition. It was an excursion of considerable difficulty and also a race against time. This, too, turned out to be an undertaking of over 18 hours.

Very laudable though these events were, and however much they may have satisfied masses of lesser climbers, a small worm still gnawed away at the ambitions of Miriam O'Brien. She was beginning to ask herself a very big 'Why?' In her book,[24] she wrote:

> Very early, I realised that the person who invariably climbs behind a good leader, guide or amateur, may never really learn mountaineering at all and in any case enjoys only a part of all the varied delights and rewards of climbing. He has, of course, the glorious mountain scenery, the exhilaration of physical aerobatics, the pleasure that comes from the exercise of skill, and these aerobatics often require skill to a considerable degree. But he is, after all, only following.
>
> The one who goes up first on the rope has even more fun, as he solves the immediate problems of technique, tactics and strategy as they occur. And if he is, as he usually is, also the leader, the one who carries the responsibility for the expedition, he tastes the supreme joy. For mountaineering is a sport which has a considerable intellectual component. It takes judgement to supply ideas, to make wise and proper decisions on the route, the weather, the possibility of danger from stone fall, avalanche, concealed crevasses, etc., and above all to know what one's own capabilities permit. This exercise of proper judgement is of more consequence than in most sports, for mountaineering is a game with a real and sometimes drastic penalty for failure. You don't have merely to pretend that it is important to play the game well.
>
> I saw no reason why women, *ipso facto*, should be incapable of leading a good climb.

As Miriam points out in these remarks from which we quote at length, women had on a 'few scattered occasions' done so. But why not make a regular practice of leading?

Male friends were ready enough to tell her that they shouldn't do so. One said:[25]

> There is more to leading than first meets the eye, a lot that must be learned, and that is best learned by watching competent leaders attentively and coming to understand their decisions. Women, however, never bother to do this. Since they know that they will never be allowed to lead anyway, they just come walking along behind, looking at the scenery. Therefore, even if they were given an opportunity to lead, they would be completely unprepared.

Miriam probably understates her reaction when she says she didn't find this argument 'too convincing'.[26]

She did, in fact, reach a much more positive decision: if a woman were really to lead, there should not be any man at all in the party! She decided therefore '*to try some climbs not only guideless but manless.*'[27]

These conclusions had been slowly formulating in her mind since the early years of her career. Even in the early Dolomite years she had insisted upon leading some of the easy stretches – 'although it did worry dear old Antonio almost intolerably.'[28] With Angelo it was different. He would let her lead all right, but the routes they were doing were usually so hard she felt the need of a rope above her.

Late in 1927 at Chamonix she made plans with Alfred for her to lead the Grépon – with him as second. The weather prevented this, but in the next season she performed the feat with Georges Cachat. It was the first time this great climb had been led by a woman. The ascent was made 'in good average time for a competent party'[29] – and was pounced upon by the press!

'Manless' on the Grépon

Still the worm gnawed. What Miriam really wanted was to climb the Grépon 'manless'. With Winifred Marples in 1929 she did her first 'manless climb': the Aiguille du Peigne. It was shorter and easier than the Grépon, but was similar in character.

Three days later, on 17th August 1929, at roughly 2.30 a.m., she and Alice Damesme, a brilliant French climber, left the Montenvers Hotel to ascend the Grépon. Three hours later they reached the Rognon des Nantillons, a prominent rocky outcrop in the Nantillons Glacier, where most parties bound for this side of the mountain stop for breakfast. Here they were joined by several other caravans bound for various peaks above.

The two women, without any accompanying male – professional or amateur – were viewed with some interest. 'Where are you going?' they were eventually asked, and when the reply came that they planned to climb the Grépon, it caused some commotion.

'You two alone?' someone asked disbelievingly. They admitted that that was their intention.

Alice and Miriam pretended not to notice the sideways glances, the barely-concealed smiles and the odd comment. After breakfast everyone stood aside to let them lead off, on to the glacier and up to the bergschrund where, as would be expected in such circumstances, the perversities of the ice caused them a little trouble in front of an audience growing in volume, interest and scepticism.

Finally, the bergschrund overcome, they moved up into the couloir. It was here Miriam began to feel they were too far to the left. 'The routes to the Charmoz and the Grépon diverged about here' she wrote afterwards,[30]

> and we might well be on our way to the Charmoz. We wouldn't have asked directions of any of these men for the world! We were playing a game and we must abide by the rules: no help from men! With a few rapid surreptitious whispers we took our decision: we would go right ahead with feigned assurance, and if we later found ourselves on the Charmoz we would traverse both peaks and pretend that was what we meant to do all along.

And there can be no doubt that should they have found themselves on the Charmoz they would have done precisely this!

Nearing the col they found that they *were* too far to the left, and had to cross steep icy rocks to reach the correct line. A party above saw their predicament and offered to throw down a rope. This superfluous rescue was declined with thanks.

At the col they found Armand Charlet and Guido Alberti Rivetti, who had just crossed the Charmoz and were heading for the Grépon. When he spotted the two women, Charlet announced to his companion that they would have lunch. At first Rivetti was astonished. It was far too early and the locality was not terribly suitable for lunch. But in a few moments he realised why Charlet wished to stop and they settled down to watch. The next pitch from the gap was the famous Mummery Crack.

The Crack, which does not lead straight up the wall from the col, has to be reached by a traverse out across the wall that plunges down into the Charmoz-Grépon Couloir and the Nantillons Glacier, 460 m (1,500 ft) below.

It was Alice's turn to lead, and (as Miriam had led the Crack the year before with Georges Cachat as second) it was an arrangement which suited admirably. They changed into light climbing shoes; then Miriam, belaying in the col, payed out the rope to her leader as Alice set off in an atmosphere of some tenseness and excitement.

The Crack is attained these days with the aid of pitons for security, by a horizontal traverse straight out from the col to reach the fissure at about its mid-height. However, at that time it was more usual for the leader to descend some 15 m (50 ft) or so from the notch, *then* traverse out to reach the *foot* of the Crack. Below this point there is nothing to break the view to the Glacier for 300 m (1,000 ft) or more.

The technique of climbing the Crack involves either jamming in to it as far as possible, which makes the ascent very strenuous, or staying out to use a bridging action, requiring the use of small holds on the outer walls. This is not so exhausting. In either case it is the bottom 3 m (10 ft) of the Crack which are the most difficult.

As Alice pondered the problem, the voice of her husband, Maurice Damesme, floated down through the mist from the Charmoz, across the gap, where he, Winifred Marples and Rene Pacard were doing the Charmoz traverse.

'Are you up the Mummery Crack?'

'Almost', was Alice's cheerful white lie – she had not even started it![31]

Reaching the Crack she attacked its overhanging base. Difficulty followed, but after a few awkward moments she worked out the moves and was away, climbing with ease and confidence. 'It was, as might have been expected, the performance of a real expert.'[32]

At the mid-point of the Crack, Alice rested, then continued up the last 9 m (30 ft) of still strenuous and fatiguing rock to gain the summit. A cheer went up from the small crowd now in the gap, and after the rucksacks had been hauled to the top it was Miriam's turn. She summed up her own effort on the Crack:

> When I had led the Mummery Crack the preceding year it had seemed surprisingly easy and I was astonished this time to find it had once again become much more laborious. There is indubitably a stimulation to going up first, it seems to me; the excitement and elation bring on a real increase in strength and skill.[33]

After the crux pitch there was no way of stopping these two. A sharp blizzard of snow could do no more than cause them to halt to put on their sweaters and mitts. The next exciting pitches followed: the Boite aux Lettres, the Rateau de Chèvre and the Grande Gendarme, a descent of 15 m (50 ft) on a doubled rope over a sensational drop. A safety rope is frequently used in these circumstances, but, to save weight, they were climbing on a light 45 m (150 ft) alpine line – with no second rope!

When they reached the flat rock that forms the summit of the Grépon they met Armand Charlet and Guido Rivetti, and all four settled down to eat.

> It was a gay lunch, enlivened by an impassioned ovation, no less, by Guido Rivetti on the humiliation suffered by a man, and a man who considered himself a good climber, at being escorted over the Grépon by a guide on a day such as this.[34]

In Chamonix that evening there were cheers and sighs.

'The Grépon has disappeared,' mourned one Etienne Bruhl,

> Of course there are still some rocks standing there, but as a climb it no longer exists. Now that it has been done by two women alone no self respecting man can undertake it. A pity, too, because it used to be a very good climb.[35]

The next season, 1930, began with a manless ascent by Marjorie Hurd of the Torre Grande at Cortina.

The Matterhorn

Later in the season Miriam and Alice Damesme, after some excursions from Courmayeur on the south side of Mont Blanc, resolved to climb the Matterhorn. Circumstances, as it happened, were against them in 1930, but in 1931 the pair of them with Jessie Whitehead, another American woman climber, arranged to meet in Zermatt for an ascent of this great peak.

Probably no other mountain is so well known to mountaineers and non-mountaineers alike. To the latter it seems to be *the* mountain, whilst to the former, however fashionable it may be from time to time to deride its ascent, the ticking-off of its summit is still a much sought after objective.

The Matterhorn, 4,476 m (14,690 ft), sits astride the Swiss–Italian border as a slightly imperfect pyramid. Four great triangular faces – north, south, east and west – box the compass, each being clearly defined by sharp bounding ridges. These are the North East, or Hörnli Ridge, which drops towards Zermatt in Switzerland (this was the ridge of the first ascent). Next to it in anti-clockwise direction is the Zmutt Ridge (these two bound the North Face). To the right, the West Face, and falling into Italy, is the Italian Ridge (up which the second ascent of the Matterhorn was made, within a few days of the first, by Whymper's great rival, the Italian guide, J. A. Carrel). Next, between the South and East faces lies the Furggengrat – the last of the four Matterhorn Ridges to be climbed.

Visually, the Matterhorn's greatest appeal lies in its elegance when seen from the Swiss side. The huge North and East faces sweep upwards in great snow-plastered planes to where the perfect symmetry of their apices has been broken by the giant hand of the great mountain sculptor, who seems to have taken the tip of the perfect pyramid and given it a playful tweak and twist between his finger and thumb to create towers and shoulders and noses a few hundred feet below the summit. It is here that the climbing is the most difficult (or was before it was swathed in fixed ropes and simplified with metal stanchions) and where the weather can be at its fiercest.

For all its relative ease and the refuges (the Solvay and the Hörnli Huts) that are to be found on the Swiss ridge, an ascent of the Matterhorn is not to be taken lightly. Statistics continue to show that the mountain weather can still exact a toll.

'Manless' on the Matterhorn

The Matterhorn, then, by the Hörnli route from Zermatt, was their objective. If they got up, it would not be the first ascent by a woman – that had been done by Lucy Walker 60 years before, and followed up by the Pigeon sisters who did the complete traverse of the mountain by going up one ridge and down the other. However, it would be the first ascent by an *all-woman party, without guides,* or any sort of male assistance to help them over the difficulties (if one is allowed to overlook the affection of the hut warden who took great pains to see that they got the best possible treatment in the hut – and start to the day).

Miriam, sensibly, realised that up to then all their manless climbing had been fundamentally rock ascents. In July, therefore, she set out to gain greater manless snow and ice experience in the Bernese Oberland, where she and Micheline Morin, another excellent French climber (of whom we shall hear more later) climbed the Jungfrau and the Mönch – routes which 'while not uneventful, still presented no great difficulties.'[36]

On 2nd August 1931, Alice, Jessie and Miriam assembled as planned in Zermatt. The signs were not auspicious: Alice was having trouble with a knee, and the weather was poor. For three weeks it remained unfavourable, though Jessie and Miriam managed in this time to ascend the Alphubel, a peak of nearly 4,270 m (14,000 ft) which lies on the southern end of the Misehabelhorner: the great range of peaks, which includes the Taschorn and the Dom, that lies between Zermatt and Saas Fee.

Jessie Whitehead, a sound climber and a sparkling wit, has left us with a number of delightful aphorisms, one of which deserves to be recalled. After their repeated set-backs in Zermatt and retreats from the Matterhorn Hut due to bad weather, Geoffrey Winthrop Young, who was in the Valley at the time said,[37] 'If you can learn to turn back you are safe to undertake any climb.' Jessie replied, 'Turning back is what we didn't learn, nothing else but!'

They passed the rest of the season trying to climb the Matterhorn.

> Jessie felt that our attempts provided the comic relief in an otherwise deplorable season in Zermatt and that the guides, in the long winter evenings ahead, could amuse themselves by thinking of the girls who had tried so hard.[38]

The weather won, despite their several attempts in 1931.

They were back again in 1932, this time without Jessie, who had to miss the season in the Alps; the weather was as before: deplorable. They went to Chamonix – the weather was no better – and then on to the Dauphiné, which being much further south, would, they hoped, give better weather. They were still out of luck.

In the second week of August it began to improve. On 12th August 1932, Miriam and Alice headed back to Zermatt and plodded once more up to the Matterhorn Hut, where they had already spent many previous nights on their abortive attempts on the mountain. Miriam wrote:[39] 'Next day we climbed the Matterhorn. It was as easy as that.'

In a way it seemed so much of an anti-climax. Little of any note happened on the way up. A guideless party of three men held them up until Miriam and Alice adroitly managed to pass them. They reached the summit at 8.30 a.m. The day was now beautiful and warm. They toyed with the idea of descending by the Italian ridge, and went across to the Italian summit of the mountain to see what conditions were like. Conditions were bad; the ridge was deep in snow. They set off back down the Hörnli at 10.30 a.m. – the descent proved to be more awkward now that the snow was soft and slid off the surface to reveal ice underneath. They put on crampons down to the Solvay Hut, and fresh snow began to fall gently on them, just enough Miriam said, 'to make us feel at home'.[40]

After their climb she and Alice were expected back in Chamonix.

> G.H.M. friends had prepared an elaborate reception at the railway station with enormous bunches of flowers, a 'band' and 'orations' in honour of the first women to climb the Matterhorn alone.[41]

Instead of returning to Chamonix she went to the Eastern Alps to join a small group of friends, one of whom was Robert Underhill. 'After that' (the last word must go to her), 'my constant companion on every climb was Robert Underhill. Manless climbing is fun for a while, but this other arrangement is better!'[42]

Miriam and Robert became engaged soon after their return from the Alps, and later married. From then on they climbed first together and then with a growing-up family, exploring some of the wildest parts of the North American high country in Idaho, Montana and New Hampshire.

Chronological list of events

1898   Miriam O'Brien born.
1914   First visited Chamonix.
1921   Pinnacle Club formed.
1922   Pat Kelly died.
1924   Traverse of Wellenkuppe and Obergabelhorn.
1926   Climbing in the Dolomites and Aiguilles of Chamonix: three attempts on the Grépon.
1927   Ascent of Via Miriam.
1928   First complete ascent of Les Aiguilles du Diable.
      First female lead of the Grépon.
      First ascent of the north ridge of the Dent Blanche, by Dorothy Pilley.
1929   First all-women's ascent of the Mer de Glace face of the Grépon.
1932   First all-women's ascent of the Matterhorn.
      Met and married Robert Underhill.
1961   Dorothy Thompson died.
1976   Miriam O'Brien died.

References

[1]Cecily Williams, *Women On The Rope* (Allen & Unwin, 1973), p. 106/[2]Emily Kelly, 'The Pinnacle Club' (*Fell and Rock Climbing Club Journal*, 1921), p. 324/[3]ibid., p. 326/[4 and 5]Dorothy Thompson, *Climbing With Joseph Georges* (Titus Wilson, 1961)/[6]ibid., p. 99/[7]ibid., p. 93/ [8]Dorothy Pilley, *Climbing Days* (Secker & Warburg, 1953), p. 130/[9]ibid., p. 130/[10]Arnold Lunn, *A Century of Mountaineering* (Allen & Unwin, 1957, p. 173/[11]Miriam Underhill, *Give Me The Hills* (Methuen, 1956), p. 14 (subsequent references denoted by *GMTH*)/[12]ibid., p. 18/[13]ibid., p. 35/[14]ibid., p. 36/[15]ibid., p. 36/[16]ibid., p. 35/[17]ibid., p. 44/[18]Alpine Club, *Dolomites East* (West Col Productions, 1970), p. 159/[19]Walt Unsworth, *Tiger In The Snow* (Gollancz, 1967), p. 48/[20]loc. cit./[21]*GMTH*, p. 62/[22]ibid., p. 63/[23]ibid., p. 65/[24]ibid., p. 149/[25]ibid., p. 150/[26]ibid., p. 150/[27]ibid., p. 150/[28]ibid., p. 150/[29]ibid., p. 151/[30]ibid., p. 153/[31]ibid., p. 155/[32]ibid., p. 155/[33]ibid., p. 156/[34]ibid., p. 158/[35]ibid., p. 158/[36]ibid., p. 159/[37]ibid., p. 160/[38]ibid., p. 161/[39]ibid., p. 168/[40]ibid., p. 169/[41]ibid., p. 169/[42]ibid., p. 169

3

Loulou Boulaz – first among equals

The inter-war years

It was in the 1920s and 1930s that female European mountaineers began to leave a very positive mark on the history of Alpine climbing.

The brilliant Alice Damesme, with Micheline Morin and her sister-in-law Nea (who occasionally regarded herself as half French!), were amongst the best from France.

From Italy came Nina Pietrosanta, Tina Bozzino and Livia Bertolini, who attacked the great Italian side of Mont Blanc: the Brenva and Peuterey ridges.

Una Cameron, a fine British mountaineer, was also attracted by the massive southern side of Mont Blanc, and the Brenva, Peuterey, Innominata ridges and the Sentinelle and Route Major were ascended by her. Dorothy 'Tommy' Thompson and Dorothy Pilley were also significant British climbers in the two decades.

From Holland, a country not hitherto noted for its Alpine traditions, emerged Anna Roelfsema, who with her brother, Roeli, made the first woman's guideless ascent of the Younggrat on the Breithorn.

However, the one woman mountaineer who, probably more than any other between the wars, has captured the interest of the climbing world was a Swiss climber. Her name is Loulou Boulaz and she was regarded by many as the finest of her generation.

In Geneva

Early in May 1983 Tom Price, André Roch and I were motoring pleasantly through Geneva's warm sunny boulevards. Tom, the then 'Great White Father' of the British Mountaineering Council, sat in the front seat alongside André, President of the Geneva Section of the Swiss Alpine Club (S.A.C.). I sat at the back.

Tom and I had been staying with André as his guests, and taking part in the less energetic activities of the S.A.C.'s International Free Climbing meeting. The meet had been a hugely successful affair. Young climbers, men and women, from many nations had been invited to attend, and climbing on the great limestone cliffs of the nearby Salève had been of a high standard. We three were largely 'observers': the only stance that older climbers can take when confronted with the incredible energy and abilities of the young (yet dreaming the secret dream that once, when we also were young, it was the same for us!)

The conversation between Tom and André, friends for 30 years, drifted backwards and forwards. I, mind in neutral, joined in the gossip as its trend leant my way, and effortlessly fell under the spell of Geneva, the most elegant of cities.

Suddenly André announced, 'I'm picking up Loulou'.

I saw her standing on the pavement in the city centre, a small, rather lonely figure. She was dressed in a long, fawn gaberdine-type overcoat, which tended to make her seem even more forlorn. Her dark hair was uncovered. It was difficult to see her as anything else but some little shopper waiting for the street lights to change and largely engrossed, one imagined, with the problems of daily survival. Could this be Loulou?

It was! The instance she got into the car, everyone's mood leapt into top gear. It was quite remarkable. Within seconds we were captivated by Loulou Boulaz, that fabulous woman climber of so many years ago.

The early years

Loulou Boulaz was born in Avenches in Switzerland in 1912, and went to live in Geneva when she was nine years old. At high school her ability and staying power – particularly at gymnastics – began to point the way to a great climbing career.

In those early years, skiing played an important part in her life. She was a member of the Swiss national team from 1936 to 1941, was the international champion of France in 1936 and 1937 and, in the same year, she came third in the World Slalom Championships in Chamonix.

But at the age of 20 she was persuaded by Raymond Lambert, the great Swiss climber who also lived in Geneva, to try climbing. Her earliest climbs with Lambert were in the Salève, where she later made the first ascent of one of the classic routes on the big cliff, Les Paturages. Soon, however, Mont Blanc claimed her attention.

On her first trip to Chamonix they climbed the Aiguille de Peigne, a summit of over 3,000 m (9,840 ft). From then onwards, all through the season, they went every weekend by bicycle from Geneva to Chamonix.

The series of *cordée féminine* climbs she did with Lulu Durand in the early and mid-'30s – the S. W. Face of the Dent du Géant, the Requin, the Grands Charmoz traverse and that of the Droites – were all first ascents by a woman.

Loulou's major climbs

Loulou's record of major climbs reads like a mountaineer's dream list. As well as her successes in the Mont Blanc massif, in the Oberland, the Valais, and the Dauphiné, she has climbed in the Dolomites, the Caucasus, the Himalayas and in the Sahara (where at the age of 65 she climbed several of the Aiguilles in the Mountains of the Air, and made the first ascent of Tour Loulou!). Indeed, many of her climbs were first female ascents – and some were particularly notable, such as the North face of the Petit Dru with Raymond Lambert, which also happened to be the second ascent by anyone, and necessitated two bivouacs. This stupendous 800 m (2,625 ft) face, first climbed in 1935 by Pierre Allain and Raymond Leininger, remains one of the great classic routes in the Mont Blanc region. It is an expedition which still defeats some of the most experienced parties.

Her list also includes the formidable South Arête of the Aiguille Noire de Peterel, the Red Sentinel and the Pear Routes on the Brenva Face of Mont Blanc, North Face of the Aiguille du Plan, the Bec D'Oiseau by the East Face (which was also a first ascent) and many others on the Mont Blanc range. Numerous ascents in the Dolomites fell to her, too, including that most unbelievably steep wall, the North Face of the Cima Grande di Lavaredo – 300 m (985 ft) of vertical and overhanging cliff.

In the Valais, the North Face of the Velan and the North shoulder of the Rothorn were also first ascents. Whilst on the mixed routes in the Bernese Oberland, ascents of the North Faces of the Schreckhorn, the Studerhorn (another new route) and the Jungfrau all became first female ascents.

The 'Last Great Problems'

The history of climbing anywhere is a saga of 'Last Great Problems'. In 1930 there were three. These were the North Faces of the Matterhorn (also known as the Cervin), the Grandes Jorasses and the Eiger. All became lodestars for the ambitious climbers of the day.

The first to 'go under' was the North Face of the Matterhorn. In July 1931 (the year before Loulou began to climb), two young German climbers, the brothers Franz and Toni Schmid, cycled out from Munich with their camping and climbing gear on their backs, and established their base below the North Face. After two days of hard climbing, the final section during a ferocious storm, they reached the summit on 1st August.

The Grandes Jorasses

The second of the 'Big Three' to be climbed was the Grandes Jorasses. It is this climb, possibly more than any other made by Loulou, that has meant so much to her. Her part in the initial exploration is intimately woven into the history of this huge face.

The great wall, collectively known as the North Face of the Grandes Jorasses, is one of the most imposing in the Mont Blanc range – indeed, in the Alps. On the other hand, the summit of the peak is not as impressive as so many others in the massif, being more a collection of knobs or points running roughly west to east, across the summit ridge.

The Central Spur
The highest of these knobs, at 4,208 m (13,806 ft), is known as Pointe Walker (after Lucy's brother, Horace, who reached it with Melchior Anderegg, J. Jaun and F. Grange in June 1868). It is only 24 m (78 ft) higher than the next one to the west on the summit ridge, Point Whymper (named after that indefatigable peak-bagger who ascended to it in 1865 mainly to get a view of the Aiguille Verte across the way). Further west still are Pointes Croz (4,110 m or 13,484 ft), Hélène (4,045 m or 13,271 ft), Marguerite (4,066 m or 13,340 ft) and Young (3,996 m or 13,110 ft). None of these in themselves presents a fearful challenge, being readily accessible by a long traverse across the summit ridge from the col in the west. However, the enormous wall falling to the north from the summit corrugations is another matter entirely.

The wall itself is not a flat plate like many limestone cliffs, but is a collection of very steep spurs, each one rising to its own particular summit knob. The two largest of these are the Walker Spur, some 1,200 m (3,900 ft) in vertical height, which rises to Pointe Walker, and the equally massive but slightly shorter Central Spur that ascends to Pointe Croz. In the early summer of 1935 this great face was still unclimbed, despite numerous attempts.

The North Face of the Grandes Jorasses, one of the last great challenges of the Alps and one in which Loulou Boulaz played a major role. *(André Roch collection)*

Beneath the face is the Leschaux glacier near to which, and named after it, is the Leschaux hut. This was the operations' base for attempts on the wall. The first serious attempt on the face was made in 1928 by a party of six, which included the legendary Armand Charlet. They attacked by way of the Walker Spur, but this attempt failed.

In 1931 a German team, Heckmair and Kroner, tried the central Couloir between the two great spurs – also without success. A few days after this attempt two more Germans, Brehm and Rittler, tried the same route and were killed. Two years later the great Italian climbers Gervasutti and Zanetti tried the central Spur. They got to 3,500 m (11,480 ft), some 400 m (1,300 ft) above the start but still a long way from the top of Pointe Croz. The following year, 1934, Armand Charlet with Robert Greloz attacked the central Spur again – but had to retreat.

Within the month there were more strong attempts. Four parties were simultaneously on the Spur. They were Peters and Haringer (German), Charlet and Belin (French), an Austrian party, and Gervasutti and Chabod (Italians). Bad weather came on. Everyone, except the two Germans, decided on retreat. Peters and Haringer continued until they, too, were turned back, even though they had climbed the crux. On the descent Haringer fell and was killed; Peters completed the descent alone.

In late June 1935, the contenders for the Central or Croz Spur once more returned to the attack. This time they included the tiny 23-year-old Loulou Boulaz and Raymond Lambert. As she walked up to the hut alone to join Lambert Loulou met her fellow Genevoise climbers André Roch and Robert Greloz coming down. These two had actually got as far as the Second Tower, one of the principal landmarks on the route, at which point Greloz had dislocated his shoulder. Even though Greloz had wanted to carry on, wisdom had prevailed and the pair decided to retreat.

Left to right: Loulou Boulaz and Raymond Lambert at the Leschaux hut prior to embarking on the mighty challenge of a first ascent on the North Face of the Grandes Jorasses in 1935. *(Loulou Boulaz collection)*

However, there was much more worrying news for Loulou. Two Germans were on the face. One of them was Rudolf Peters (of the previous year's attempt), with another climber, Martin Meier. They had been on the face for two and a half days. If the weather held, there was every chance Peters and Meier would make it to the top.

At the Leschaux Hut there were also Gervasutti and Chabod, the very strong Italian team. Lambert and Loulou discussed plans with them, and in the early hours of 1st July 1935 the four of them left the hut and headed for the Central Spur. After two days and one night of epic struggle, battered by storm, they finally emerged onto the summit ridge. There they saw, by the tracks, that undoubtedly Peters and Meier had reached the summit first. This was corroborated by the entry in the Hut log book, which showed clearly that they had been beaten to the first ascent by two days. Nevertheless, as Chabod said, it gave them the first ascent by a woman!

The Walker Spur
The Walker Spur held out for a further three years – almost to the day – when another Italian team led by Roberto Cassin picked this 'Last Great Plum' in three days.

The Walker Spur is, wrote Rebuffat in *The Mont Blanc Massif:*[1]

> A route to dream of, perhaps the finest in existence. But, once again, if the climber wants to live up to his dreams, he must climb to the highest standard. Success is not a matter of scrambling up anyhow.

Seventeen years after the second ascent of the Central Spur (and its first female ascent) Loulou Boulaz was again at the Leschaux Hut with five companions intent upon an ascent of the Walker Spur. To save time it was decided to climb on two ropes of three. In the first rope were Eric Gachat, Loulou and Pierre Bonnant; in the second were Marcel Bron, Raymond Dreier and Claude Asper. If they succeeded, this, too, would be the first ascent by a woman.

The day began fine and dry; all was well except for the sheet lightning that streaked across the southern sky. 'The first real problem is the Rebuffat Fissure – it's a grade 6 pitch but it's the open sesame to the ascent,' Eric told them.

The day was very cold and their rucksacks were heavy. There were problems with rhythm, and their will had to be screwed up to the limit. Loulou tried to avoid communicating her thoughts to her companions, but the same reaction was written on all their faces: 'If it's like this here, at the start, what's it like higher up?'

As it happened, the crucial 75 m (250 ft) diedre and the diagonal abseil higher up, which they were dreading, were overcome without fuss. Above them was a sheet of very steep slabs – the Black Slabs – about which she mused as she stared up at them:

> neither the guidebook nor anyone else has been able to give us an exact description. To 'climb as best you can' is strange advice for pitches of the sixth grade.[2]

Loulou felt a distinct comfort in the knowledge that she was placed in the middle of the rope, with good climbers above and below. But the 'moment of truth' was at hand. Eric led straight up, then began to move right. 'That's a cow of a pitch ... I don't know where to go next', she heard him mutter. The rope passing through her fingers hesitated, then continued moving; again it halted, then again moved upwards.

'Three metres [10 ft] of rope left . . . One metre [3 ft] left. No more rope,'[3] she called.

Eric's reply came back, 'Start to climb, but I can't secure you from here!'

She began the ascent, heart thumping, but mentally assured by the intermediary pitons between Eric and her, despite their obvious precariousness. The Slabs yielded, and at last all three were above them, and Eric was still climbing strongly.

Higher up they reached a narrow platform, and below them they saw the second rope struggling upwards – but it, too, arrived safely on the platform. It was the point where Cassin made his second bivouac on the first ascent. Nightfall was not far away, and they decided to spend the night at Cassin's bivouac spot.

Suddenly, just as they settled into their sleeping bags, there was a crash of rock from high above and then around them. Pierre Bonnant began groaning in his sleeping bag, his face twisted, his body shaking with convulsions. A large block of stone had hit him full in the chest, just as he was dozing off. 'I was seized with fear and panic,' Loulou confided. 'What will become of him when we have to set off again?'

To add to the fears, the weather began to break. The lightning was now accompanied by thunder, nearer at hand – and lightning always means that a storm is brewing. The snow began to fall at about 5 a.m. They knew for certain that to survive they had to keep going upwards, that there was no way back down. Pierre's condition gave great concern. They tried to protect him as best they could. He kept repeating, mechanically, 'It will be all right, it will be all right.' They decided that despite the inconveniences and delays, it was better that the whole party form one rope.

The next section was a sweep of slabs – superb in fine weather, but now covered in snow. To climb it was a desperate fight. They moved slowly. The morning had almost gone before they were all up the steep wall above the bivouac. 'In *good* conditions it is all sixth grade (or plus) climbing. But now the snow makes it much harder.'[4] Finally, they emerged onto a small triangular area of snow – The Triangular Névé as it is called – below the final huge step. It was crossed without too much trouble.

Above the Névé the wall rears again into the vertical. This has to be climbed delicately to reach the chimney-crack system known as the Red Chimney. Eric Gauchat, still in front, was forcing the wall, belayed by Marcel Bron. Raymond Dreier was twenty metres (65 ft) lower, with the rope passed through a doubtful peg; Pierre and Loulou, at the entrance to a gully, were tied to an ice piton; Claude Asper, at the rear, stood some 10 m (33 ft) below them.

Suddenly, from high up came a cry, 'Look out!'. A large block which Eric had been using came away, and both he and the block were seen crashing downwards. Miraculously, he succeeded in catching one of his ropes (which he had passed through a piton) and managed to stop his fall. The other rope was cut to pieces by the block. The rest of the block hurtled straight down towards Loulou and Pierre, smashed into the rock a short distance away from them and broke into pieces. The flying debris scored a direct hit, and both Loulou and Pierre were swept off their feet to hang 'like puppets on a string'[5] on the doubtful ice piton in the gully. Loulou's forehead was cut by a flying splinter, but she knew, despite the flow of blood, that the cut was only superficial.

Eric, who had led from the start and was badly shaken by his fall, now relinquished the leadership to Marcel Bron.

The long rope was stretched to its limit in the Red Chimney. The snow fell ceaselessly and curtains of powder swirled about them. Everything that fell from above was channelled towards them. Progress became slower. For hours on end, it seemed to her, Loulou stood on a small ridge, a little sheltered, exchanging from time to time a few words with Claude Asper who was not far below her.

'A huge indifference overcame me,' she said,

> Condemned to doing nothing and incapable of influencing events, it was with complete detachment that I saw, passing me, a small rope, a glove, a hat . . . What a struggle they must be having up there![6]

Not far away Raymond was reassuring Pierre, who was having great difficulty in crossing a large overhang. Pierre was very nearly at the end of his strength. He and Raymond had been under the avalanche for hours; snow had accumulated in front of them and had covered them, pushing them backwards.

From above came a cry. Most of the sounds were lost in the mist, but they knew what was happening. Exhausted, conquered by the cold, Marcel had slipped and fallen a few metres. They could not go on. Night was on them once again. It was essential to bivouac – but where? In the Chimney, where everything was vertical and where rocks were glazed and would hardly hold a piton, a bivouac was impossible.

Finally, they discovered a sort of sloping traverse where, hanging by a piton one against the other and incapable of movement, they prepared to spend the night.

The snow stopped, but it was replaced by a probing north wind to which they became an easy prey. The temperature dropped lower and lower. Wet clothing was now case-hardened with ice. They were attacked by cramp as well as by cold, and the wall resounded to their groans and curses. Their teeth chattered. That dreadful night seemed eternal.

Finally, the first dawn light tinged the sky. The cold was even more intense, but gradually the sun touched the wall and moved down towards them.

It was time to move. Claude Asper, being very experienced on mixed terrain, took the lead. Normally it would have been Pierre, a great master on ice, who would have taken over. But Pierre was incapable. He had held out with admirable courage and extraordinary endurance, at what cost and by what depth of resources of human spirit no one could tell. His distant air worried Loulou.

She had now been relegated to the last position on the rope, where her primary job was to recover the pitons that had been hammered into rock or ice. It was two hours before she was able to evacuate this place which, she declared, she both wanted and feared to leave.

Above, her friends were engaged in forcing the wall. They were invisible to her, but she could hear their shouts – and they were not comforting noises. Yet, despite it all – the cold, the weariness – they pushed upwards, and the angle eased into the sun. Its warmth plunged them into a state of utter exhaustion. This, as every mountaineer knows, is the greatest danger period: when one relaxes from concentration and when, on easy ground, one can trip over a stone or a bootlace and plunge over an edge.

This became suddenly apparent when Claude Asper yelled, 'Look out, move aside'. In his arms was a huge block which he was trying to hold back. Its weight forced him to let go – but no one moved! Miraculously, it passed them by. The event produced no reaction from any of them.

They fell asleep whenever they stopped, and each one in turn had to be

Loulou Boulaz on the Au Col d'Argentières in 1951. *(Loulou Boulaz collection)*

awakened by the shaking of the rope from the companion above – and sometimes, when they finally ascended to the person who was supposed to be securing them, it was to find that he, too, was asleep.

They crossed the summit cornice almost in a daze.

> We were alive, we had won. But not one of us felt the sensation, the staggering sensation of victory[7]

Loulou was to recall later.

We remained sitting down, without a thought, watching the sun go down, all idea of time gone. An hour passed this way, whilst it seemed to us that we had been there only a few minutes. Then we began our descent.

Pierre Bonnant, completely dehydrated, stopped at each thin trickle of water to drink. How is he still standing?[8]

Night fell again. They were forced into another bivouac within an hour's distance of the hut, too tired to search the way. And Eric, 'in his young, never satisfied vitality says, "I'm hungry".[9] But they had had nothing left to eat for a long time. In the night Loulou was troubled by a nightmare of frozen feet and frost-bite; unfortunately, it was no dream!

At last the dawn came, and the weary party set off on the final short step to attain the security of the hut without further incident.

The Eigerwand

Success does not come easily at the top end of climbing endeavour. There are many times when it doesn't come at all; such was the case for Loulou with the Eigerwand.

This huge North Face of the Eiger was first climbed in July 1938. It was the climax of one of the most sustained attacks on any of the 'Great Problems' in the Alps. The whole saga of the Eiger was one of storms, avalanches, death, heroics and ambitions, before Harrer, Kasparek, Heckmaier and Vorg achieved success. Many lives have been lost on this ferocious face – and still are!

Some four years after the first ascent, Loulou and Pierre Bonnant made their next attempt. Bad weather forced their retreat. A year later the same two were back again, and the story was the same as the year before.

Again, in 1958, Loulou returned with Michel Vaucher, still without success. She went back a fourth time with Michel and Yvette Vaucher and Michel Darbellay in 1962; still the Eigerwand had not been climbed by a woman. On this occasion they went higher than she had ever been before. But again, atrocious conditions – avalanches and bad weather – caused their retreat.

In Geneva, 20 years later, she laughed as she talked about it. 'Four times we tried the Eiger, four times we had to retreat. But,' and her eyes twinkled, 'I'm still alive!'

The ascents to which she aspired were prodigious problems by anyone's standards, and at the time she was involved with them, her peak years, she stood alone amongst women and shoulder to shoulder with the best of male equals – to the wonder of many of them, and an inspiration to her women contemporaries and generations yet to come.

Chronological list of events

1912 Loulou Boulaz born.
1921 Moved to Geneva.
1932 Began climbing on the Salève and at Chamonix.
       First all-female ascent of Dent du Requin, with Lulu Durand.
1933 First all-female ascent of Dent du Géant, with Lulu Durand.
1935 First all-female traverse of S.W. face and N.W. ridge of Grands Charmoz.
       First all-female traverse of Les Droites.
       Second ascent and first women's ascent of Central Spur of Grandes Jorasses.

1936   Second ascent and first female ascent of North face of Petit Dru.
1936 & 1937   Loulou became French International Ski Champion.
1936–41   Member of Swiss national ski team.
1937   Third in World Slalom Championships.
1941   First ascent of Zinal Rothorn.
1952   First female ascent of Walker Spur of Grandes Jorasses. Aiguille Verte.
1959   Cho Oyu.
1977   Montagnes de l'Air, including first ascent of Tour Loulou.

References

[1]Gaston Rebuffat, *The Mont Blanc Massif* (Kaye & Ward, 1974), p. 230/[2]Loulou Boulaz, 'Dans La Face Nord Des Grandes Jorasses' (7-page essay, not folioed, written 15 Jan. 1966) (Birkett Collection)/[3]ibid./[4]ibid./[5]ibid./[6]ibid./[7]ibid./[8]ibid./[9]ibid.

4

Nea Morin – a family affair

If the fundamental definition of a mountaineer is one who is skilled in climbing mountains, then there can never be any doubt that Nea Morin was such a person. However, the more one gets to know of her, the more inadequate the term becomes. That she was a fine mountaineer (and many, like Charles Marriott, would say she was the greatest British female mountaineer between the wars) is never in question, but her relationship with mountains did not begin and end with a demonstration of her skills in the climbing of them. In essence, she loved mountains – to be amongst them, to scale them, to climb rocks and to teach others to do the same, to introduce beginners, to foster and develop this love in her own family so that mountains took a major position in all their lives. This was something of what mountains meant to Nea Morin. But it went so much further . . .

Mountains sustained her at times of great personal difficulties and loss. When physical adversity and increasing years beset her, and when by far the majority of other mountaineers would have opted out, Nea continued to climb. Few climbers have won the respect and affection accorded to Nea Morin.

From Harrison Rocks to Arlberg

In a way her introduction to mountains was easy, even though on Tunbridge Wells Common close to where she lived, there is nothing that would warrant the title of a 'peak'. But there were rocks, Harrison Rocks and others. Her father was a member of the Alpine Club, and the family doctor was Claude Wilson, the Club's one-time President. Her first trip to Switzerland was made when she was six, but the onset of World War I stopped further visits (though not her climbing on the nearby rocks around Tunbridge Wells). It was not until 1922, when she was 16 years of age that she began to climb *real* mountains. It was in the Tirol at St Anton am Arlberg (now a great ski resort, but hardly renowned, even then, as a mountaineering centre, even though the peaks are around 3,000 m (10,000 ft) and snow-covered) that Nea Barnard, as she then was, became a mountaineer. To someone nurtured on Harrison Rocks, the peaks of Arlberg were 'pure heaven'.[1]

This was just the beginning. In 1923 and 1925 she returned with her family to the scene of her first childhood scrambles, Diablerets. With her elder brother, Mordo, she set off to climb the Diableret (3,246 m or 10,650 ft) by the Paprioz Glacier. The expedition was guideless, and developed into a test of judgement on the descent. Neither trusted that of the other! These were early lessons for her in route finding and assessment.

Chamonix and Fontainebleau

1926 was to prove to be the year of destiny. In that year, with her companion Winifred (Jo) Marples, she made her first trip to Chamonix. It was a splendid season for them. It included the traverse of the Grands Charmoz and Aigs. du Mummery–Ravanel, ascents of the Grépon and the Dent du Requin; but more importantly, as it turned out, they met at the Couvercle Hut one of the best-known climbers of the day. His name was Jean Morin: a highly experienced mountaineer, and a founder member of the very prestigious *Groupe de Haute Montagne.*

The following year Nea and Jo were invited by Jean to join his group in Chamonix, one other member of which was Micheline, Jean's sister. At the end of that season Jean and Nea became engaged, and were married several months later. In 1931 Nea's daughter Denise was born, and four years later her son, Ian.

After a brief sojourn in London, the Morins moved to Paris, and here Nea became included in the 'Bleau' group. This comprised climbers who frequented the rocks at Fontainebleau on the outskirts of Paris, which was then, as it still is, a ferocious training ground for rising stars. Micheline climbed there, and it was at Bleau that Nea met Alice Damesme, with whom a deep and lasting friendship developed. Later, these three – Alice, Micheline and Nea – were to leave a very significant record in the pages of women's climbing history.

In Britain at that time, leads of the great classic rock climbs were being ticked off. In 1926 Mabel Barber made the first women's ascent of what was probably Britain's greatest challenge: the Central Buttress of Scafell. Thirteen years later this splendid route was led for the first time by a woman, Alice Nelson (better known as 'Jammy' Cross). Phyl White (now Mrs A. E. Wormell) made the ascent of the climb nine times. All of these were remarkable performances on a crag which, at the time, was considered to be the most serious undertaking in the Lake District, if not in Britain.

Also, there had been a determined struggle by women for recognition, particularly in the field of politics, but any success achieved here did not necessarily permeate the family structure.

Jean and Nea were both very conscious of the objective dangers of climbing: they were not unfamiliar with the sadness attending the death of good climbing friends in the mountains. They decided, because of their young children, it would be to the family's advantage to climb on separate ropes where possible.

En cordée féminine

To what extent this decision influenced their plans in 1933 we cannot say, but in that year Alice, Micheline and Nea secretly discussed a possible traverse of the Meije in the Dauphine Alps (and the last major peak in the Alps to be climbed). Their route was to be *en cordée féminine* – a women-only rope. In the meantime tragedy struck, at first on Mont Pelvoux, where a fellow member of the Groupe de Haute Montagne (G.H.M.) had been killed, and a short time later to a small party who were traversing the glacier just below the Morins. Involved in the unsuccessful attempts to get the body of the leader out of the crevasse into which he had fallen, the experience did little for their morale.

> It now seemed doubtful whether Alice, Micheline and I would ever get Maurice (Damesme) and Jean to consent to our proposed *cordée féminine* on the Meije.[2]

Consent of a male spouse was still considered necessary in 1933!

However, the traverse was made. The husbands reluctantly agreed to give their consent to the venture. A few days later, after parting from Maurice and Jean, the three women ascended to the Promontoire Hut. It is at the foot of the

Left to right: Micheline Morin, Nea Morin, Alice Damesme in 1933 at the Aigle hut after the traverse of the Meije 'en cordée féminine'. *(Alpine Club Library collection)*

main ridge up which the ascent of the Meije is made. Here, despite having parted from him a few days before, they found Maurice

> unable to keep away. He told us that the day on which we had intended to traverse the Meije was an unlucky date for him. Now that it was safely passed he wanted to come along too.[3]

Despite argument they set off with Maurice and *three* friends (enough to help – should and when it be required!) in close attendance.

Technically speaking, this was the first traverse of the Meije by an all-women party, but it was not quite the victory they would have preferred. Nevertheless, it was their first major *cordée féminine* climb. Nea's appetite was obviously whetted. Things would be different next year!

The Aiguille de Blaitière

In that year, 1934, they decided to 'do' the Aig. de Blaitière. The excitement 'at going off without husbands and brothers' was delicious.

Alone at last! Alice, Micheline and I found ourselves on the terrace of the Montenvers Hotel, having just speeded our male friends and relatives on their way to the Requin Hut, thus accomplishing by far the most difficult and trying part of our programme.

All summer we had hoped to do a climb really on our own, but the way of the would-be 'man-less' climber is fraught with many an obstacle unknown to the general mountaineering public. Several times we had been together on a rope, but always with a party of friends near at hand . . . and under such conditions more than half the sense of adventure is lost.[4]

Much of the organisational success that had been achieved on this occasion was due to Micheline. The men had proposed a big expedition with the women being allowed to follow *en cordée féminine*, where they could be under constant supervision as surreptitiously as possible. They hoped the women, if they used their imaginations, could pretend they were on their own!

Micheline had other ideas. When they all assembled to sort out the details Micheline, 'with a warlike glitter in her eye', blandly told the menfolk that the women were going off to do something else, totally on their own. It was very much a case of 'lump it or leave it'.

Alice and I sat tight waiting for the inevitable explosion, for on these occasions Micheline was the spokesman [sic] of the party. Throughout the season Maurice had manoeuvred successfully to keep his wife in sight, so it was little wonder that he was not pleased with the plan. Micheline had hard work to obtain the required permission, but as a valiant and experienced manless climber she had all the answers.[5]

This, of course, was 1934 – a far cry from 1984 or, for that matter, even 1954.

One finds it hard, at this distance, to comprehend the shackles placed upon these three women climbers (and many others like them) – three climbers who could be rated amongst the best of their time.

As it happened, the expedition turned out to be a marvellous day. Everything went right: weather, form, making good time. At one stage they caught up with a guided party.

They seemed surprised to see us, and still more surprised when we politely declined their good-natured offer of a rope up the next pitch, and in consequence had to try to look as professional and dignified as possible while giving the leader a shoulder up. We were touched by the fatherly eye kept on us by the guides; more than once they offered us aid or tips as to what to do, though of course with the condescending masculine amuse-yourselves-as-much-as-you-like-and-we-are-always-at-hand-to-come-to-the-rescue smile.[6]

Their climb went splendidly: all three summits of the Aiguille were reached, and then a cheerful descent to the Nantillons Glacier and eventually down to the Montenvers Hotel completed the outing.

At the Montenvers we met friends nearly all returning from successful trips, but no husbands or brother. A few minutes before the last train to Chamonix, Maurice turned up bathed in perspiration and ready to be furious had we not been there. He had raced down from the Requin Hut, in something less than half the usual time, saying to himself, if they do the three peaks they are sure to miss the last train, and then won't I scold them! I think he was almost disappointed to find us washed and brushed and cool, comfortably installed drinking tea with friends.[7]

The climb, although far from being the hardest they had done, had given them enormous satisfaction.

The Second World War

Two more excellent seasons were to follow, in the Dolomites and again at Chamonix . . . then came World War II.

Nea took the children to Britain to where Jean escaped when the fall of France was imminent. In 1943 he was killed on a mission with the Free French Forces.

Nea hid her grief and turned even closer to the mountains. In Wales, where she now lived with the children, she climbed extensively.

She later wrote:

> Since 1940 Wales and the Welsh mountains have played such a large part in my life that, although I love the Alps and always long for the high peaks and glaciers, it is, I think, to Wales that I would return for comfort and understanding . . . these very old hills somehow gave me confidence, a deep feeling of security, of peace and hope even in the face of tragedy.[8]

On the Welsh rock, her Fontainebleau-developed technique paid dividends. In Wales she met and climbed with the best climbers of the day – and not merely to hold their ropes.

In 1941, with J. Menlove Edwards as second, she made the first ascent of a climb on Clogwyn Y Grochan (one of the three cliffs which became a focal point of Welsh climbing for decades). The climb was called 'Nea', after her. It was one of the very few first ascents at the time to be led by a woman; even today, when so many more people climb, and when such a welter of new climbs are made each year – albeit, for the most part, short, one pitch gymnastic problems – there are few first ascents which are led by women! 'Nea', which the 1981 guidebook[9] called a 'Magnificent route of great character', is 70 m (230 ft) high and is graded Severe.

She also made, with John Barford as second, an ascent of the Curving Crack on Clogwyn du'r Arddu (the Black Cliff), which was considered by many climbers of the day (at least the Welsh-based ones) to be the most ferocious cliff in Britain. This female lead was certainly one of its best in Britain at the time, and most probably a first lead by a woman climber.

The post-war years

In 1947 Micheline and Nea returned to Chamonix to attend the International Climbing Meet. It was a star-spangled gathering. Micheline was one of the organisers as well as a representative of the G.H.M.; Nea described herself as 'a hybrid British–French representative for both the B.M.C. and the G.H.M.'[10] Jean Franco and his wife Jeanne, the leaders of the Meet, presided over a wonderful atmosphere of goodwill and enthusiasm. Some fine climbs were done – and Micheline and Nea climbed the Dent du Requin *en cordée féminine*!

That year had a more significant turn of events: Denise, now 16, and Ian, 12, joined her in the Alps. It was the beginning of many family climbing days, and the forerunner of what proved to be one of the most successful mother/daughter climbing teams in climbing history.

In 1953 in particular, Nea and Denise enjoyed some fine climbs: the north face of the Cima Piccola di Lavaredo, the traverse of the Vajolet Towers in the Dolomites, and the Traverse of the Weissmies, by the North Ridge and the Ordinary Route with Charles Marriott. These were all led by women.

In North Wales they had been attacking the great classics, including Long-

Nea Morin outside an Alpine mountain hut in 1953. (*Janet Adam Smith collection*)

land's climb (Denise leading) whilst it was snowing. Overhanging Bastion, on Castle Rock of Triermain in the Lake District also fell to them (when, in the 'pre-protection' days of 1955, it was still considered to be a fine achievement).

However, an ominous crack was developing in the armour of this remarkable woman, now nearing 50 years of age. On an excursion from the Schönbühl hut over the Col d'Hérens and down to Arolla with Janet Adam Smith (now Mrs Janet Carlton), she noticed a strange ache in her hip and back. Whatever the pains of the troublesome hip Nea still climbed.

The South Pillar of the Ecrins, the Dent du Géant and a *cordée féminine* ascent of the Mer de Glace face of the Grépon led by Denise, were the best climbs of 1955. In 1958 she returned to the Dauphiné once again, this time with Janet Adam Smith. Their chosen route was the Traverse of the Meije, guideless. It was to be, as she said, her last big climb in the Alps – but far from the end of her climbing life.

Left to right: Nea Morin and Micheline Morin descending from Aigle in 1958. (*Janet Adam Smith collection*)

Nea Morin outside the Weischorn hut in 1953. *(Janet Adam Smith collection)*

In the Himalayas

In 1959 she was invited to join Emlyn Jones' expedition to the Himalayas to climb Ama Dablam. She accepted the invitation and, despite a knee injury sustained on Harrison Rocks a few days before departure date, left London in mid-March for Delhi. From Delhi she flew to Kathmandu.

Her knee was still badly swollen when the time came to embark on the 240 km (150 mile) trek into the Base Camp at 5,000 m (16,500 ft), some 1,830 m (6,000 ft) below the summit of the superb pinnacle of Ama Dablam. She feared she would need to withdraw from the expedition almost before it started, but Fred Jackson, the expedition doctor, handed her an elastic knee bandage and said 'Here, try this!' She accepted the instruction and the bandage, and set off.

The journey was gruelling, but despite the added pains of blistered feet she arrived at the Base Camp, lighter in weight but able to participate. The attempt on the North East ridge of Ama Dablam is now history. Four camps were set up on the ridge above the point known as the 'Notch', where difficulties commence. On the 19th May Mike Harris and George Fraser set off from Camp IV intending to establish Camp V, from which to make a summit bid. They were seen next day preparing the way to the top of the wedge of ice and snow, known as the Pyramid.

On the 21st they were seen on the Pyramid going well. The day was fine and all seemed set for success. On the 22nd the weather became warm and the air was full of the rumblings of avalanches. Later came thick mist and snow flurries; then the weather broke. Mike and George were never seen again, and the little expedition, now reduced to four, set off with their sherpas on the long haul back.

For Nea physically it had been a very demanding exercise. Yet, as she said:

I learned how the body can adapt itself to conditions that one would normally consider crippling, and yet still capable of great physical effort . . . And even had I been able to foresee that it would end my climbing days, I still think I would have taken the opportunity to go.[10]

Still climbing at 70

After her return from the Himalayas Nea developed osteo-arthritis in her hip, and in 1963 had an operation which resulted in one leg being shorter than the other and a stiff hip.

It was characteristic of the woman that she still continued to climb. Hill walking, especially downhill, was difficult, but she could still get up climbs of Hard Severe grade. Each climb, even old familiar ones, had to be re-learned.

At 70 years of age this remarkable climber, complete with stiff leg, again ascended 'Nea', her first ascent of 1941.

Barbara James, herself a very fine rock climber and mountaineer with an impressive record of British, Alpine and Himalayan achievements to her credit, said:

When I first met her she was already an old lady in climbing terms. It was at the Pinnacle Club Hut and the first thing that struck me was the awe and obvious esteem in which she was held by members. At first, all I saw was a very thin lady with a stick and a limp and I wondered why! It was in the Dolomites where I found out.[11]

Nea Morin on the Mer de Glace face of the Grépon in 1955. *(Nea Morin collection)*

Despite her infirmity she returned time and again to the Alps, mostly in groups which included her old contemporaries. In 1971 she was climbing in the Maritime Alps. Then, in 1972 she attended a club meet at the Sella Pass (Dolomites). Here Nea climbed a grade 2/3 route on the Cinque Torri. She was unable to bridge across a chimney because of her hip, but by falling across the chimney with her hands together on one wall and feet together on the other, she was able first to move her feet up until she was nearly horizontal, and then to work her hands up on the opposite wall until she approached the vertical again. She also developed an ability to see and assess the holds and know how to make use of them, without resorting to several energy-wasting attempts to find out.

On this meet with her old friends she made the traverse of the Fünffingerspitze, which is Grade 4 in parts. First she took the ski-lift up to the Demetz Hut; then, with the help of her walking stick, she got down the scree from the Hut and across to the base of the climb. Once on the rocks she was in her element. Even the very steep corner near the top did not present insuperable problems. The traverse completed, the party descended by long abseils to the Demetz Hut. On their arrival at the col, they met up with a large party of Italians who stared in disbelief at these elderly women, including one with a limp and a walking stick, who came off the end of the abseil rope.

There were three happy journeys, with Margaret Darvall, to join the Rendez-vous Haute Montagne – an international women's climbing meet – at Engelberg, Kranska Gora in Yugoslavia, and Zermatt. Although Nea didn't actually climb, she considerably enjoyed the company of the many kindred spirits from several countries.

Nea did, in fact, return to the Himalayas in 1978 with younger friends on a trekking trip to Kashmir. From Pahalgam and Sonamarg they walked into the hills, sleeping at rest-houses. During all this time Nea, suffering from a doctor's prescription that suppressed her appetite, was in considerable discomfort. This ability to suffer pain, the price she paid to be in the hills, was a source of wonder for those who knew of her courage.

But the cards had not all been dealt for Nea Morin: sadly, there was one card still in the pack. In 1982, at the age of 76, she suffered a devastating stroke which not even her indomitable will could conquer.

The respect and admiration that Nea Morin engendered is shared by great numbers of climbers – men, as well as women. Janet Adam Smith, her old companion of the Meije Traverse, has said:

> Her two most striking qualities as a climber – moral climbing qualities, I should say – were her utter lack of prima-donna attitudes and complete unselfishness.
>
> She was ambitious as any good climber is, to extend her range, do something yet more difficult, etc., but you never felt she was building herself up as a Great Climber, who had to display her climbs as trophies.
>
> And when she could have been off with her equals or near-equals, gaining new laurels she would spend much of her climbing time with people far below her in prowess, helping them to become better climbers and setting them possibilities of new achievements they hadn't thought they could manage . . .
>
> She certainly made me a much better climber, largely because when she was leading, one had such complete confidence in her judgement as well as her physical skill (and in her confidence in oneself) that, to one's amazement, one found a climb, that had seemed well out of reach, to be not too hard at all! I think particularly of a little climb in 1958, some days after she'd led me over the Meije, of the Aiguillette that looks down on the Lauzon Valley above Briançon. 'Not for me', I said, when I heard it was 'Cinq Sup' or some such. 'Rubbish', said Nea, 'you'll enjoy it.' And I did.[12]

There are mountaineers who have climbed harder and higher than Nea Morin, but there are none who have shown such a love of mountains for so long, who have overcome so much to express that love, or who have remained so faithful to the spirit of the game for so many years.

Some climbs by Nea Morin

Year	Ascent	Fellow climbers	Achievement
1927	Aig. de Roc	Jo Marples, Jean Morin, Robert Tézénas du Moncel, Paul Fallet	2nd ascent (1st guideless)
1933	La Meije (traverse)	Alice Damesme and Micheline Morin	1st female party
1934	La Grande Casse (traverse via North Face and Glacier des Grands Couloirs)	Alice Damesme and Micheline Morin	1st female party
1934	Aig. de Blaitière (by Rocher de la Corde)	Alice Damesme and Micheline Morin	1st female party
1937	Guglia de Amicis (Dülfer route)	Maurice Damesme	1st female lead
1938	Aigs. Mummery-Ravanel (traverse)	Maurice Damesme	1st female lead
1938	Punta Fiammes, S.E. Spigolo (Dimai route)	Maurice Damesme	1st female lead
1938	Aig. Qui Remue	Alice Damesme and Micheline Morin	1st female party
1941	Lorraine (Britain)	J. A. Barford	1st ascent
1941	Nea (Britain)	J. M. Edwards	1st ascent
1947	Dent du Requin	Micheline Morin	1st female party
1947	Aig. du Moine (S.W. ridge)	Micheline Morin	1st female party
1947	Aig. du Diable (traverse)	Micheline Morin	1st female party
1950	Les Cineastes (traverse)	Micheline and Denise Morin	1st female party
1951	Aig. du Grépon (by C. P. and Lochmatter Slab)	Tom de Lépiney and Etienne Bruhl	1st female lead
1951	Aig. du Chardonnet (by Forbes Arête)	Tony Moulam	1st female lead
1953	Matterhorn (Hörnli Route)	Ian Morin	1st British female lead
1953	Weissmies (traverse, North Ridge – Ord. Route)	Denise Morin and E. H. (Charles) Marriott	1st female lead
1953	Cima Piccola di Lavaredo (North Face)	Denise Morin	1st female party
1953	Vajolet Towers (traverse – Winkler, Stabeler, Delago)	Denise Morin	1st British female party
1954	Aig. de Sialouze (traverse)	Rie Leggett	1st female party
1955	Aig. du Grépon (Mer de Glace Face)	Denise Morin	1st British female party
1958	Dente del Cimon (via Langes)	Denise and Micheline Morin	1st female party
1958	La Meije (traverse)	Janet Adam Smith	Nea's last big Alpine expedition and the 1st female British party

Chronological list of events

1906 Nea Morin born.
1911 Climbing on Harrison Rocks with her father (A.C. member). First trip to
    Switzerland.
1923 Small climbs in Diablerets
1926 First trip to Chamonix, with Winifred (Jo) Marples: met Miriam O'Brien
    and many others.
    Traverse of the Charmoz, ascents of Grépon, Mummery Ravanel, Dent
    du Réquin.
    Met Jean Morin at Couvercle.
    First female ascent of Central Buttress of Scafell by Mabel Barker.
1928 Married Jean, went to live in London.
1929 Chamonix, Paris and Fontainebleau.
1931 Daughter Denise born.
1933 First all-female traverse of the Meije.
1934 All-women ascent of the Aig. de Blaitière.
1935 Son Ian born.
1939 First female lead of Central Buttress of Scafell by Alice Nelson ('Jammy'
    Cross).
1941 First ascent of 'Nea' on Clogwyn Y Grochan.
1943 Jean Morin killed.
1947 President of Ladies' Alpine Club.
1947 International Climbing Meet at Chamonix: *en cordée féminine* traversed the
    Aiguilles du Diable.
1948 Translated *Climbs of My Youth*.
1952 Translated, with Janet Adam Smith, *Annapurna* and *The Last Crevasse*.
1953 Ascents by Nea and Denise of north face of Cima Piccola di Lavaredo;
    traverses of Vajolet Towers and the Weissmies.
1954 President of the Pinnacle Club.
1955 Overhanging Bastion in the Lake District.
    South Pillar of the Ecrins, Dent du Géant and Mer de Glace face of
    Grépon.
1955 Translated, with Janet Adam Smith, *A Mountain Called Nun Kun*.
1957 Translated, with Janet Adam Smith, *Gervasutti's Climbs*.
1958 Guideless traverse of the Meije.
1959 Ama Dablam expedition.
1963 Operation for osteoarthritis.
1968 Autobiography, *A Woman's Reach*, published.
1972 Cinque Torri and Fünffingerspitze.
1976 Ascent of 'Nea'.
1981 Elected honorary member of The Alpine Club.
1982 End of climbing career (suffered a stroke).
1986 Died.

References

[1]Nea Morin, *A Woman's Reach* (Eyre & Spottiswoode, 1968), p. 108 (subsequent references
denoted by *AWR*)/[2]ibid., p. 63/[3]ibid., p. 64/[4]ibid., p. 65/[5]ibid., p. 66/[6]ibid., p. 68/[7]ibid., p.
71/[8]ibid., p. 89/[9]Geoff Milburn, 'Llanberis Pass' (*Climber's Club Guidebook*, 1981), p.
25/[10]*AWR*, p. 108/[11]ibid., p. 245/[12]Personal correspondence Janet Adam Smith/Peascod 1984

5

Gwen Moffat – freedom to climb

Kern Knotts Crack

It was a beautiful day in August, 1947. Bert Beck, George Rushworth and I had walked up to Kern Knotts, largely with the intention of introducing George to this beautiful, compact little crag on Great Gable, near the top of Sty Head Pass in the Lake District.

Bert and I knew Kern Knotts well. We had done all the climbs on the crag before, some of them a number of times. A great deal of variety is to be found there on its perfect rock: steep fingery cracks, strenuous chimneys, delicate face climbing, and of course that little climb, the Buttonhook route, which was the hardest one on Great Gable for many years – and of which we had made the third ascent in 1940 a few weeks after Jim Birkett had led the second. George had only recently begun climbing, but already he was shaping up into a very fine climber. He had reached the point in his development where exposure to short, steep, difficult climbs which take one's technique for an airing was just what was needed.

We began with Kern Knotts Crack, the old O. G. Jones classic, and after descending the enormously popular and nail-worn Chimney, ascended the West Buttress (Sansom and Herford's old climb) before winding our way back through the large boulders at the foot of the main face to reach the eastern wall before the sun had swung round too far. Innominate Crack would be good for George, we said.

The east face of Kern Knotts is not very high – only about 20 m (70 ft) or so. It is a very flat face, fairly steep and smooth, and cut by a deep continuous crack near the left hand end. This is Jones' Kern Knotts Crack (K.K.C.). At the other end of the wall is a very large overhang of rock beneath which, in those days, was a huge block split off from the main face to form a superb lay-back corner crack. This was called the Sepulchre, after the cave that existed between the top of the layback block and the roof of the overhang.

Between Sepulchre and K.K.C. the face is uniformly smooth, rising at a continuously steep angle. It is split by a series of thin cracks which offer small but reasonably good holds for strong fingers, and demands sound technique if it is to be climbed properly. This is Innominate Crack.

Scrambling round the base of the buttress we suddenly discovered we were not alone. Whilst we had been on the other routes a couple more climbers had arrived. They were roping up at the foot of Innominate Crack.

One was small and lightly built, probably in her early twenties. Her dark-coloured jump suit had seen better days. Her feet were bare.

Her companion was male, large and awkward in comparison.

She began to ascend the crack, strong fingers and bare toes making light of the technicalities. Her climbing was effortless.

Bert, George and I stood in line at the foot of the crag transfixed. We had never seen anything like this on the hills before.

She was poetry in motion. Her laughter echoed around the cliff. We stayed watching until she had disappeared over the top of the wall, then we too climbed Innominate Crack – but it was not the same. Compared with the smooth, flowing rhythm of the woman's climbing, our efforts left much to be desired.

This was my first meeting with Gwen Moffat. As time went by I began to realise that on that day something different hit the crags. I had never seen any other woman climb as effortlessly as Gwen.

Her climbing in bare feet impressed me enormously. But isn't it logical enough, I realised afterwards? One does not wear gloves on the hands to give a better grip. The flesh friction is as perfect as one can expect, and the contact with the rock is at a maximum! If one has tough enough feet, why cannot bare feet give the same sureness of contact? But it was not just bare feet that made her climb well.

After that the name of this woman climber began to filter through more and more into the wilds of Lakeland – not because of the hard climbs she did, but because of what she stood for.

A product of changing times

Gwen Goddard (later to be known as Gwen Moffat) was a product of the rapidly changing times before and after the Second World War. She was born in Brighton in July 1924. During the war years she went from school into a newspaper office, but after a few months joined the Land Army. Tending animals had little appeal at the time, and for someone whose war-time dream was to be a guerrilla, it hardly gave the 'charge' for which she longed. She gave a false age, after working the Land for a year and a half, and joined the A.T.S. (Auxiliary Territorial Service).

Army life in Stoke on Trent left much to be desired. One day, below Cader Idris, she met a conscientious objector. His conversation fed her imagination and attracted visions of a carefree existence free from troublesome rules.

Early in 1946 she returned to North Wales on three weeks leave, and with her friend from Cader Idris made her first rock climbs on Idwal Slabs and Tryfan, and went up Crib Goch in a freezing, southwesterly gale.

Later she met her friend's companions. She rediscovered a freedom, however temporary and illusory, that war service had repressed. The minimal rules imposed by the small social group into which she had moved were in sharp contrast to the often inexplicable and sometimes implacable strictures of Army life. When the time came to return to Camp, doubts assailed her. That evening she deserted and made her way north – she was on the road for months.

Eventually she returned to Wales and threw in her lot with the friends from the cottage. From Wales she tramped and hitched lifts to Cornwall with a dog she called Thomas that had taken charge of her on the road. She slept in barns, deserted cottages and under caravans. Longing for Wales again, she begged a lift on a sailing boat and then trudged back to Nantmor.

Climbing, in its fullness, had not touched her deeply up to now. However, with Thomas she walked the ridges of Snowdon, Tryfan and the Glyders; it was on the latter, she recalls, that she realised she had 'come home'.[1]

That year she met the hard core of the climbing group in North Wales: Scottie Dwyer, Dickie Morsley, Yappy Hughes and others, and she began to climb regularly. One of the climbs, Holly Tree Wall, marked the end of what she calls her 'initiation phase'.[2] Many mountaineers will recall such a phase: when enthusiasm sometimes overrides judgement; when every hand hold and foot hold and the air beneath one's feet becomes joy and wonder and discovery; when the realisation is driven home, that what one really and truly wants to be, what one has been searching for all this time without knowing it, is this – to be a climber. This is what Holly Tree Wall meant for her that day. Now she says,

> I was completely converted to climbing and wanted no more beards and sandals and James Joyce. To me everything was in watertight compartments; it never occurred to me that a climber might read Joyce.[3]

But inside her all was not well; she gave herself up to a military policewoman on Chester station. By early 1947 she had served her time and the penances inflicted upon her for her former escapades, and was officially demobbed from the A.T.S. It was the beginning of her first great season.

Climbing, working and mothering

On her £50 gratuity she settled in North Wales, and took on a job over Easter as assistant warden at the Capel Curig Youth Hostel. That done, she then pitched her tent in Idwal. She climbed every day, with friends, acquaintances, strangers picked up on the roads or at the bottom of crags. When all these failed she climbed solo.

She was offered the use of a stone cottage on the moor above Bethesda until July. She survived by picking up odd jobs to augment her dwindling savings. From the security of a roof above her head and a base to which to retreat, her climbing skills developed at a remarkable speed.

By the end of July, she had done most of the 'Very Severe' routes in Idwal and had climbed on that most 'tigerish' of cliffs, Clogwyn d'ur Arddu.

In August she left her cottage, and with David Thomas went north to the Lakes. This (as Glencoe, Ben Nevis and the Cuillin in Skye still were) had been nothing more than a distant dream. Now she found the Napes and Kern Knotts, the Great Central Buttress of Scafell, Moss Ghyll Grooves, Pillar Rock and Dow Crag . . .

The next discovery had to be Scotland. There is nothing in Britain more wonderful than the rough gabbro of Sron na Ciche in the Cuillin of Skye in fine hot summer weather. The weather was perfect, and they revelled in it. Then it broke and they returned to the mainland and Ben Nevis.

Her money had now completely gone, and she began to look for work in Fort William. She got a job with the Forestry Commission, and was sent to a bothy in the Great Glen. Her companions on the job were all Scottish women who had no time for Gwen's off-the-job activities: climbing adventures, swimming nude in Loch Ness in winter, eating vegetarian food, writing short stories in a corner of the bothy.

She was leading, as she said, a normal, quite respectable life complete with pay-packet on Friday. But it was a shallow respectability. For the first time, after months of wandering, sleeping rough and grabbing happiness where she could, she began to feel the lack of a home life. There was little of it in the Forestry Commission bothy. She stuck the job until Christmas, then resigned and made her way to Glencoe, where she was due to meet David Thomas.

At the hostel she met another man; he was short, wiry, witty, 'with sparkling eyes and the agility of a monkey. His name was Gordon Moffat'.[4] A day together on the hills, and Gwen knew she had met a kindred spirit.

Eventually the two of them went to live in a cottage in Skye where, amongst other things, they did the traverse of the Main Cuillin Ridge. They spent 39 hours

The Black Cuillin Ridge on the Isle of Skye, along which Gwen Moffat made the record for the slowest traverse! *(Bill Birkett)*

on the gruelling ridge walk through some of the most exciting craggy mountain scenery in Britain, and put up a record for the *longest* time taken for the venture.

Later that year, after a visit to Chamonix, Gordon and Gwen were married and went to live in a cottage in Ro Wen in the Conway Valley in North Wales. By the new year of 1949 she found herself pregnant. This did not immediately slow down her mountain activities. In the meantime she decided to apply for membership of the all-women Pinnacle Club, and was invited to climb with its members at Easter. When she happened to mention at the top of the climb that she was pregnant and the baby was due in July, the news created consternation in the kindred ropes on the cliff.

In the summer of 1949, growing larger with child, she began to help Gordon to restore an old hulk they had found in the Conway estuary. It was a race against time to make the boat habitable for the arrival of the baby. Their daughter was born in August, and was named Sheena. Five days later they were all living on 'Lady Kathleen'.

Now came an additional problem to be sorted out: before climbing expeditions could be undertaken, Sheena had to be considered. Friends helped out. A problem less easily resolved was to follow: money was in short supply; no work was to be had. Gordon searched for employment in the Highlands and around Edinburgh, but could not find anything.

The distress of trying to exist against oppressive financial odds became intolerable. They lived in poverty, broken now and then by talks, including one on Skye, she wrote for the B.B.C.

She managed to climb occasionally, but these few experiences and the odd sale of her writing were not sufficient to stave off her sense of being trapped.

Gwen and Sheena went to live with Gwen's mother in Sussex. From here her life and Gordon's took their separate paths. With a little more security from her occasional sale of scripts and a job with a theatre company in Brighton, her mountain career began to expand.

In 1951 she made her first visit to the Swiss Alps and the Dolomites, where amongst other things she did the first female ascent of the Andrich Route on the Civetta, the Via Tissi on the Torre Trieste, the Marinella Couloir on Monte Rosa and the Rothorngrat. On her return from the Alps she and Sheena once again moved to Wales.

It was now Easter 1952. Gwen and Sheena found accommodation in the Pinnacle Club Hut in Cwm Dyli (they stayed six weeks). After spending Good Friday on Lliwedd with Charles Marriott, Gwen and one or two of the others repaired to the Pen y Gwryd Hotel. There she met a long-legged, talkative man who was to play a very large part in her life over the years. It was Johnnie Lees. Johnnie at the time was in the R.A.F. Mountain Rescue organisation. He was a very fine climber with considerable experience of all weather conditions and climbs throughout the U.K., and was an acknowledged expert on mountain rescue techniques.

Soon after this meeting, still desperately fighting the spectre of want, she applied for the job of resident warden at the Ro Wen Youth Hostel. She was given the job, and for a time Gwen and Sheena once more knew the security of a home.

Sheena was well cared for by helpful neighbours and hostellers, or by Gwen's mother, who visited them periodically. Gwen packed in climb after climb.

Under Johnnie's guidance she began to *think* on rock; the days of supreme confidence only last for a limited period! She learned better rope management and climbed in nails, which meant climbing on her feet – properly.

Guiding

During the winter months when the hostel was quiet and she was involved in a long run of prolific but financially unsuccessful writing, with a considerable number of rejection slips to her credit, the suggestion was put to her to become a guide. The idea was first advanced by Geoff Sutton, a fine climber of the post-war years. Mentally, she compared her own achievements and abilities with those of the only guides she knew: those in the Alps, Geoff and Scottie Dwyer. Her first reaction was to write the idea off as a temporary aberration on Sutton's part, and she did not talk about it again until the following spring. To her surprise, when she mentioned it to him, Scottie took the idea seriously and urged her to pursue it with all speed.

> I began to realise the enormous advantage of possessing a guide's certificate. There were women instructors working for the Central Council of Physical Recreation. With a guide's certificate behind me I could work full time at what was, to me, a fabulous salary. Sheena, who needed the company of other children, could go to a boarding school.[5]

The idea took deep root.

She planned and put into operation her programme to increase her knowledge, not only of climbing but of associated skills. She was invited to become a member of the Alpine Climbing Group: a group whose objectives included mountaineering of the highest standard. The only other women members were Denise Morin and Nancy Smith. In Wales and the Lakes she pushed up her standards. By the end of the following year she was exhausted. But she had worked hard to gain the necessary experience, and decided to put in her application to the British Mountaineering Council for a Guide's Certificate.

Some time later, whilst recovering in hospital from an operation, she received a letter from the B.M.C. She had been granted both of their Certificates; one was Grade I for rock climbing, and the other was Grade 2, for mountaineering. She became the first qualified female rock climbing and mountaineering guide in Britain, and one of only three instructors in Wales.

Becoming a qualified guide presented immediate problems if she was to take advantage of the qualifications. The first was to find work, and the second involved breaking up their secure retreat at Ro Wen. However, the decision had to be made; Sheena went to boarding school, and Gwen went to Scotland to recuperate and get into form after her six weeks' hospitalisation.

The winter was spent around Ben Nevis – good climbs were recorded – and she returned to Wales.

By Easter, her first guiding season began in earnest. She hitched up Langdale in the Lake District and took on her first group. She wrote[6]:

> On the first morning, I took them up Middlefell Buttress: five of us, all on one rope. It was slow, cold and boring. They climbed faster than I did, surrounded with an almost visible aura of masculine resentment. So I took them to Gwynne's Chimney on Pavey Ark, and as they struggled and sweated in that smooth cleft, with sparks flying from their nails, and me waiting at the top with a taut rope and a turn round my wrist, I knew that I had won. The atmosphere – when we were all together again – was clean and relaxed . . .
>
> I was no longer a woman with a reputation, but an instructor with a technique superior to theirs, and now we could settle down to work.

In the winter months Gwen worked hard at her writing; in the summer, she guided. In 1955 the summer was superb, until she cracked a bone in her ankle when she fell off a boulder.

It happened at a time when she was nearing the end of a series of courses that required her to give an assessment of the participants. After the slip, Johnnie took leave from his R.A.F. station and helped out with the practical business of putting the students through the routine. Gwen felt that she must do the assessment herself, and limped up to the foot of Idwal Slabs with her lower leg and foot in plaster. The plaster encased most of her foot, but by breaking away the front part of it she found she could free her toes sufficiently to get a grip on the rock.

Thus accoutred she led her party up Hope and Lazarus, some 150 m (500 ft) of rock, and found out, as she put it, 'What the students were like and could write a report with a clear conscience'.[7] There must be a record of *her* assessment of the *students* – there is no way of knowing what they thought of *her*! To be led sagely and sedately up a long climb is one thing – but being taken up by a leader with one leg in plaster is another!

Instructing

Gwen differentiates between 'guiding' and 'instructing'. The latter, she contends, is much harder. The best climbers are not necessarily the best instructors, and as anyone who has spent much time at the job will know, because instructing means getting down to a beginner's level over a prolonged period of time, it tends to bring down one's own climbing standard. On top of this is the weariness of it all. At the end of the week the clients go home to tell their friends all about it. The instructor/guide has to saddle up for a new group, rehash the introductory talk and get down again, for the 'umpteenth' time, to basic principles of rope management – and push the weariness into the background.

Brede Arkless, a highly experienced British mountaineer who lives in Wales and who holds the prestigious full Guides' Carnet. *(Bill Birkett)*

Since the days of Gwen Moffat, women have been included as instructors on the staffs of outdoor pursuits organisations. However, there is only one Briton who has attained the rigorous standards required of the U.I.A.G.M. (the International Union of Mountain Guides) for the award of the *carnet* as a *Bergführer*. She is the highly experienced Brede Arkless, who lives in Wales. On the continent there are others, such as the brilliant Martine Rolland of France, and Renata Rossi and Serena Fait of Italy; whilst in Switzerland the young Nicole Niquille is heading towards being the first ever Swiss woman guide.

Writing and exploring

In June 1956, Johnnie and Gwen were married. The honeymoon was spent in Skye and on Ben Nevis. The next year they visited Zermatt, and amongst other things, the Younggrat of the Breithorn, one of the great classic ridges in the Pennine Alps. It was one of the high points of her climbing years.

The winding down of Gwen's active climbing days saw an upsurge in production in her literary work. *Space Below My Feet*, *Two Star Red* and *On My Home Ground* were all published in the 1960s, and dwelt largely on her climbing career.

Her marriage to Johnnie Lees ended in 1969 and she became involved in conservation. From her new home in North Wales she voiced her concern on the pollution problem, wrote activist articles and 'Survival Count', and worked for several years on the British Mountaineering Council's Welsh Committee. For two years she was environmental columnist and book reviewer for *Climber and Rambler*. Her list of crime novels began in 1973.

Essentially a mountaineer who responds to rock climbing, ice climbing, ridge walking and exploration in equal measure, Gwen Moffat is probably best remembered for her mountaineering autobiographies, and the fact that she was Britain's first qualified woman rock climbing and mountaineering guide.

She has always been very much of a loner: someone who enjoys the solitude of the open spaces. When guiding seemed to be too organised, when it began to take on the trappings of a trade union, it was time, she felt, to turn her face again to the lonely trail.

In the late 1970s she was commissioned to write about and follow the pioneers of the overland trail from the Missouri River to California. As she had done many times before, she slept out in the open, alone, for six months or so. Out of the experience came *Hard Road West* and (her favourite book) *Buckskin Girl*. The mountains are never far away.

Again, from 1982 to 1984, she journeyed through the desert country of the South West, living near Joshua Tree in the early months, and spending the second winter researching and writing *Grizzly Trail*. This time also saw many explorations on her part into the mountains between the Rockies and the Pacific, into the Gros Ventres and Taylors and Spanish Peaks in Wyoming and Montana.

'Settling down' is a term foreign to Gwen Moffat's vocabulary. To her life is adventure: there might well be something happening over the next hill; there are more deserts and forests and above all mountains to explore, to look at and walk round and dream upon.

So, essentially Gwen Moffat was (and is) an explorer. From those early years, the mountain environment has been the lodestone of her explorations. In his foreword to *Space Below My Feet*, her first book, (Sir) Jack Longland wrote: 'Gwen Moffat is probably the best all round woman mountaineer in this country'. The

Gwen Moffat talking with Bill Peascod, April 1984. *(Bill Birkett)*

'Best This' and the 'Best That' are usually fairly debatable terms when applied in the context of mountaineering. Sufficient to say that she was regarded very highly as a climber by some of the ablest mountaineers of those years. Some of the grandest climbs of the period fell to her, either as leader or as follower.

In the mid-twentieth century, women were not free to abandon their 'domestic duties' whenever they felt like it, and rush off to the hills. But Gwen Moffat did just this, defying social conventions of the day to prove beyond doubt, though at some personal cost, that women could be as free as men to climb.

Chronological list of events

1924 Gwen Goddard born in Brighton.
1946 Began climbing in Wales.
1947 Began climbing seriously.
1949 Daughter Sheena born, married Gordon Moffat.
1951 Climbed in the Alps and Dolomites. First female ascent of Andrich route on the Civetta; Via Tissi on Torre Trieste; Marinella Couloir on Monte Rosa; Rothorngrat.
1952 Met Johnnie Lees.
1953 Became the first female qualified climbing and mountaineering guide.
1956 Married Johnnie Lees: honeymoon on Skye and Ben Nevis.
1957 Younggrat of the Breithorn.
1961 *Space Below My Feet* (Hodder & Stoughton) published.
1964 *Two Star Red* (Hodder & Stoughton) published.
1968 *On My Home Ground* (Hodder & Stoughton) published.
1969 Second marriage ended; became involved in conservation.
1972 *Survival Count* (Hodder & Stoughton) published.
1972 Began writing crime novels.
1978 Commissioned to follow and write about the pioneers' trail west.
1981 *Hard Road West* (Gollancz) published.
1982 Researched next series of books in U.S.A. until 1984.
1984 *Grizzly Trail* (Gollancz) published.

References

[1]Gwen Moffat, *Space Below My Feet* (Hodder & Stoughton, 1961), p. 42/[2]ibid., p. 43/[3]ibid., p. 44/[4]ibid., p. 83/[5]ibid., p. 183/[6]ibid., p. 213/[7]ibid., p. 248

6

Claude Kogan – the route to respect

Women in the Himalayas

Women had been climbing in the highest peaks long before Claude Kogan went to the Himalayas in the 1950s (Fanny Bullock-Workman had been there 50 years before, Annie Peck had been to the Andes at a similar time, and Una Cameron had climbed Mount Kenya in 1938). However, it was Claude's successes that caught women's interest in the high peaks on a grand scale, and so in the mid-'fifties there occurred a remarkable series of explorations by women in the Himalayas.

In the early part of 1955 the first women's expedition left for Kathmandu: a small group from members of the Ladies' Scottish Climbing Club. The expedition was modest in size and ambition, but it accomplished a great deal – not only glacier exploration and the summit of Gyalgen Peak (6,400 m or 21,000 ft), climbed by Monica Jackson and Betty Stark, but most importantly the proof that women could set up their own expeditions to remote places. They came back, not only alive, but with successful achievements to their credit.

Other all-women expeditions followed rapidly. In 1956 a small group comprising Joyce Dunsheath, Hilda Reid, Eileen Gregory and Frances Delaney – all from the Ladies' Alpine Club – went to the Kulu area of the Himalayas. Cathedral Peak (6,100 m or 20,000 ft) and Chapter House Peak (5,820 m or 19,100 ft) fell to Eileen Gregory. The Kulu area saw in 1961 yet another small team, Jo Scarr and Barbara Spark. They described themselves, rather tongue-in-cheek, as the Women's Kulu Expedition. This was mainly because it was felt by their friends that with some official title, however presumptious, they stood a greater chance of receiving financial and material support. This proved to be correct! Besides handling a welter of organisational problems, they made the first ascents of Central Peak, Lion Peak and Unnamed Peak, all in the Kulu Basin area and all around 6,100 m (20,000 ft).

The following year, after 'wintering' in India, they joined up with Countess Dorothea Gravina's all-women expedition to Nepal. The Jagdula Expedition, so named because of its intention to explore and climb in the Jagdula River area, comprised a strong team of six climbers. The other three were Denise Evans, Nancy Smith and Pat Wood. It was a very highly experienced team, and six peaks, the highest being Lha Shamma in the Kanjiroba Himal (6,400 m or 21,000 ft), were climbed. Bigger and even more successful expeditions were to follow.

Failure on Cho Oyu

On 26th October 1954, Claude Kogan, Raymond Lambert, Denis Bertholet, Jean Juge and two sherpas, Wongdi and Ang Namgal, occupied Camp IV in preparation for the second ascent of Cho Oyu (8,201 m or 26,906 ft) in the Himalayas – one of the prestigious eight-thousand metre (26,250 ft) peaks.

An Austrian team which was also on the mountain had had (following an 'agreement of honour' with the Swiss) two attempts at the peak. After being repulsed by high winds and low temperatures at the first attempt, the team finally reached the summit on its second one on 19th October 1954.

Lambert's party began its attempt on the second ascent soon afterwards. Despite being a highly successful expedition in scientific and exploratory terms, things had not gone as well as they might have done on the climbing front.

The Swiss team had comprised five climbing members but, for a variety of reasons, when the time came to make the summit bid only Kogan and Lambert were fit. In *White Fury*[1] Lambert says:

> I was surprised to see how enfeebled the expedition was becoming, with the exception of Claude Kogan and myself. Our companions were no longer putting up a fight; they could hardly struggle against the cold and were letting death creep upon them without striking a blow to defend themselves . . . the wind was sweeping all before it corrupting moral strength as well as physical.

All, that is, except that of the great Lambert – one of the all-time giants of the climbing world – and a woman of utterly indomitable courage, Claude Kogan.

The next day, after a fearful night spent in an ice cave hacked out of a shallow crevasse, Juge, Bertholet and the two sherpas had to go down. This left Lambert and Kogan in the crude shelter. They had decided that the summit bid should be made the following day.

Lambert wrote:

> The day passed quickly. Outside the sky was clear but violent gusts were tearing the snow from slope and ridge – all of it seemed to be flung down on us in minor avalanches. But we were no longer surprised at that. If one can fight altitude one can fight the rest. And we were fighting – against wind and cold, especially against cold.[2]

In these circumstances, Claude's steady uncomplaining attitude and her unshakeable determination to climb the next day were a tremendous support to Lambert. Throughout the day of waiting she quietly went about the necessary survival duties of cooking, tidying the snow cave, and blocking up holes to try to keep out the wind.

She worked in that camp, Lambert recorded later, like a sherpa. Next day they left Camp IV at 9 a.m. and after lashing on crampons, and roping up, headed for the summit, 885 m (2,900 ft) higher. The wind, already strong, began to increase in ferocity:

> It smote us continually, forcing us to climb one at a time belaying each other with the rope . . . when the worst gusts struck us it was fall flat on the stomach or be blown away. But we kept moving upward.[3]

The wind increased to such a velocity that they were reduced to crawling up the slopes on all fours, running out 18 m (60 ft) rope lengths at a time, alternating the 'leads'.

> I wanted to yell at this stubborn wind that it was useless to go on making life impossible for us,

wrote Claude in *White Fury*,

> Because we were just as stubborn as it was . . . It was better to stop worrying and try and advance methodically. I tried to make the wind help me by leaning forward on it – but immediately it dropped and I found myself face downwards on the snow with

all my breath gone and my mouth wide open gasping desperately for oxygen. Never have I had so furious a struggle with the elements.

At every gust we shut our eyes tightly and the whipped up snow lacerated our skin, its frozen dust stifling us and penetrating every chink in our clothing. But we went on, bent double, step by step, willing ourselves onward.

We spoke little. 'All right?' 'All right!' And that was all.

Once more Raymond stopped to refasten his crampon. And this time he looked at his watch and the altimeter. I knew what he was going to say and I dared not look at him. We had reached 25,600 feet [7,800 m].[4]

It was 2 p.m. They needed at least three hours to reach the summit, and time and the wind were against them. A bivouac meant almost certain frostbite and loss of limbs – even worse! The danger was clearly very great, and in the end the decision was reached to descend to Camp IV.

After an intense struggle Cho Oyu had won.

Recalling this battle by the Swiss on Cho Oyu shows Claude Koyan to be a very special person and a very courageous mountaineer. It is prudent, now, to commence her story from the beginning.

Europe, the Andes and the Himalayas

Claude was born in 1919 and began climbing in the Belgian Ardennes which she, like so many others, was forced to leave when the tides of war washed into their valleys. When the Germans overran Western Europe and occupied the Channel and Atlantic coasts, Claude moved south to the sun and the mountaineering community around Nice, where she eventually built up a small business designing and manufacturing women's swim wear. Climbing with the locals on the surrounding limestone walls and peaks became more than an escape from the Occupation, and her skills developed very rapidly. It became very obvious that the young woman from the north was a climber of outstanding potential.

One member of the group with whom she climbed was Georges Kogan. He, too, was a very fine mountaineer. In 1945 they were married. When the war ended and movement became less restrictive, the team of Georges and Claude Kogan began making impressive ascents in the Dauphine and Chamonix, and became members of the élite Groupe de Haute Montagne. Two of their best climbs at this time were the North Face of the Dru in 1946, which had been climbed first some 11 years earlier by Pierre Allain and Raymond Leininger (husband of her friend Nicole) and in 1949 the South Ridge of the Aiguille Noire de Peuterey ('A name of legendary quality, a ridge profiled against the sky, a great reputation, magnificent climbing, all these combine in a route from which dreams are made,' wrote Gaston Rébuffat in *The Mont Blanc Massif*.[5]

Claude led all the way. It was the first feminine lead. Although they were impressive climbs, they merely signposted the path that was to lead to the Andes and Himalayas.

The Andes

In the Andes in 1951 Georges Kogan and Raymond Leininger, with two others, made the first ascent of Alpamayo (6,120 m or 20,079 ft). Within a week their two wives, Claude Kogan and Nicole Leininger, went higher on the second ascent of Quitaraju (6,180 m or 20,276 ft). It was an occasion worthy of great celebration, but sadness lay over the horizon for Claude. Six months after their return from

Some contemporaries of Claude Kogan; from left to right: Fernand Gros, Raymond Lambert, Erika Stagni. They are standing by the Tour Rouge hut on the Grépon, with Aiguille Verte beyond.

Claude Kogan on Ganesh Himal in 1955. *(Alpine Club
Library collection)*

South America, Georges fell ill; within days he was dead. Her loss seemed merely
to strengthen her determination to climb.

In 1952 she returned to the Andes. With Bernard Pierre, a rope mate of Gaston
Rébuffat, she made the first ascent of Salcantay (6,250 m or 20,500 ft).

The Himalayas

The following year she was in Kashmir. This time Nun Kun (7,130 m or 23,400 ft)
was the plum – another first ascent.

With such a record she was an obvious choice for Lambert's expedition for the
attempt on Cho Oyu. On Cho Oyu she reached 7,800 m (25,600 ft), the highest
point ever attained by a woman. It was a record that stood for many years.
Although Cho Oyu did not fall to the party, some excellent exploratory work was
done in the area around Gaurisankar and Menlungtse.

The next year, 1955, it was again Nepal, and with Lambert and E. Gauchat the
first ascent of Ganesh Himal was made. It seemed that success now touched
everything she did; but her greatest moment, according to many, came elsewhere
in 1955!

In that year the Alpine Club held a joint meet with the Ladies' Alpine Club.
Cecily Williams wrote:[6]

Never in all the ninety-eight years of its existence, had the Alpine Club ever contemplated such a revolutionary suggestion as a *joint* meeting – the founding fathers must have turned in their graves. The Alpine Club was munificent; both Presidents were in the Chair. Claude Kogan spoke to a packed house about her climbs ... Most of these climbs established records but they paled into insignificance beside the fact that Claude was the first woman ever to lift up her voice in the sanctuaries of the Alpine Club.

It was a sentiment echoed by many others. One cannot help but think that somewhere the spirits of 'A. and E. Pigeon' would be nodding their heads in approval.

Death on Cho Oyu

Claude was elected an Honorary Member of the Ladies' Alpine Club, and at the Jubilee dinner of the Club she suggested a Women's International Expedition. Two years later, in 1959, the Expedition went to the Himalayas; the objective was Cho Oyu! The choice of peak was Claude's and was totally in character. Cho Oyu had been her one magnificent failure (if that is the correct expression for such a remarkable effort!). What better place for her team to show its strength?

Cho Oyu, a splendid Himalayan giant, lies on the main chain of the Himalayas, some 24 km (15 miles) north west of Everest, on the border between Nepal and Tibet and overlooking the Ngozumpa Glacier – the principal glacier system lying immediately west of that of the Khumbu glacier, the gateway to Everest.

It was a very powerful and experienced team. Claude was the leader; other members were Eileen Healey (née Gregory), Dorothea Gravina, Margaret Darvall, Loulou Boulaz, Claudine Van der Stratten, Jeanne Franco, Colette le Bret and Micheline Rambaud. These were joined by two daughters and a niece of Sherpa Tensing, the first man with Edmund Hillary to climb Everest.

There was every chance, if the weather held, that Cho Oyu would be the highest peak climbed by women. Everything was progressing well, and hopes were high. On the 29th September Claude and Claudine left Camp III to establish Camp IV. On 30th September everything seemed set for an attempt on the summit within the next couple of days. A note from Claude said she and Claudine would occupy Camp IV on 1st October and, if the weather was good, make a summit bid the day after. That night the weather changed; it had become unpleasantly warm, and the mountain's skin began to creak and disintegrate. Avalanche after avalanche thundered down Cho Oyu's mighty flanks. Contact was lost with Camp IV. All the camps below it were evacuated to Base Camp. The avalanches continued throughout the night.

On the 3rd October the weather improved somewhat. Gradually the camps were reoccupied. The exploration party found that Camp III had disappeared. When they reached the site of Camp IV where Claude, Claudine and Ang Norbu had been sheltering, 'there was nothing, absolutely nothing – it was swept completely clean ...' The vengeful rivers of snow had brushed away every trace of humanity; Cho Oyu had exacted its toll.

Many beautiful things have been said about Claude Kogan. Certainly, talking to those who knew her, and reading her writings and those of others, reveal her as a magnificent climber who felt deeply and endeared herself to many. Perhaps Raymond Lambert described her best, in 1955 whilst she was still alive, when he said:

petite, slim, graceful. But hidden beneath this frail outer shell is one of the most forceful wills I have ever encountered. Set in a smiling face crowned with rebellious fair curls, two blue eyes dance with a tiny but very brilliant light . . . I know of no other woman so rich in contrasts, so strong in determination. She never bows before adversity. She dares the highest summits and the fiercest storms with the same serenity, with the same rather shy smile . . . Her real purpose in life is to climb mountains.

I will add, to complete the picture, that she possesses a keen sense of observation, an ever-wakeful critical intelligence and . . . a lyric taste in adventure. For her an expedition is not an athletic feat; it is an essay in the poetics. She brings to it the same passion that filled the first seekers of gold or the companions of Magellan. For Claude, mountaineering is one long search for the Route to the Indies.[8]

At the British Mountaineering Council's International Conference in Buxton in 1984, I talked to Walter Bonatti who is regarded by many as the greatest Alpinist of all time.

'Did you know Claude Kogan?' I enquired.

'Yes,' he answered.

'What was she like?'

His eyes pierced mine. Quick as a flash the reply came – firmly and with total sincerity in two simple words – '*The Best*'. There was nothing more that needed to be asked.

Chronological list of events

1919   Claude born.
1945   Married George Kogan.
1946   North face of the Dru.
1949   First female lead of South ridge of Aiguille Noire de Peuterey.
1951   Second ascent of Quitaraju.
       George died.
1952   First ascent of Salcanty.
1953   First ascent of Nun Kun.
1954   Failure on Cho Oyu.
1955   First ascent of Ganesh Himal.
       Elected Hon. Member of Ladies' Alpine Club.
       Addressed Alpine Club.
       Ladies' Scottish Climbing Club Himalayan expedition: Gyalgen Peak.
1956   Ladies' Alpine Club expedition to Kulu area: Cathedral Peak and Chapter House Peak.
1959   Claude Kogan died on Cho Oyu.
1961   Women's Kulu Expedition: first ascents of Central Peak, Lion Peak and Unnamed Peak.
1962   Jagdula Expedition to Nepal: Lha Shamma.

References

[1]Raymond Lambert, *White Fury* (Hurst and Blackett, 1956), p. 148/[2]ibid., p. 149/[3]ibid., p. 150/[4]ibid., p. 161/[5]Gaston Rebuffat, *The Mont Blanc Massif* (Kaye & Ward, 1975), p. 182/[6]Cecily Williams, *Women On The Rope* (Allen & Unwin, 1973), p. 165/[7]ibid., p. 184/[8]Raymond Lambert, *White Fury*, p. 19

7

Yvette Vaucher – endurance on the great North Faces

The great classic Alpine routes also came in for serious attention in the 1960s. In the forefront of the wave of attack was a brilliant Genevoise climber, Yvette Vaucher. She was a friend of Loulou Boulaz and wife of another great mountaineer, Michel Vaucher.

Yvette's successes on the North Faces of the Matterhorn and Dent Blanche are now history, although success was not easily won. Despite several attempts, she and Loulou were beaten to the earliest female ascents of the most notorious of Alpine faces – the North Wall of the Eiger. Daisy Voog, with Werner Bittner, accomplished the first female ascent in 1964, and Christine de Colombel made it the second woman's ascent two years later.

By 1970 Simone Badier had launched her exceptional Alpine career and women climbers from countries not usually known for their mountaineering interests began to attract attention. A Japanese women's party made the ascent of the North Face of the Eiger; two other Japanese women, Junko Tabei and Hiroko Hirakawa, climbed Annapurna III (7,555 m or 24,787 ft). In 1962 women climbers from Austria, Britain, Czechoslovakia, France, Germany, Holland, Italy, Poland, Switzerland and Yugoslavia formed the organisation known as *Rendez-Vous Hautes Montagnes*, whose purpose was to bring together those who climb because they love mountains.

The 1971 International Expedition

Finally in 1971, at a time when women's reputations stood very high, Yvette Vaucher was invited to join an International Everest Expedition. Although it was a bench mark for women, the big day was still to come, and did so in 1975 when the diminutive Junko Tabei became the first woman to climb Everest.

Early in 1971 a large expedition converged on the Western Cwm, the great hanging valley between the South–Western Face of Mount Everest and the Nuptse-Lhotse ridge to the south. Known as the 1971 International Expedition, it had been put together by Norman Dyhrenfurth, a very experienced mountaineer from a well-known climbing family, and it included some of the most accomplished mountain climbers of the day.

The 22-member team that Dyhrenfurth had assembled was as star-studded as any that has ever set out for a high mountain. The British participants were the powerful little Lancastrian Don Whillans and the determined Scotsman, Dougal Haston; from Norway came O. Eliassen, J. Teigland; from U.S.A. were Dr D. Peterson, G. Colliver, D. Isles; from Italy was Carlo Mauri; from France came Pierre Mazeaud; the Japanese representatives were Reizo Ito and Naomi Uemura; Toni Hiebeler was from West Germany; Wolfgang Axt and Leo Schlömmer were Austrian; and from Switzerland came those fine mountaineers the Vauchers.

All were climbers of indisputable ability. Also attached to the expedition was an eight-strong television team from the B.B.C., and a *Sunday Times* journalist, Murray Sayle.

There were two other interesting facts about this expedition: firstly it was the first really *internationally* organised expedition to Everest, and secondly, one of the Vauchers was a woman. Her name was Yvette; she, like her companions, was a climber of outstanding ability and achievement.

Brave assaults on Everest

It is now history that things went badly wrong in the eyes of some (but not all) of the members of the 1971 International Expedition. Many did, in fact, have a good expedition and formed lasting friendships. But for the so-called 'Latins' – Mazeaud, Mauri, the two Vauchers – things did not go the way they would have wished. For Bahaguna it was the ultimate expedition: he died.

It had been decided fairly early on that there would be two separate assaults on the mountain. One was to be by the South West Face and the other by the West Ridge. On the walk in to the Base Camp, Dyhrenfurth invited the team members to choose the route they wished to climb. Whillans, Haston, Ito, Uemura, Hiebeler and Schlömmer, with the two Americans Colliver (who later retired with an eye infection) and Petersen, selected the South West Face.

Axt, Mauri, Mazeaud, Michel and Yvette Vaucher, Bahaguna of India, Teigland and Eliassen of Norway, Isles of the U.S.A., and Steele, the British doctor with the expedition, headed for the West Ridge.

In the early stages of the twin assaults there were very few problems, and considering the size of the expedition and its international character there were remarkably few communication difficulties. All appeared to go reasonably well until, whilst trying to set up Camp II on the West Ridge, Bahaguna got into difficulties. At this time the weather began to turn bad, which did not help Bahaguna in his plight, and on the retreat from the Camp II site, the Indian died from exposure.

Conditions became fairly desperate. The team members, regardless of nationality or any personal reservations they may have had about the way the expedition was developing, gave of their best, but despite their valiant efforts it took two weeks to recover Bahaguna's body. Because of the delay and the protracted recovery operations, it was becoming clear that the difficulties of maintaining two major attempts on the mountain needed serious reappraisal, and the West Ridge project was called off.

As an alternative, Mazeaud, Mauri and the Vauchers wanted to climb the ordinary route to the summit but, as Dyhrenfurth pointed out, it had already been climbed by '23 climbers of six nations', and reality demanded that all resources should be concentrated on the South West Face project. Tempers flared. Mazeaud, Mauri and the Vauchers felt they had been cheated of an attempt on the summit – even by the easiest way – when it was announced by Lt Col. 'Jimmie' Roberts, the second-in-command of the expedition, that all efforts must be brought to bear on the South West Face attempt, and that anyone who didn't agree could leave.

For some reason Mazeaud's fury centred on Don Whillans who had, in fact, been high up on the South West face for most of the time, pushing up the high camps with Haston and the two Japanese. When Whillans cleared out the last remaining camp set up by Mazeaud's group in the West Cwm, it was more than the latter could bear. Insults and accusations were traded. Mazeaud, Mauri and the Vauchers left the expedition soon afterwards, feeling victimised (Yvette it is said actually vented her feelings by throwing snowballs at Dyhrenfurth). They were convinced that they had been pawns in some conspiracy to give preference to the British. Don Whillans maintains that:[1]

> This was positively not correct: there were *no* pressures, nor had there ever been during all the development of the expedition, by either the climbers, the leaders or external forces such as the B.B.C. and newspapers, to put a British team up on top of the mountain in preference to any other.

Many years afterwards Whillans said[2]:

> All worked well up to the death of 'Bag'. There was no squabbling until after this. Bad weather and the delay made it clear there weren't enough resources to maintain two teams. It was after this that dispute arose and the Continentals were out-voted.

It was a sad end to what could have been an exciting and fulfilling occasion for Mazeaud, Mauri and the Vauchers.

Walt Unsworth[3] says of them:

> They had seen it wrongly, as a way to achieve personal ambitions – Mazeaud would have been the first Frenchman to climb Everest, Mauri the first Italian and Yvette Vaucher the first woman.

There was no personal 'first' for Michel, but as Unsworth says:[4]

> Vaucher was one of the ablest climbers on the expedition and his rightful place was on the Face, with Whillans and the others.

Whether one agrees with Unsworth's summation or not, it was indeed sad that such a breakdown in communication and goodwill had occurred between the lead climbers in the team. It was easy to see how superficial this breakdown really was when attempts had been made to rescue the dying Bahaguna. On that occasion Mazeaud, Whillans, Vaucher, Mauri, Eliassen and Steele with the sherpa, Ang Phurba, had battled through the storm and risked their own lives in a prodigious effort and with great team spirit in an abortive attempt to rescue the dying man.

The reverberations of the furore in the 1971 International Expedition were latched onto by British journalists. Images were coloured and distorted out of all recognition – none more so than that of Yvette Vaucher, whose great contribution to mountaineering has been largely overlooked by English-speaking climbers because of the controversy on Everest in 1971. Her great climbing career needs to be seen more fully.

A Swiss childhood

Yvette Pilliard was born in 1929 in Vallorbe, some 80 km (50 miles) north-east of Geneva on the Franco–Swiss frontier. Her schooling in Geneva led to an interest in gymnastics and skiing.

Like so many other mountaineers, chance played a big part in her development as a climber. She was 22, she says, when it all started. Studying a map of Switzerland, she spotted a very small point marked Ferpècle, at the end of a long valley. There was no road up to Ferpècle, only a footpath. For some reason it attracted her, and she went there for her holidays. 'That summer of 1952', she said later, 'I discovered both the Valais and the Val d'Hérens which I have never stopped loving from that moment.'[5] She went on long walks, crossed her first glacier and visited the Rossier Hut. The mountain majesty overwhelmed her, particularly the sight of that great summit, the Dent Blanche, a massive rock and snow peak of 4,357 m (14,300 ft), which was to feature so much in her career.

In the spring of 1953 she went ski touring and climbed her first 4,000 m (13,120 ft) peak, the Grand Combin. It was tiring, it was cold, but it was very beautiful – and there was much to learn, not only about clothing and equipment, but about where to go and how to improve her technique. In Geneva she joined a climbing club that went to the trouble to help newcomers with these problems. With her new found friends and increased knowledge, she returned later in the same year to the Val d'Hérens. Amongst several ascents she climbed her first summer 4,000 m (13,120 ft): the mighty Dent Blanche.

Two years later she left Geneva to live in Neuchâtel, and somehow, for five years, lost touch with summer climbing. Temporarily she found a new excitement; she took up free-fall parachuting. 'I made over a hundred descents,' she said,[6] 'It was intoxicating. But they were over too quickly; and they were expensive; and gradually, there were too many people around!'

Climbing successes

By 1960 she had made contact again with her mountaineering friends. 'Ideas for climbs began to pile up'; and the person arranging the programme was a climber who was to play such a large part in her life: Michel Vaucher.

> We formed a team. I found I could do climbs, each one as unbelievable as the other. I never realised I had so much strength.[7]

From then onwards it was climb, climb and more climbing in summer, and skiing – cross-country and alpine – in winter. Her record of ascents is a mountaineer's dream list; on rock peaks, big walls and great ice faces there seemed no end to her success. With Michel, sometimes with others also but often enough just the pair of them, they embarked on and ascended the greatest climbs known in the Alps at the time: the breath-taking north faces of the Matterhorn (first female ascent), the Grand Jorasses by the Walker Spur, the Badile, the Triolet and the Drus. On the latter also, were ascents of the Bonatti Pillar and the 'American Direct' (also known as the Voie Hemming) on the West Face of the huge pinnacle – a great wall over 1,000 m (3,280 ft) in height.

On the stupendous Brenva Face of Mont Blanc they climbed the Sentinel and Pear routes (great classic climbs on rock, ice and snow), a repeat of the Bonatti-Gobbi route of the Pilier d'Angle and of that very hard route, the Frêney Pillar. The latter is considered by many to be the last of the really great 'last problems' of Mt Blanc. In the Dolomites she repeated, amongst many other climbs, the classic Comici Route on the appalling North Face of the Cima Grande, and did the second female ascent of the very hard French route on the neighbouring and equally fantastic Cima Ovest, the Carlesso on the Torre Trieste. It is still regarded as one of the hardest routes in the Dolomites. She also made the first female ascent of the Maestri Baldessari Route on the South West face of the Roda di Vael. All of these, and a number of others which she climbed, are Grade VI or VI+ with difficult 'aid' sections, where total reliance has to be placed on pegging.

A hard and brilliant rock climber, she loved the great limestone walls of western Europe: the Salève (near to Geneva, and where she did her first rock climbs), Buoux, Verdon, the Calanques, Vercors, and so on. Overseas, she climbed Mt McKinley in Alaska by the West Ridge and various peaks in the Cordillera Huayhuash in Peru; in the Yosemite Valley, the 1,000 m (3,280 ft) Nose of El Capitan and Half Dome were ticked off.

One could annotate the ascents at length, but the list itself will speak volumes to most mountaineers. However, two climbs call for greater detail. In the record of all her North Face routes these stand out: the Eiger and her first love, the Dent Blanche.

The Eiger

In August 1962 Yvette was poised for what she describes as 'my first great alpine adventure'.[8] With her were, as she says, 'the three best contemporary climbers in the world', Michel Darbellay, Michel Vaucher and Loulou Boulaz.

The story is best left to Yvette:[9]

A dream that I do not dare dream and there I am roped to Michel Vaucher on this huge face with its legendary crossings: Hinterstoisser traverse – the three névés (snowfields) – the Flat Iron – Death Bivouac – the Ramp . . . water and rock falls. Rapid progress. Suddenly bad weather paralyses us.

A long bivouac in the 'Ramp' on our haunches and on the tip of our crampons. We are soaked to the skin. The throbbing whisper of the snow, falling continuously, camouflages everything.

At last dawn; in this opaque dawn we look at each other questioningly. We know that up to now no one has gone down again alive from so high up on the wall. There is no safety higher up. There is too much fresh snow in the Traverse of the Gods and avalanches in the Spider. As the altitude changes, the cold bites deeper; there is a danger of serious frost-bite.

What then?

We have to act quickly before the stones pepper our faces. One solitary long rope – Darbellay sets off in the mist and fixes the ice screws in the vastness of the névés, Loulou and myself are in the middle and move together, Vaucher retrieves everything in a nightmare.

At last security.

Groping we finally reach the Pilier Fissuré bivouac, it is night-time. Shivering, exhausted, hungry, thirsty but alive we sink into sleep, at last sheltered from everything. Next day the descent continues without further incident. At the Petite Scheidegg Hotel, the managers Heidi and Fritz Von Allmen, unaware of the identity of the four climbers they had been watching through their telescope most of the day before, offered their hospitality and their friendship and the comfort of their luxurious hotel.

After that episode on the Eiger, Yvette and Michel were married. 13 years later she was once more back on the North Wall of the Eiger, this time to achieve success. Before that she had retreated three times from the face; 'the Ogre has defended itself well!'[10]

The Dent Blanche

The story of another fearsome expedition has been told in detail by Michel Vaucher. It is the story of the first direct ascent of the North Face of the Dent Blanche, 9th to 12th July 1966. Michel wrote[11]:

I have been thinking of the Dent Blanche now for a good five years, and the idea of making a direct route up the north face was suggested to me by my wife. A great

Yvette Vaucher attempting the first women's ascent of the North Face of the Eiger in 1962. (*Yvette Vaucher collection*)

lover of the Val d'Hérens and of the peak she had climbed twice before by the normal route, Yvette said: 'I don't think anything has been tried on the north face. Isn't that odd?'

Michel and Yvette asked of the locals and the guides and got the same kind of reply. One reply, from the great Armand Charlet of Chamonix caused them concern. 'I think two Austrians have done it . . .'

He sowed seeds of trouble in our minds,

Michel continued:[12]

First or not, the ascent of this face could be ranked only among the routes of the great north faces.

Early in July they went to stay in the Val d'Hérens, surrounded by the mountains Yvette loved so much. It rained most of the time!

On 9th July the good weather arrived. Quickly they got in their supplies and sorted out their gear, then headed off by truck as far up the valley as they could.

We want to arrive at the Col de la Dent Blanche before night. We have to do it.[13]

Up to 3,500 m (11,480 ft)–1,300 m (4,265 ft) of ups and downs were covered before darkness fell. They made it and bivouacked on the Col before the light failed completely. It was fine, but cold.

The north face which we can see in the half-light is very impressive. Where will we be tomorrow?[14]

At six the following morning they left their bivouac and descended by abseil the unstable rocks below the Col that led down to the snow-field below the great north face. Half-way across, a cone of soft snow caused by avalanches served as a

Yvetter Vaucher on the first ascent of the direct route on the North Face of the Dent Blanche. (*Yvette Vaucher collection*)

point of departure. The bergschrund was not high, about 3 m (9 ft), but it had an overhang at the top, and the snow was very bad. The climbing was a mixture of rock and ice. In 300 m (985 ft) they arrived at a vertical slab of rock which offered substantial resistance to progress. First they tried to the right and then to the left. With slabs overlapping in the wrong direction, glistening with glazed frost, everything was vertical or overhanging. It took two hours to cross the five metres' traverse.

> Two doubled ropes hanging, pitons that won't find a cleft, everything is blocked, unfit for climbing.[15]

The traverse gave access to the median névé, but the ramp itself projected outwards in a great thirty metre overhang.

> I don't believe I have ever crossed over anything as dreadful. Two bad pitons allow me to heave Yvette up. I am a little anxious to see how she is going to get herself out from there. She recovers the pitons, swings on a small cord which she pulls from her pocket, the whole thing done so smoothly. She arrives at my side, still fresh and feminine. Our confidence in each other is immense. What luck we have, to be able to make an attempt together.

Time was getting on. It was now 4 p.m. They found a small spur of rock which was sheltered from rock falls, and decided to bivouac. They drove in 'pitons in every direction, but not one [was] any good.' It was a constricting, sitting-bivouac which started to get uncomfortable in 15 minutes – and the weather was becoming worse.

Next morning they were alarmed to notice a considerable pressure drop reading on their altimeter. More bad weather was on the way! They began moving upwards as early as they could. By 10 a.m., just as they were about to launch their attack on the head wall, it was snowing.

Ice stuck to the rock – rock which doesn't accept pitons. It's hard to do these 40 m [130 ft] by rope without safety and to tell yourself that the slightest error is fatal . . . We climb up a gigantic river of powder snow. Visibility is nil. I soon find my way blocked in the middle of a slab. About 30 m below me is Yvette tied on to a laughable piton! I feel that above I will not be able to get through: it's smooth and there isn't the slightest fissure. I have to descend. It takes me more than an hour to knock in a bad piton. This doubtful support allows me to return to our resting place. Yvette is there, curled up with cold. On her shoulders a very heavy bag. We look at each other. Without saying a word I set off again, taking with me the memory of that eloquent look.

– This time it's serious . . .

– 'Yvette, we have to bivouac. I can't continue in this weather, I can't see a thing.'
'Do you want to bivouac standing up?'

The question has sense. Twenty metres [65 ft] from us is a sheet of ice. Perhaps by cutting out a platform? On my arrival at the spot I find with joy that the sheet is thick enough. I cut away with what remains of my strength. A ledge 80 cms [30 inches] by 30 cms [12 inches] will be our seat; rock lies deeper. Four steps for our feet, two ice screws and Yvette can leave the resting place she has been inhabiting for three good hours. Let it not be me who says women suffer the cold badly! We get out the duvets, we are soaked. The bivouac tent isolates us a little from the storm, but we can't remove the crampons and will keep them on throughout the night and the next day . . . We succeed in making soup . . . I am very worried and I don't know how it will all turn out in the end. About 1900 hours we listen in to the weather on our small transistor – 'Bright intervals in Valais' – that's a point for us. Then there's the news of the Tour de France – Jacques Anquetil has given up because of a chill. We find the joke a bitter one. A chill, the poor man! A pop singer follows the sports news.

We prefer to chat and turn off the voices of these people living in comfort and safety. Night falls slowly . . . Tomorrow, the summit perhaps? I try to eat dried meat and vomit immediately.[16]

At 5 a.m. on 12th July they continued their ascent without breakfast, eager to find out what lay ahead.

Slabs even more upright, sheets of ice like glass, a bad resting place, a stretch of 80 m where the complete absence of safety begins to weigh heavily . . . I concentrate deeply. It seems unthinkable climbing for such a long time without making a mistake.[17]

A crampon strap broke and was noticed just in time. A temporary repair was carried out on the job. A short time later a second strap went, needing another hasty repair.

The summit could not be far away now – only about 30 m (100 ft) to the Quatre Anes arête which sweeps up from the left to the summit.

I go very slowly. So near to our goal, it would be stupid . . . Then, onto the arête in bright sunshine. It is too beautiful! In her turn Yvette appears, handing me two pitons retrieved with ease. We sit down and make some tea. It has a taste that is quite new. Again we join those humans capable of listening to pop singers on the

The North Face of the Dent Blanche. The direct route was first climbed by Yvette and Michel Vaucher over four days, from 9th to 12th July 1966. (*André Roch collection*)

Yvette Vaucher has achieved success in skiing as well as in climbing. *(Yvette Vaucher collection)*

radio. About midday it's the summit. And while we embrace each other I cry like a child . . . Tears give place to joy, in spite of feet I cannot feel.[18]

It was 7 p.m. by the time they completed a delicate descent over snow-covered slabs on the ordinary route to the Hut. In its safety, they examined their feet, fearing the worst. Michel's socks were frozen on, his toenails were black and fingers were blue. Yvette's were in a better condition. Michel wrote:[19]

Despite her lengthy waiting at resting places and the bivouac, she has endured the cold much better than I have. Tourists offer us a glass of wine. We dry out our boots, then a little dazed, we stretch out on the bunks for a restless night.

Next morning Michel's feet were distended and painful, and he found it difficult to move on them. Yvette's, too, were in pain, and her face was badly swollen with the wind, but she was able to hobble around. Three young climbers abandoned their climb for the day and helped them down to the valley.

My feet were a terrible sight,

Michel tells us,

Huge purplish-blue swellings, nails half off . . . we return that same evening to Geneva.[20]

The morning after their return Michel visited his doctor, who had had a good deal of experience of frost-bite cases:

'It's bad, third degree, you will lose four to five toe-joints on each foot.'
Then . . . 'The Dent Blanche, was it worth it?'
With no hesitation I reply 'Yes'.
'They are all the same', says the Doctor laughing.[21]

The current picture

Yvette Vaucher is certainly the same. Today she is a quiet, unassuming (almost retiring) woman of medium height, firm of handshake, of slim build and trained for cross-country skiing to a very high level of fitness. Her hard climbing days may be behind her (one might guess), but she is still achieving spectacular success in ski racing, and is a qualified long distance skiing instructor and an expert downhill skier. Yvette is also an Honorary Member of the Swiss Alpine Club, and still maintains links with old companions of the hills, – although she and Michel are no longer together.

In a recent interview[22] she was asked what she thought of climbing and femininity.

> I think that femininity does exist in a virile sport . . . and that sport has an influence on contemporary life. A sportswoman will not clutter herself with too much trumpery, but at the other extreme it is not necessary for everything to become utilitarian. I believe that a woman who is not feminine *in* sport is not feminine *outside* sport.

And her best memory?

> They are all good . . .

And if she stopped climbing?

> I would still like the mountains even if I did not pursue the sport of mountaineering. I like the naturally beautiful setting even in the worst of weathers. Everything seems to be in place. The locals in the mountains are still independent; their individuality has not yet been blunted . . . They still know how to make a fire, choose the wood and look for water. Each gesture is vital (as on a climb). I cherish with all my heart the small hamlet of Sepec, below the way to Ferpècle.

And of climbing:

> Every gesture is important; there is no artificial limit; no man-made rules. There is the scenery! No ego kicks. I'm very happy when success does come along, but not because of any external thing. Every climb has its own story; companions, events.

And, in private correspondence she has said:

> I am often told, 'you must be brave to do all that, etc., etc. . . .' In my opinion you don't need courage to do what you like doing. Living with obligations that are not of your choosing, *that* takes courage!
>
> If I love mountains, mountaineering, it's precisely because the laws of the game have not been made by man. Your commonsense tells you what it is good to do and doesn't bully your instincts. I love this shedding of one's outer self. Only natural sounds limit the silence. Why put music onto films of mountains? Beautiful images – beautiful music, it's too much . . . and takes away any sense of concentration and remoteness. The rhythm of breathing says so much more.
>
> To climb with someone you love is a happiness that I shall never forget . . . I do not like to philosophise nor to remove the mystery of what I believe in.

After talking to this remarkable climber and reading what she has to say about the hills and the climbing of them one begins to feel, with increasing certainty, that there is far more to her as a mountaineer and an individual than has been painted for us in the stories of controversy and snowball throwing on Mount Everest.

Chronological list of events

1929   Yvette Pilliard born in Vallorbe.
1951   Began climbing at the Salève.
1953   Began ski touring: climbed Grand Combin and Dent Blanche.
1955   Moved to Neuchâtel: tried parachuting.
1960   Formed climbing team with Michel Vaucher.
1962   *Rendez-Vous Hautes Montagnes* formed.
       Failure on the Eiger.
1964   First female ascent of North Wall of Eiger by Daisy Voog.
1966   Second female ascent of North Wall of Eiger by Christine de Colombel.
       First direct ascent of North Face of Dent Blanche.
1970   Ascent of North Face of Eiger by Japanese women's party.
       Ascent of Annapurna III by Junko Tabei.
1971   International Everest Expedition, ended in failure.
1975   First female ascent of Everest by Junko Tabei.
       Success on the North Wall of the Eiger.

Some of Yvette Vaucher's more important climbs

Alps
North Face   – Matterhorn – First female ascent
North Face   – Grandes Jorasses – Walker Spur
North Face   – Piz Badile
North Face   – Triolet
North Face   – Drus
North Face   – Dent Blanche – First direct ascent
North Face   – Eiger
Fou   – South Face (Second female ascent)
Drus   – West Face – Hemming Route
Drus   – Bonatti Pillar
Grand Capuchin – Bonatti Route
Aiguille Noire de Peuterey – West Face – Ratti Route
Brenva Face   – Sentinelle Route
               The Pear
               Pilier d'Angle – Bonatti/Gobbi
               Frêney Pillar

Dolomites
Tre Cime, Cima Grande, North Face – Via Comici
Tre Cime, Cima Ovest – North Face – French route (second female ascent)
Tre Cime, Cima Ouest – Squirrels' Ridge
Torre Trieste, The Carlesso
Civetta, North Face – Philip/Flauim
Chima Su Alto, North West Face – Gabriel/Livanos
Crozzon di Brenta, Aste Dièdre
Roda di Vael, South West Face – Maestri/Baldessari (First female ascent)

Zaire   Ninagougo

Alaska   Mt McKinley – West Ridge

Peru	Yejupaja Pujoc	Cordillera Huayhuash
U.S.A.	El Capitan – The Nose Half Dome – North Face	
Nepal	Everest – 1971 International Expedition	
Other areas	Salève, Buis les Baronies, Buoux, Verdon, Calanques, Vercors, Chartreuse, etc. . . .	

References

[1]Personal correspondence Whillans/Peascod (1984)/[2]ibid./[3]Walt Unsworth, *Everest* (Allen Lane, 1984), p. 420/[4]ibid./[5]Yvette Vaucher, *Les Alpes* (Swiss Alpine Club, 1967), number 1, pp. 11 and 14/[6]Interview Vaucher/Peascod (August, 1984)/[7]Yvette Vaucher, *Les Alpes*/[8]ibid./[9]ibid./[10]ibid./[11]Michel Vaucher, *Les Alpes – First Direct Ascent of the north face of Dent Blanche* (Swiss Alpine Club, 1967), number 1/[12]ibid./[13]ibid./[14]ibid./[15]ibid./[16]ibid./[17]ibid./[18]ibid./[19]ibid./[20]ibid./[21]ibid./[22]Interview Yvette Vaucher/Peascod (August, 1984)

8

Junko Tabei – 'Everest mother'

Mount Everest

On the 26th May 1953 Edmund Hillary and Sherpa Tensing reached the summit of Mount Everest, the highest mountain in the world. They received, deservedly, world-wide public acclaim.

Cold and aloof, yet dangerously inviting, this mountain has a fascination to the mountaineer that transcends even its beauty. Constantly blasted by high winds, it is subject to frequent storms, and any ascent is always a race against time and the oncoming monsoon. The route taken by Junko Tabei was that followed by Edmund Hillary and Tensing Norgay, which involves negotiating the notorious Khumbu icefall to gain the uncertain sanctuary of the Western Cwm. Dougal Haston describes it as:[1]

> a mentally exhausting journey. In some places the only possible route was under overhanging shaky seracs. Frequent crossings of this type of passage are more wearing than big wall climbing. You cannot even take the normal safety precaution of going when there is no sun as the sun is on the icefall for most of the day. One can only go in and hope. On some occasions complete sections of the route were destroyed by movement of ice. When one finally comes out of this icy mess into the Western Cwm it is like being in a newer, brighter land.

From this point the South Col is gained via steep ice slopes; from the wind-torn shoulder, which offers only small respite from the surrounding verticality, the summit can be reached.

The personal qualities required to ascend a mountain such as Everest are of course many. They include courage, great physical and mental stamina, mountain craft, technique and the ability to acclimatise. For the last of these it is necessary to have indepth experience of high-altitude climbing. A brilliant climber at lesser altitudes, even a superb Alpinist, may physiologically not be able to function above 6,400 m (21,000 ft). If the climber does not have the ability to acclimatise, if his or her blood and lungs cannot extract enough oxygen from the thin, cold air above 6,400 m (21,000 ft), then that mountaineer will not be able to climb the high Himalayan peaks. There are many climbers who have learned their mountain craft and technique at lower altitudes only to find, to their frustration, that they cannot adapt their bodies to function at higher ones.

The scale of Everest determines that the above requirements are not all that is necessary of an individual. Teamwork is also very important. It is essential to live and climb harmoniously with others under the most difficult conditions imaginable and for long periods of time. If, in the teeth of a ferocious blizzard, huddled in your tiny tent, your companion spills soup in your lap, you must smile. Your very survival depends on a good relationship and a mutual understanding. However, possibly the greatest requirements are those of determination and commitment. Both are essential for safety and, ultimately, success.

A Japanese upbringing

Junko Tabei was born in 1939 in an area which gave her an immediate passport to the hills. It was here that the seed of the desire to climb germinated in her character. Miharu Machi, in the Fukushima prefecture, is a very pleasant little market town surrounded by hills and attractive countryside, and with a topography not unlike the highlands of Scotland.

At ten years of age, on a school holiday, she scaled her first real, 'non-green', mountain. This was the 2,000 m (6,562 ft) Yumoto, and the group walked with enough provisions to spend the night out. The trip made an impression on her that was to affect 'her very being'.[2]

As she touched the ground she was intrigued to find that it was warm. The teacher explained that this was a volcanic mountain, and the source of the hot spring water feeding the village spring baths. But Junko felt as though she alone had made the discovery, and that this source of heat was hers. Junko wanted to know more about mountains, and these beginnings helped her to grow up with dreams, ambitions and the ability to look at the world around her.

Junko's adolescence and early adulthood were unhappy. The realities of life, its disappointments and difficulties, were rapidly introduced to her. She was accepted only for her second choice of university in Tokyo: at the Showa Women's College, social life was severely restricted and the classes were academically uninspiring.

Junko developed a nervous illness and went home. When her father died, she decided to return to college, but to find herself new accommodation and lead a self-sufficient life. Her strength of mind was taking form.

Now there were no restrictions on her social life, and she found Sundays free for her own pleasure. She visited a climbing area near Tokyo. It was her first contact with the mountains again.

The smell, the colour, the grass, the earth and rocks, the coolness of the air intoxicated her. She said:[3]

> All excited my heart, it was like some vital organ in my body had started to function again. This was the real me and I discovered myself by climbing mountains. I felt a great sense of freedom that I'd done it with my own free will.

The start of a climbing life

This return to the mountains marked the start of her climbing life: in 1962 she joined the Hakurei Mountaineering Club. Promising herself never to fall in love with anyone, her whole ambition became to climb white mountains. Junko's 'white mountains' are the high, challenging snow-covered summits, whereas her 'green mountains' are the easier and friendlier lower peaks.

On graduation she found a job with the Japanese Physics Society, editing the Journal of European Physics. She found herself with much more time available than before, and was soon training for her first white mountain on the iced slopes of Mount Fuji. Fuji, the Sacred Mountain, is the highest in Japan at 3,776 m (12,388 ft), and is under snow and ice for eight months of the year. Ice-axe braking down the icy slopes, she scratched her face repeatedly – but she did not mind. (Ice-axe braking must be practised for use in the event of a fall on a snow slope. On steep snow the only way to stop is to hold onto your ice-axe correctly and fall in a manner such that all your weight is pressing the axe into the snow.

You lie face down with the ice particles rushing past your face.)

It was her first experience of winter on the mountain: the shrieking wind, the intense cold and the threat of those steep, icy slopes constantly waiting for an error of judgement. The combinations of intense emotions generated by fear, the physical pain of frozen digits, and the satisfaction of learning a craft were manna to Junko.

Her first true white mountain climb, Goryu Dake, was soon to follow. She was 22 years old. Her excitement in anticipation was to be fully satisfied in reality. She was learning quickly and thoroughly the lessons which were necessary to be a competent mountaineer, those of preparation, clothing and technique – but she learned something else which was to be even more important. Expecting to be vastly inferior to her experienced male companions, she found to her surprise she was at least equal in strength, and better in stamina and technique. Junko had that gift which cannot be gained with practice or experience: natural ability.

More hard peaks followed in rapid succession. Soon she had that familiar problem shared by many keen and talented climbers: her companions began to hold her back. Looking to new horizons, she changed her club to the Rhyu ho toko, a club with only seven members – but every one of them a tiger. Junko was the only woman in the club, and she made a conscious effort to stay away from all emotional relationships. Nothing was to prejudice her climbing, and there was no other motive to her activities.

She proved herself in her own right, and was soon climbing with the club's top climber, Yokoo San. ('San' means Mr, Mrs or Miss and is applied to all persons regardless of sex.) He had a very forceful attitude, and she soon realised what a

Junko Tabei in the Japanese Alps. (*Junko Tabei collection*)

difference a good, keen partner makes. She was attracted, purely platonically, to all his qualities: balance, strength, positive attitude and consideration.

Facing death together, with the mutual respect known between climbers, they could communicate as equals. With no traditions or put-downs by social doctrine to interfere, they were two people on the same level. This was the true relationship that Junko had always wanted with life and people.

Despite all this, Junko felt that Yokoo San was compromising himself, his own ability, by climbing with her. She did not want anyone playing a protective man's role in her climbing, although she did not feel this directly with Yokoo San. So, when she met Rumie Saso, Junko put it to her that they should climb together and the idea appealed.

She was now spending 110 days of the year climbing, and accurately and meticulously planning her expeditions. In 1956 Junko and Rumie made the first all-female winter ascent of the Central Buttress (Ichino-kura) on Tanigawa-Dake. They set off in the dark, illuminated only by a head torch, because the ice was hard and suitable for climbing. It was snowing, and the moon had disappeared. The childhood game of 'Janken' (scissors cut paper, stone blunts scissors, paper wraps stone) decided who was to take the first lead. The first pitch was hard, and the rope whipped wildly in the wind as the ice-axe shattered thin ice to reveal bare rock below. Conditions were trying, and the ascent involved a bivouac hanging from two pitons driven into the rock, but they won through.

Around this time she met the man she was to marry three years later. Masanobu Tabei was an able climber out on a works trip with Honda engineering. Junko now told herself that marriage would not interfere with climbing, and in fact her climbing has received nothing but encouragement and support from Tabei San. Their philosophy to marriage is that each partner should give something to the other, and each should be a better person after the marriage.

It was not easy for Junko to marry Tabei San: her mother was set against it. She could not see a mountaineer wishing to ascend the social ladder, and he was therefore highly undesirable.

Around the time of Junko's marriage, her climbing partner Saso San was killed whilst attempting to save her falling second. Dragged from her belay, Saso San fell to her death through no error of her own, but the second climber was saved by a tree. Saso San had been in bad spirits and she had felt a sense of guilt over the death of a novice from the same club, who had slipped and was killed exactly 49 days earlier. The significance here is that in the Buddhist religion, the spiritual 'after death' lasts for 49 days. It is a period of prayer until the spirit departs. To Junko it seemed as though the very sage and experienced Saso San had been fated to die in this way.

Masanobu Tabei went off to climb in the European Alps. During an attempt on the North face of the Matterhorn he was caught in a storm, and was forced to bivouac for three days on the face. He suffered frost bite, and ultimately lost four of his toes. He was insured, and so the compensation he received bought them both land outside Tokyo and enabled them to build their own house. 'It's an ill wind that blows no good.' 'We bought the house for four toes', Junko laughed.

Annapurna III

None of these incidents deterred Junko, who was now climbing more than ever before. But where was her next challenge to come from? Unexpectedly, the telephone rang, with Eiko Miyuzaki asking the question: 'Do you wish to join an all-women expedition to climb Annapurna III [7,555 m or 24,787 ft] in the Himalayas?'

Initially there were 14 women intending to make the trip, but by the time the group reached Kathmandu in March 1970, the party numbered only eight climbers and one doctor. Needless to say, Junko was one of the eight. There had been troubles and disagreement, with five members withdrawing from the expedition. Even so, there was a total of 138 people involved in the climb: eight climbers, one doctor, one reporter, 14 sherpas, and 114 porters to carry the necessary equipment and supplies. In short, it was no small organisational feat. The climbers raised the money themselves to fund the trip and it cost each of them personally 700,000 Yen (approximately £2,000).

It took the party four days to reach the foot of the mountain and Base Camp. On their way in they had to pass through the sacred village of Chomlon. Junko entered nervously, for no women were supposedly allowed in this holy area. In 1965 a German expedition utilising some women as porters were turned back. (Porters carry the expedition loads up to 27 kilos (60 lb), and are often women accompanied by their children. It is not unknown for them to walk barefoot, even across the snow and ice of the lower regions of the mountains.) But Junko and her fellow climbers were welcomed with smiles and voices of greeting. Afterwards Junko felt worried – perhaps they had not been recognised as women!

Even at Base Camp the high altitude started to exact its toll, and the party suffered from nose-bleeds, headaches and vomiting. Morale was low, but Camp I at 4,350 m (14,370 ft) and Camp II at 4,800 m (16,830 ft) were established without undue difficulty. It was only at Camp IV, 5,000 m (16,400 ft), that Junko began to have real fears about the effects of high altitude climbing. Would she be able to cope, could her body acclimatise satisfactorily? Her period pains were tremendous, yet some of the others were faring even worse, for they had stopped menstruating altogether. The adverse psychological effects were enormous.

Junko felt drained:

> I felt a woman cutting steps with an ice-axe was like being an ant on the side of this great mountain. I desperately wanted strength.[4]

She felt she had to retreat but that she had not enough strength to get down. Her body would not function correctly and she developed haemorrhoids. Miyozaki, the expedition leader, ordered Junko to rest, recuperate and descend. Sherpas took over the cutting of steps in the ice, and eventually Camp V was established on the Col. The altitude was 6,800 m (22,300 ft), and from here the summit could be reached.

Gaining the summit

It was on the 16th May 1970, with the camps adequately stocked with food and equipment and the weather looking promising, that Miyazaki San, the expedition leader, had to announce the final assault team. On large Himalayan mountains (because of prevailing weather conditions, individual fitness and the complicated logistics of stocking and supporting high, remote camps), only a limited number of the expedition's climbers can generally reach the summit. These climbers are known as the final assault team. The leader of the expedition must make the vital decision of whom to select, after carefully considering all the factors. It is always a difficult and usually controversial decision; obviously, all climbers on an expedition wish to reach the summit themselves. It is their prime motivation. In such circumstances it is easy for one's emotions to unbalance sound judgement.

Miyazaki announced the assault team: Team no. 1 (the first to attempt the summit) would be Junko Tabei, Hiroko Hirakawa and Sherpas Gilmie and Passan. Team no. 2 (which would have a second chance if circumstances so allowed) was to be comprised of Eiko Miyazuki (the leader herself), Reiko Sato and Sherpa Kutile.

There was uproar at the announcement, with other expedition members threatening not to take part in any further attempt on the summit, or to assist those who had been chosen. Junko accepted the decision; she was of course on the assault team. If it had been otherwise, I am sure she would also have accepted this decision and provided the necessary support. As it was, Junko felt her position was very vulnerable, and she was genuinely concerned that the all important back-up would not be there if required.

The Himalayan game is a serious one. The line between commitment and misadventure, between adventure and tragedy, is very fine. Weighing the circumstances carefully, looking deeply into her own ability, Junko became determined to attempt to reach the summit.

The ascent was arduous, and drew upon Junko's last dregs of energy. But at 1.30 p.m. the team made the plateau a little way below the summit. Here, where the strong Himalayan winds had stripped the snow to reveal a complicated jumble of rocks and boulders, Junko could see two humps of which the second one would be the top. After struggling up snow that was so hard it could not be dented with the ice-axe, she gained the summit of Annapurna III, 7,555 m (24,787 ft) at 2.45 p.m. on the 19th May.

There was no second assault team: Miyazaki and Sato were suffering from altitude sickness, and the mountain was abandoned as quickly as possible. On returning to Kathmandu Junko, significantly, purchased her return ticket to Japan.

The first woman to climb Everest

'Let's go to Everest', Miyazaki (who later married and became Mrs Eiko Hisano) put the idea to Junko. 'But you must be leader this time'. Junko was keen to go, but what would her husband think? He was happy for her to proceed, with one condition: he wanted a child first. Junko commented: 'I also wanted a child but it's not like laying an egg'.[5]

However, as was the case with earlier generations in Europe, Junko felt that if requested by her husband to have a child, then this was the correct and proper thing to do – her duty, in fact. In Japan, husband and family come first with, traditionally, the wife and female children playing a subservient role.

Junko was four months pregnant when official permission for the expedition was requested in April 1972; her daughter would be 2½ years old when the attempt took place in May 1975.

Climbing Everest was a daunting proposition. Junko knew there to be, from her experiences at altitude on Annapurna III, great differences in male and female strength:[6]

> It's more than I want to believe but it's there, the speed of walking, running, placing pitons with a hammer, all show the difference.

Olympic sports are, of course, divided, but in the mountains there is no artificial division or handicap system. It is the natural physical realities that define the game.

Junko's philosophy on going to Everest was that whatever the physical difficulties, whatever the financial position, if the spirit was willing to go then the dream could become reality. As joint leader she shouldered a tremendous responsibility and work load. To organise the expedition, to equip it and to find the means to fund it were her several problems.

When Junko decided to climb Mount Everest, she and her friends were alone in expedition circles. There were no 'silver spoons' available. They had to organise the whole event themselves.

The next three years of Junko's life were dedicated to this end. Imagine a working Japanese mother in a male-dominated society, preparing, on her own initiative, to scale Everest. The difficulties were enormous, but she overcame them. She and her all-woman team organised the expedition and raised the necessary finance in a climate of disinterest, almost of disbelief.

Trying to convince the Japanese business world that it should sponsor the expedition was not easy. Most considered the attempt to be futile; ten women to try to climb the highest mountain in the world – absolutely ridiculous! Failure was 99 per cent certain, or so they thought; the odds were too great, so why waste the money? At the 'eleventh hour', a major newspaper and a television company decided they would back the expedition. Whether or not they expected a sensational tragedy and good media coverage, or provided support because they thought the enterprise was going to succeed, I would not like to speculate. Anyhow, the team's persistence had finally been rewarded, and Everest 'was on'.

Planning

Junko, Eiko and their team (Eiko was overall leader, Junko was climbing leader) spent much time planning the logistics and the necessary equipment and supplies. They economised as much as was practicable; the resulting tight budgetary control they exercised was remarkable. As an interesting comparison I will give some approximate costs, converted to sterling:

1973	Italian expedition	£600,000
1974	Japanese Mountain Association	£200,000
1975	Japanese all-female expedition	£86,000

Their scheduled menu was economic, consisting of basic non-luxury dishes, but it still consisted of 190 different kinds of food. A typical plan was as follows:

Base Camp menu

Gyoza (*stuffed pastry with pork, Chinese cabbage, ginger, garlic, sesame oil and Chinese onion*)

Egg soup
Gomaku/Zushi (*rice dish*)
Bamboo shoots and potato – braised
Kanappe (*stuffed bread*)
Tshumami (*roasted potatoes*)
Fruit jelly
Sake (*Japanese rice wine*)

Breakfast menu
Boiled rice
Miso soup *(bean paste soup)*
Mezashi *(fish)*
Fried egg
Dried seaweed – braised

Evening meal
Boiled rice
Omelette
Miso soup
Sausage and vegetables – stir fried

Camp II breakfast
Bread *(freshly made at Base Camp)*
Butter and jam
Tinned ham
Cheese
Tea

Camp II morning
Zoni *(thick soup and rice cake)*
Pickled vegetables
Green tea

Evening
Takikomi gohan *(rice pilau cooked with chicken and vegetable)*
Miso soup and seaweed
Salad
Dried instant mashed potatoes
Pickled vegetables
Tea

With all the problems that had to be faced, and with 14 prospective climbers actively involved in the organisation, one could not reasonably expect in the three years it took that everything would proceed smoothly. Within the group, Junko was severely criticised for not dedicating enough time to the expedition. However, she felt that her role in the family should not be neglected: she was determined to climb Everest, yes, but she was equally determined to support her little girl and husband.

To Junko this was all part of being a woman, but she thought it should not detract from her being a mountaineer. Both were her natural, god-given functions:

> Birth, children and family are a woman's natural problem, this must be accepted. Men, too, have problems, they must support a family or at least attend their job. So the problems are different but this must be accepted and understood – to a mountaineer the real purpose is still to go to the mountains.[7]

Summoned to a joint meeting, Junko carried her little girl on her back in the rain to drop her off at her sister's, and she felt very sad. She questioned herself – is

Junko Tabei playing koto with her daughter, Noriko. *(Junko Tabei collection)*

it really worth it? The meeting lasted two days. Junko cried inside with frustration and pain, but she would not beg for inclusion; it was up to the others whether to accept her philosophy or not. They accepted.

Until the time Junko left for Everest she was training hard and keeping fit. Running three times a week, she was covering 19 km (12 miles) per session. Her husband and daughter would follow in their car, shouting encouragement when her pace flagged.

Finally, before she left, Junko made a tape recording of herself and Noriko to act as a record if she were not to return. Noriko was to stay with Junko's sister, and her grandmother said, 'Don't worry, we will bring her up beautifully'. These words touched Junko's heart.

The Japanese Women's Expedition to Everest was under way, and consisted of:

Leader: Eiko Hisano (formerly Miyazaki)

Climbing leader: Junko Tabei

M. Manita, F. Nasa, Y. Watanabe, S. Kitamura, M. Naganuma, S. Fujiwara, T. Hirashima, Y. Mihara, R. Shioura, F. Arayama, S. Naka, Y. Taneia and Dr M. Sakaguchi.

Sherpa Sirdar Ang Tschering

The ascent

From Camp I conditions entering the Western Cwm via the great ice maze of the Khumbu ice-fall were very difficult. After discussion it was decided to let the sherpas, with their superior knowledge of the ice-fall (gained on previous expeditions), find the best route through. Camp II (advanced base camp) was established in the Western Cwm on the 8th April 1975. Camp III and Camp IV were established in bad weather, but without incident.

The strong winds and spindrift (icy snow particles) made conditions almost intolerable. Basic survival was a fight; Junko commented that going to the toilet was absolutely frightful. Because of the shortage of jumars (a jumar is a mechanical device which slides up the rope but will not slide down, so assisting the climber to move up fixed ropes), they were having to pull hand over hand up the fixed ropes. Camp II (advanced base camp) contacted Junko on the radio at Camp IV: 'Next all female club meet is to be held in Hawaii'. Junko to Camp II: 'OK! Hawaii – but with plenty of jumars'.

With sherpas again in the lead, Camp V on the South Col was established. However, they became trapped at Camp IV in worsening weather. Oxygen was used to sleep, but during the day supplies were conserved. With body and mind rapidly deteriorating due to the altitude and severe conditions, Junko felt she was going crazy. On the 3rd May it became possible to retreat to Camp II in order to rest and recuperate.

On the 4th May they were awakened by a terrible noise. 'Avalanche! We've had it!', shouted Junko. Then she found she could not move. Somebody was on top of her. A face was directly over her's. Junko shouted, sounding incredibly loud, 'Are you all right?' Silence answered. Managing to free her right hand, she reached a knife hanging from a string round her neck; opening it with her teeth, she requested Miss Mihara to cut open the tent. Then she started to lose consciousness; Junko remembers thinking that if she died there, her daughter would be sad and lonely. Pictures of Noriko, playing happily, floated through Junko's troubled mind.

She felt a great force on her body and found herself lying on the snow next to Mihara. On one side she could see the feet of her rescuer, on the other she could hear the tiny voice of Mihara praying.

The sherpas had dug them out, and miraculously everyone was safe. Junko was, in fact, the worst injured, with her legs badly bruised and hip joints stretched; she had been pulled out by her legs.

Everyone at Base Camp and all the non-climbers, e.g. reporters, T.V. cameramen etc., had now written off the attempt. But, with the backing of fellow climbers at Camp II, Junko withstood the tremendous pressure to abandon the expedition. There were threats to pull her physically down the mountain to recover at Base Camp; but she would have none of it.

With only limited time to the start of the monsoon, Junko knew full well that to go down would mean the end of the attempt. There simply was not enough time to descend, recover and reascend.

After three days she began to walk again! On the 10th May Eiko Hisano announced the assault party. It was to be Junko Tabei, Y. Watanabe and Sherpa Sirdar Ang Tschering. Everyone congratulated Junko and shook hands; the scene was somewhat different from that on Annapurna some five years earlier.

The summit

As they fought their way back up the mountain, it was decided by Hisano that one of them would have to drop out of the attempt on the summit because of the resource situation. Apparently there was not the supply capacity for three. It was Watanabe who descended, but with no hard feelings towards Junko.

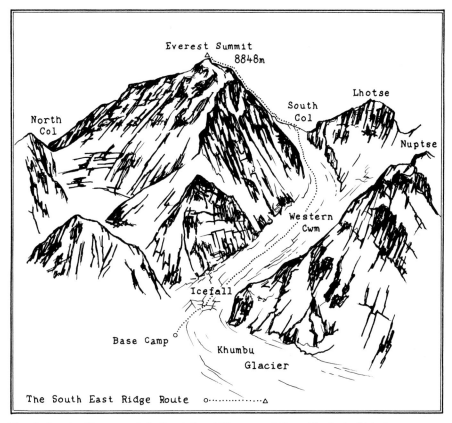

Sketch showing Everest and the South East Ridge route followed by Junko Tabei.
(Martin Bagness)

So, Junko Tabei and Ang Tschering set off from the South Col (Camp V) on
the summit attempt on the 15th May. At over 8,000 m (25,250 ft) they sat on a
narrow ledge to rest. Ang Tschering smoked a cigarette, and looked for all the
world as though he were in some down-town café – a café with the finest view in
the world!

Continuing to traverse steep ground, they stopped on a rock/ice ledge the size
of a single tatami mat. The height was over 8,500 m (27,890 ft) and they were
level with the summit of Lhotse. They cut ice with their axes, clearing enough
space to erect their tiny tent and make Camp VI. In this threatened, confined
space Junko recalls that the Sirdar behaved as a perfect gentleman, holding the
rope from the inside of the tent as she went to the toilet.

On May 16th, after three cups of coffee, with a superb panoramic view of
Makalu, Lhotse and Pumori, they set off for the summit. Deep powder snow
made the going very arduous. After reaching the South (lesser) summit they
followed the ridge, which became increasingly knife-edged, to the technical crux,
the Hillary step (a small, but very steep snow couloir, named after its first
ascensionist, Edmund Hillary).

The crest of the ridge was too narrow to walk on, so they traversed below it on
one side, using the edge itself as a handhold. Junko noted that if she looked over
the edge, her head was in China and her chest in Nepal!

A slip here would have been fatal, but soon the Hillary step was reached. This proved very difficult, with soft, new snow overlaying ice. Junko was acutely aware that to reverse this would be even more difficult.

Resting many times, taking only one step at a time, she willed that there would be a last step. The sherpa's words: 'Tabei San, this is the top', were just reward for her effort. This was the culmination of 1,400 days of preparation and team effort.

On the 16th May 1975, in International Women's Year, Junko Tabei, a 36-year-old Japanese woman, and Sherpa Sirdar Ang Tschering stood on Everest's summit. Junko Tabei was the first woman to climb Mount Everest; it was a magnificent achievement.

Their feat was only sparsely reported in the Western climbing and mountaineering press. Junko has regrets about Everest and, to a great extent, resents the publicity and ballyhoo in Japan that followed:

> Others try to make me into something I'm not, I'm just the same person now as before I went to Everest. They said it was a fantastic achievement for International Women's Year, but myself, I didn't even know such a thing existed. It wasn't until I got back home and read the newspapers that I realised.[8]

Headlines read 'Japanese women are strong' and 'Japanese success for International Women's Year'.

> It was ironic that people who had said it was impossible before, and would not back us financially, were now sending congratulations, etc. The parties, the prizes, the luncheons, I thought were all very artificial.[9]

When I talked to Junko in Tokyo, she made one comment in good humour, but which was meant seriously. She said, 'I can't understand why men make all this fuss about Everest – it's only a mountain'.

To Junko, Everest was only a stage in her climbing career; it was not the ultimate goal. The good thing to her about conquering Everest was that the planning and team work were rewarded, and she regards the ascent to be the achievement of 14 people, not hers alone.

Junko has ascended many mountains since Everest, including another of the exclusive eight thousanders, Xixabangma (8,012 m, or 26,286 ft). She has plans for many more.

True mountaineers will always return to the mountains; it is their life. As Junko said,

> Technique and ability alone do not get you to the top, it is the willpower that is the most important. This willpower you cannot buy with money or be given by others – it rises from your heart.[10]

No matter what Junko Tabei had done before, what she has done since and what she will no doubt yet achieve, it will always be the first ascent of Everest by a woman for which she will remain famous.

Chronological list of events

1939   Junko Ishibashi born.
1949   Climbed Yumoto.
1962   Graduated from Showa Women's College.
        Joined Hakurei Mountaineering Club.
1965   First all-female ascent of Central Buttress on Tanigawa-Dake.
1967   Climbing partner (Saso San) killed.
        Married Masanobu Tabei.

1970   Annapurna III, Damavand (Iran).
1972   Daughter Noriko born.
1975   First woman to climb Everest.
1977   Yellow Peak (Himalayas).
1978   Son Shinya born.
1979   Mont Blanc.
1980   Kilimanjaro.
1981   Xixabangma.
1983   Sepchukan (Bhutan Himalayas).

References

[1]Walt Unsworth, *Everest* (Allen Lane, 1981), p. 7/[2]Junko Tabei, *Everest Mother* (Shinco-Sha, 1982/[3]ibid./[4]ibid./[5]Interview Junko Tabei/Birkett (November 1984)/[6]ibid./[7]ibid./[8]ibid./[9]ibid./[10]ibid.

9

Molly Higgins – new dimensions

The Russian High Pamirs

It was July 1974 in the Russian High Pamirs, and Elvira Shataeyava was to lead seven other Soviet women on the first all-women ascent of Peak Lenin. Their aim was to traverse the peak up from the east on the Lipkin ridge to the summit and down the Razdelny on the west.

Elvira was a striking individual with an accomplished climbing record. She possessed a lively intelligence and sported a personality which was both attractive and dominant; she was undoubtedly the darling of the twelve-nation, Soviet-organised, international meet in the remote, beautiful and dangerous Pamirs.

At Base Camp the reported large storm was showing its presence with heavily gusting winds and blowing snow. High on Peak Lenin the Scot, Ronnie Richards, urged the women to descend. Elvira's reply was emphatic:

> We are strong. We are Soviet women. It is late and we are tired. We will camp here and go down to Razdelny tomorrow.[1]

The following day at 7,165 m (23,400 ft), following heavy snow and gale-force winds, the Soviet women reported (on their radio to Base Camp) that they had had a bad night with the winds destroying two of their tents, so there were now four in each of the two remaining tents. The tents themselves were hopeless, with toggle fasteners letting the snow enter easily, and wooden poles which had a history of failure even at Base Camp.

From Base they were ordered to descend; their reply over the radio, all but obliterated by the roaring wind, was not encouraging. At 5.00 p.m. the Soviet women called Base: one had died, two were ill. The Russian woman translator at Base commented to the anxious waiting and helpless climbers, 'It is like a dream; she doesn't seem to realise what is happening to them.'[2]

On the 6th August at 8.30 p.m., Elvira transmitted again; the storm raged in the background, frequently drowning her voice, but the message was clear enough: two more had died, and a further tent had been obliterated by the savage wind. Elvira maintained her composure (it seemed unreal to those below), only faltering when referring to her dead companions.

At 8.00 a.m. on the 7th, Elvira came on the radio again: weak, tired and disorientated, they were cold, had eaten nothing and had little strength left.

> 'Three more are sick; now there are only two of us who are functioning and we are getting weaker. We cannot, we would not, leave our comrades after all they have done for us. We are Soviet women. We must stick together, whatever happens!'

At 10.00 a.m.:

> 'We are holding on. We cannot dig in, we are too weak. We have had almost nothing to eat or drink for two days. The three girls are going rapidly. It is very sad here where it was once so beautiful. We will carry on and talk again soon. Over.'

At 12.00:

'We will go down; there is nothing left for us here. They are all gone now. The last asked "When will we see the flowers again?" The others earlier, asked about the children. Now it is no use! We will go down.'[3]

Four were dead, two were dying; Elvira and one other still struggled to survive.

At 3.30 p.m. Elvira called Base; a lull in the storm enabled all to hear someone beside her weeping:

'They are all dead; what will happen to us? What will happen to the children? It is not fair, we did everything right.'
    'We are sorry, we have failed you. We tried so hard. Now we are so cold.'

At 6.30 p.m., Elvira radioed:

'Another has died. We cannot go through another night. I do not have the strength to hold down the transmitter button.'[4]

At 8.30 p.m., the receiver clicked as Elvira bravely attempted to press the transmitter button.

'Now we are two. And now we will all die. We are very sorry. We tried but we could not . . . Please forgive us. We love you. Goodbye.'[5]

High on the mountain the American, Jeff Lowe (some 1,525 m or 5,000 ft below the Soviet women's camp in a rescue team comprising Doug Scott, Tut Braithwaite, the two Soviet coaches, Boris and Kostya, and four French climbers) recorded Elvira's last message:

'The others are all dead – I am too weak to push the button on the radio any longer – this is my last transmission – goodbye.'[6]

The radio crackled, and then there was only the roaring of the cold, unforgiving, wind.

The large, multi-national collection of climbers gathered in the Base Camp were unable to assist. They were effectively imprisoned at the lower altitude by atrocious conditions and logistical problems. Amongst them in Base Camp the young, inexperienced, Molly Higgins had just witnessed one of mountaineering's saddest tragedies. Higher on Peak Lenin, eight Soviet women mountaineers had died, one by one; so near, yet so inaccessible.

At Base Camp they had been helpless to prevent the disaster, with nothing Molly, or anyone else, could do by the time the magnitude of the situation had dawned. In all, on that ill-fated, storm-besotten climbing expedition to the Russian High Pamirs, 15 climbers eventually lost their lives. It had been a terrible expedition, with extreme conditions of bad weather and earthquake all resulting in unpredictable snow and avalanche.

Climbing in Colorado

Molly was born at Bryn Mawr, Pennsylvania on 16th February 1950 and was raised in a conservative and wealthy suburb of Philadelphia. When she left for Colorado College, in 1968, it was like a great breath of fresh air for this 18-year-old, rather wild, rather extrovert teenager. Philadelphia had begun to stifle her:

You couldn't be your own person and people would say things to me like 'Molly you're not with it – when you dance you totally let yourself go – you have got to keep a hold of yourself, you've got to keep cool.'[7]

She studied botany, and on graduation was out of school for five years. After this time, during which she taught at the Outward Bound school, she sat first a B.Sc. degree and then a Medical Technologist's degree. She is now, by profession, a medical technologist.

Colorado with its mountains and tolerant atmosphere gave Molly the room in which to find and express herself. She joined the College Mountain Club and immediately became enchanted with the sport of rock climbing.

She started to lead climbs right from the beginning. With her boyfriend she tackled an 18 m (60 ft) climb on sandstone (about 5.6 in difficulty). After two hours he had not even got off the ground, so she led it. It was her first lead and she was terrified, but she made the following exciting comments about it:

> The feeling of getting on top was just euphoric and from that first day it was always assumed that I would take my part doing the leading. In fact I always climb better leading. You know – if your neck's on the line you make sure you're doing it right.[8]

By 1968 she was leading reasonably high standard rock climbs (5.7–5.8, VS–HVS) and also pioneering new routes locally. A year or so later, in 1970, she received two sharp and timely reminders that rock climbing can indeed be dangerous.

The first was a fall from a climb named Snuggles in the 'Garden of the Gods', Colorado Springs. She was 20 years old and 4.6 m (15 ft) out from her last pin (protection point/running belay), and was reaching to clip her rope into the karabiner she had placed on the next pin. She could not reach it, so she pulled the rope and held it in her teeth ready for the next attempt to clip. Then she fell 9 m (30 ft), and the rope zipped through her mouth:

> . . . and the teeth were sticking out but the worse thing was a couple of guys came up and they said 'Oh it doesn't look so bad, Moll' – I mean it looked like holy hell. Blood and white teeth sticking out all buckled and stuff – but they just got pushed back in and wired.
>
> The fall was so painful and I found it difficult to start leading again. So in order to get over the fear I told myself that my boyfriend would never let me lead something I could not do. After that it was OK. Having passed off all that two months later I fell 85 ft [26 m] off the East Face of Long's Peak (Stetner's Ledges), just bouncing off the ledges; I really nearly did myself in.
>
> It brought home to me later that you have to learn to climb responsibly. I think a lot of people climb with others more responsible than themselves and they never learn their own inner parameters of what they're willing to do and how they are prepared to time the sport and I think that's very, very necessary to be a good climber and to be a happy climber.[9]

Hardly surprisingly after this last, almost fatal fall, her boyfriend had had enough and refused to climb with her. She did not climb again for another two years. Age 23, she again felt the need to climb:

> But then I realised how famished I was for it and how happy it made me – so I started out climbing again – with a girl friend who was not any kind of climber. We started out on the 5·0's and the 5·2's and it felt like a big deal. We'd take some little canyon with no guidebook or anything and we'd just do it and then get drunk at night and have a great old time.[10]

Yosemite

During this time (1971 to 1976) she taught both summer and winter courses at the Colorado Outward Bound School, and was building up a great deal of fitness and stamina. Then in the spring of 1974 (May) she first went to the Yosemite Valley. She scratched around leading the 5·0 climbs, but knew she had to climb harder to be able to do the better routes.

A female friend, who also had taken a 9 m (30 ft) fall and broken her wrist, and who wanted to be a good climber, gave Molly the following advice:

'If you really want to be a good climber you have to spend every spring and every fall in Yosemite and you'll get good.'[11]

Her friend was Barb Eastman and that is what they did. It was a brilliant partnership. Together they achieved the first all-women ascents of some of America's hardest and most famous rock climbs.

After that rather aimless first spring in Yosemite, just finding her feet, Molly was invited to the Pamirs. On the expedition a number of considerations shaped her future. One, of course, was the bitter experience of seeing these climbers, including her heroine Elvira, just die hopelessly. Another, I think, was the resentment, dissent and resulting loneliness she was subjected to by other team members. They regarded her as totally inexperienced, a threat to their grandiose plans, and nothing more than a 'token American female' on this international mixed expedition. Possibly also, as she displayed her gregarious character and her considerable strength and fitness, she may have presented just a little threat to their male egos.

On the expedition in 1974 Molly was a liberated 24-year-old, who, two years out of college, taught at an Outward Bound Centre. Quiet and demure she was not. If her fellow team members wanted an elegant, soft-spoken, 'sweet little thing' to flatter them along to great things, they were in for a rude awakening.

Certainly, she was inexperienced on high peaks, but her job at Outward Bound had physically prepared her for the workload involved. Added to this, her enthusiasm and energy were boundless.

Krylenko

Prior to the Soviet women's disaster, Molly had succeeded in climbing Peak Lenin, 7,132 m (23,399 ft), but she also wanted to do a technically more demanding climb. Accordingly, she signed up to attempt Krylenko along with other members of the American team. The Krylenko Pass was heaving with international activity, with parties both ascending and descending. With the words,

'Oh God damn those steps are so far apart. Who the hell put them in?'[12]

Molly entered the camp at 5,180 m (17,000 ft) on Krylenko. 'Just cussing a blue streak', having 'whipped the arses' of her male companions, she was firmly making the point that she was fit and strong; indeed, stronger than they were. The Englishmen Doug Scott and 'Tut' Braithwaite were already there, sitting on their sacs, ready to move further up the mountain. On their return the next day they were to find the entire camp obliterated by an avalanche. Scattered amongst the debris they found Molly's diary, and they assumed that Molly had perished. In fact, she had been incredibly lucky and had survived.

Doug returned her diary, the only object to be brought down from that camp, and they became friends. Perhaps it is wrong to describe such an event as luck; perhaps our destinies are written, our fate irrevocably planned. Molly described[13] the incident thus:

> I stooped down against the wind and covered my face, remembering everything I'd ever learned about avalanches. The roar of the avalanche lasted a long time; I knew that it might be safer in the crevasse, but I was doing fine where I was and was unwilling to go moving about, maybe getting into a worse position for all I knew. The snowfall from the avalanche back-spin was so thick that I could not see. After 30 or 45 seconds, I was only buried to my ankles and realised that I might make it. I noticed Chris Wren by my side, I think he might have been there the whole time. I told him to cover his face, which he did. We were crouched down, side by side. The avalanche lessened and stopped.
>
> I was amazed that I was alive. More amazed that upon looking about, everyone else was alive and fine, too.[13]

The decision to be a climber

Despite, or perhaps because of, this devastating experience, Molly Higgins was to emerge as one of the greatest American women climbers. The total expedition experience shaped her thoughts and reinforced her resolve. At the end of the expedition Molly made that essential mental decision, the decision that makes someone not just good or even very good, but the best. The expedition equipment was being sold off to the individual members:

> I bought some screws [ice screws – used on steep ice] and ropes and other things. Some of the men laughed and said 'Oh you're going to put it on your mantlepiece, hey, Molly?' and I just went steely inside. I knew that I wasn't that talented, and it was going to take a lot of work, but I really loved doing it and was going to take time and do it.[14]

On her return to the U.S.A. she made a far reaching decision.

> When I got home I turned to my sister and said 'I'm going to be one of the best women climbers in America.'[15]

It was an interesting decision, because she decided specifically to climb, and to concentrate on the great rock walls of America, particularly the vertical granite world of Yosemite Valley. This is a totally different world from that of the high mountains. It is no more or less challenging, but it is very, very different. In terms of absolute strength in the arm, it certainly requires more, and in terms of pure technical difficulty it is harder, but there are no avalanches and few team problems.

At that time in Yosemite an enthusiastic new climbing scene had rapidly developed. Names that have now become legend – Chouinard, Harding, Kor, Pratt and Robbins – had pioneered rock climbs up the most awe-inspiring cliffs on earth. Molly was determined to make the step and impress her personality on the world of 'big wall' and free rock climbing.

The profound experiences both of tragedy and isolation catalyzed the already fizzing Molly Higgins into achieving great things. Pushing the limits, along with Barb Eastman, they began climbing routes that no other women's team had ever dared to tackle before. On the Pamirs' expedition Doug Scott had said to her: 'Molly, you can do the Nose'.

The Nose

Yosemite Valley, California, gives its name to the 93,000 km^2 (35,900 mile^2) Yosemite National Park. The Valley cuts through massive domes of granite, leaving spectacular and beautiful rock faces towering, on average, 610 m (2,000 ft) above the winding Marced river. The 60 m (200 ft) high pine trees on the Valley floor are dwarfed by the cascading waterfalls and huge sweeps of pure, multi-coloured rock reaching to the sky.

The Nose is situated here and is, arguably, the most famous rock climb in the whole of America, possibly the world. It rises directly from the pine-clad Valley floor to the top of El Capitan: a majestic and breath-taking 915 m (3,000 ft) of sheer, unbroken, granite.

Today on the Valley floor, in the meadows of Camp 4 (the climbers' camp), amongst the prowling bears and hungry racoons, the climbers eye the vertical world above. The features of the exfoliated granite, its cracks, chimneys, dièdres, flakes and friction slabs make the apparently impossible into a challenging, but tangible, experience. The present state of modern rock climbing owes much to Yosemite, for it was here, in climbing these great walls, that many of today's specialised techniques and equipment originated and were refined and perfected.

In 1958 The Nose of El Capitan, the biggest feature in the Yosemite Valley, was first climbed by the indefatigable Warren Harding with Wayne Merry and George Whitmore. Forty-seven days were spent climbing, leaving fixed ropes, descending and reascending, spread over a period of 17 months.

On her return to the Valley in the autumn of 1974, Molly Higgins was determined that she would climb The Nose.

> But it was obvious that unless some guy dragged me up it I was going to have to get pretty damned good in order to do it. So Barb and I by 1975 were leading 5·9 cracks pretty consistently day after day. We decided to start off on the South Face of Washington Column [Grade V – 5·7 A2] and Barb's famous line is 'Molly you may do The Nose one day, but I never will.'

Another thing she joked was,

> 'I'm just going to borrow this junk we need for Washington Column because I'm not really sure I like this stuff.'
>
> But The Nose was our big goal and just for two years dominated my life, every move I made – stacking newspapers, working jobs that required strength, every time I looked at something it was the stove leg cracks going free in my mind.[16]

(The stove leg cracks are a notable feature of the climb. They were originally ascended using the hollow metal legs of stoves, sawn off and hammered into the crack. Today they are climbed free, without recourse to aid, and offer perfect hand jamming cracks in which you insert your hand, lock it, and pull up on it.)

> 'Stove leg cracks, stove leg cracks' it was a wonderful kind of thought and every spring and every fall we'd climb another big wall.[17]

The N.W. Buttress of Half Dome and Steak Salathe – on the Sentinel they climbed in a day – were all first women's team ascents. They began chalking up routes every season, always with The Nose in mind.

> Finally, in 1976, Barb said, 'Moll I'm so sorry! I'm not ready for The Nose'. It required a great deal of patience because we waited for one another and we really nurtured one another along.

A head-on view of The Nose on the stupendous 3,000ft/915m high wall of El Capitan in the Yosemite Valley, USA. This is possibly the most famous rock climb in the world. The first all-women's ascent was made by Molly Higgins and Barb Eastman in April 1977. *(Iain Williamson)*

The attitude was that Barb at that time wasn't as talented a free climber, but was very solid and very safe. A lot of people thought us too safe, but we had both almost killed ourselves in big falls and were determined, and loved climbing enough, not to have that as part of the game. If that was part of the game we didn't want to play it – so I really loved climbing with Barb because you knew her belay anchors were solid – you could drop elephants onto them.

So by 1977 we were finally ready to do The Nose and we spent two weeks climbing for practice. Meanwhile El Capitan just loomed like a black cloud over our heads – we'd go out and say OK today six pitches of 5·9 or 5·10 – we'd do three and break for tea and that would be that.

Oh God, how are we going to get up this thing? It took us four days and three nights – and those Stoveleg cracks were as beautiful as anyone had ever said. Just cracks, 9 pitches. I was so tired at the end of the day; we'd been hauling a 50-pound [23 kg] Sac, I would put my hand in a crack and 'wham' out it would slide, and I'd have to jam my forearm in and just muscle my way up. I was so tired – beyond tired. I wanted to stop before our destined bivouac ledge (at Dolt tower) but Barb said 'No Mol, we're doing 3 more pitches to El Cap Tower'. I had been so focused on the 'Stovelegs' and looked up at the rest of the god damned wall and thought 'Oh no I've still got to climb the rest of this thing, it's not just the Stoveleg cracks.'[18]

There was still 610 m (2,000 ft) of climbing above them. They made the El Cap Tower that night, but Molly was sick and they slept badly.

'Would you pass me a bag, I think I'm going to be sick,' I said.
Barb reached across the ledge and retrieved some paper bags from the haul sack. 'Are you going to be okay?' she asked.
'I'm so tired,' I answered. 'I've been living to climb El Cap for two years and I'm sure glad I didn't get here any sooner. I couldn't possibly have done this last year!'
Barb awoke early in the morning with the swallows, and as they darted and dived about us she passed out our allotment of granola bars, Tang, and one apple. She was in a typically cheerful mood. Barb was always like a little kid in the morning and especially optimistic on walls, as if that type of endurance and commitment most suited her strong body and will.
'Thanks to you, we made El Cap Tower in one day,' I said. 'You did a great lead in the dark.'
'And we climbed the Stovelegs almost entirely free!' Barb exclaimed.
Those beloved Stoveleg cracks! For the last two years every crack I'd climbed had been a gesture of training for those cracks, and I was sad that they were over.
'Now all we have to do is climb the upper 2,000 ft of the route,' I said. It seemed like a long way to go.[19]

Molly was tired, and found the next day very tedious. It involved a series of technical rope manoeuvres, pendulums and horizontal traverses. By the time they reached the next bivouac site, known as 'Camp 4', they were extremely tired.

By the time we'd got to camp 4 we were tired, yeah! A little bitty ledge about this big.

(She indicated the size of this minute rock ledge with her hands.)

We switched places you know – who gets the inside, who gets the outside – I got the outside. My butt was literally hanging over 1,500 ft [460 m] of space – and we slept like babies.[20]

The sleep was needed, and the next two days on the face went well.

Everything had gone so well, but we both knew the story about the guy whose rope broke when he fell on the last pitch of El Cap.

But no, Barb and I were too thorough for such a misfortune. We topped-out safely, leaving us to descend the wooded paths together, down to my tent in Camp 4 where I found a note pinned to the door.

'Congratulations: first team of women up the Nose!'[21]

An historic occasion, it must have been a tremendous feeling for Molly to 'top out' [make the final lead to the top]. But there were other emotions also:

and a feeling too that there was a change coming in my life because I knew that I was going back to college that summer and knew in two months' time my life was going to totally change. I really freaked out because I knew I was going to get much more responsible and not be spending six months at a time just climbing. Just climbing had been a little too empty, I needed more.[22]

Wider experience

Until the 1980s Molly probably did as much climbing as in those early hard hot rock years in Yosemite, but she began to widen her experience. During the summer of 1978 she visited Canada with Larry Bruce; they climbed the North Face of Mount Athabaska, which consisted of a 610 m (2,000 ft) face of ice at an angle of 50°, and they soloed Sky Ladder on Andromeda. They also climbed the North East Face of Mt Temple and traversed the mountain. This was a fantastic 18-hour day expedition and she began to get really into mountaineering. The next winter she spent much of her time doing winter climbs in the Rocky Mountain National Park.

1979 was no less fruitful, with major ascents in North America and Colorado. These included Enclosure Couloir in the Grand Tetons with Sue Giller; Bugaboo Spire, East Face (V – 5.9 A2) with Larry Bruce; and The Diamond (D1) face of Long's Peak, one of America's biggest walls, with Barb Eastman and Sue Giller. She also returned in the autumn to Yosemite, and with Sue Giller climbed the very hard East Face of Washington Column. A brilliant rock climb, she described the route as having 'elegant and wonderful pitches the way the hell up there'!

The geology of America is wonderfully diverse and for the climber offers an almost infinitely varying selection of both rock type and scenery. Molly enjoyed this inheritance to the full. West from Colorado one hits Utah, the great American desert, and on its eastern edge where the Colorado river, from its birth in the Rocky Mountain National Park, crosses the great sandstone beds, it cuts a deep and impressive gorge. (This is well before the Grand Canyon – in the state of Arizona.) Here Molly, along with Larry, made a first ascent of a route which they subsequently named 'Artist Tears'. It was an aid climb, climbed using pitons driven into the rock to assist upward progress.

If the one piton Molly had been pulling on had ripped out of the fragile crack, then all the others below would have zipped out in turn: so poor were the piton placements in the soft red sandstone. She described her emotions on making the climb:

The feeling of tension builds the higher you get and you know if one piton rips you're gone.

(She snapped her fingers.)

It's not like free climbing when you know positively how the holds are going to perform. You get a real streak of adrenalin going. It was pretty thrilling and clipping into the belay felt a lot like that first lead I ever did – you know you could crawl up on the summit and kiss it.

However, Washington Column marked the end of hard rock-climbing for Molly (to date); the enjoyment was beginning to disappear. Her reputation meant that everyone expected top performances all the time. This she did not relish. She climbed for enjoyment; to be at one with the rock, to appreciate her partner, both giving and receiving in a worthwhile relationship. In 1980 she married Larry Bruce and they moved to Aspen, where they could pursue her other great passion: cross-country ski racing.

She described cross-country racing as in many ways similar to climbing:

It requires much the same kind of concentrated movement that climbing does. When you're skiing well, especially when racing, you're training at a very high level and you think about the most minute things, like how am I coming off the ball of my foot, how hard the knee is coming through, how high is my hand – push and pull with your stomach.

Because she was very fit from her mountaineering exploits, she entered racing at a high level. Even given this start, she excelled at her newly chosen sport. In 1983 she won the 20 km (12½ mile) World Masters Championship, and was 11th in the U.S. Birkebeiner. In 1984 she became the 30+ Colorado State Champion.

Makalu and Peak 3

Despite her incredible dedication to ski racing and her professional responsibilities as medical technologist at Aspen Valley Hospital, the mountains were never that far away. Late in 1982 Doug Scott (Molly's friend and well-known Himalayan climber from Britain) invited her and Larry on his 1984 expedition to Makalu.

Situated in the Nepalese Himalayas on the Tibetan border, only 19 km (12 miles) south east of Everest, Makalu is the world's fifth-highest summit at 8,470 m (27,790 ft). Molly and Larry decided to climb North America's highest mountain, Mount McKinley, 6,194 metres (20,322 ft) high as a training exercise. She described it thus:

We knew if we stood any chance of going we had to do McKinley this spring, which was desperate after 3 years of not really climbing; to get psyched up to spend all that money and prepare all the equipment required. I was a very happy little ski racer; it seemed just absurd.

We got on that little aeroplane in Talkeetna and took off from the Alaskan Swamps and there over the trees are Mount Foraker, McKinley and Hunter as big as lions and we land on a little glacier, just the two of us, and it was totally uncomplicated. No other people's egos, ideas or anything to consider – it was just a marvellous experience together.

They ascended the west rib which had not been their initial objective, but the climb went well.

The next day we made 4,000 ft [1220 m] in 4 hours. Just cruising up this thing we felt great. He was very sweet to me, which was necessary. I don't like to be left behind especially on big ice couloirs – I hate them. He stayed with me because he knew I

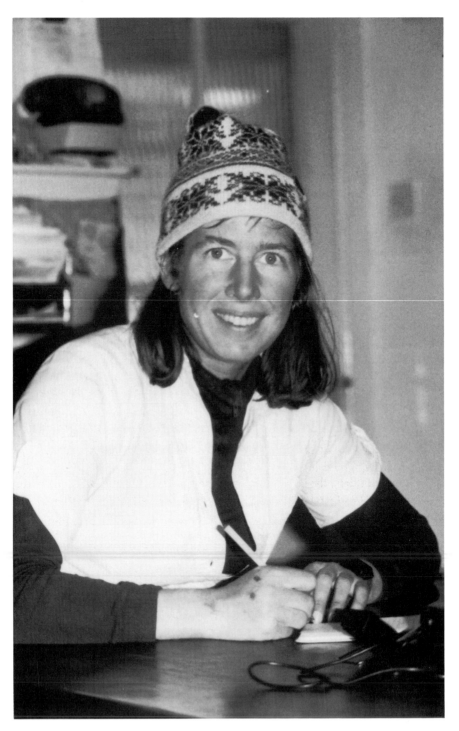

Molly Higgins, April 1984. *(Bill Birkett)*

wasn't mentally attuned to McKinley as he was. But by the time we got to the summit ridge we were both on our knees. We held hands and walked the last 10 ft together. The fact two of us had put so much into it and gotten there together was really marvellous.

Molly is illustrating here another very important quality of climbing or mountaineering: that of comradeship/companionship. This aspect can be one of the most rewarding of the whole climbing/mountaineering experience. For it is on the hills, away from the pressures of society and restrictions of conventionality, that a well-balanced team can communicate as equals. To share a common appreciation of a beautiful environment and to face the challenges together, knowing that one's survival depends on the other, is to know a great joy. In these circumstances, as in no other activity, climbing brings forth a sincere love for one's fellow human being.

1984 saw both Molly and Larry on the Doug Scott expedition, and they climbed 'Peak 3', taking the icy East Ridge to the South East Summit. It was the first ascent of this virgin peak (6,300 m or 20,670 ft). Unfortunately, time ran out, and they had to return to their respective jobs before an attempt was made on Makalu. In any case, it transpired that no one was to succeed on Makalu on this expedition. Doug Scott, Stephen Sustad and Frenchman Jean Affanessieff barely made it back to Base Camp safely after finding themselves too stretched and exhausted near the summit. (Doug Scott was actually intent on the summit, but Jean Affanessieff made the decision to descend.)

To Molly, climbing is strictly for fun, 'It's just not worth dying for', but she has left an indelible mark on the history of American rock climbing. I am quite sure whatever Molly Higgins next decides to do, she will do it determinedly and at the highest conceivable level.

She has a theory about women in climbing which is important to the development of women's climbing. From her own experiences she knows that women usually start off as less capable climbers than men. They do not have the innate strength, they cannot do pull ups, and so they have to learn how to use their natural abilities, those of agility and balance. Additionally, to compensate for this initial lack of strength, they must develop their climbing technique.

> It takes them much longer to start out on the 5·0's and 5·3's but by the time they are 5·9 and 5·10 climbers very often their technique is better than any man's. At that point with strength training they can then advance because they already have a lot of good technique.

The above realisation of fact is a very important landmark for women in climbing; it is the appreciation, gained through experience and personal courage, that women could successfully advance into the world of highly strenuous and technically hard rock climbing. Molly pointed the way, putting her theory into practice. From a vision, through application, she had the satisfaction of climbing the Nose of El Capitan. In the 1980s numerous American women rock climbers are proving the point dramatically, by training intensely and regularly leading 5·13's (America's hardest rock climbing grade to date). But it was Molly and Barb who took that first huge stride, proving it possible and breaking the all-important psychological barrier.

I already knew the answer to the final question which I asked Molly: did she ever doubt that she was going to succeed on the famous Nose of El Capitan?

> Ah. We were always going to make it. Some cool weather moved in and some clouds but there was *never* any question. I think it was because of the two years of

preparation in getting there. We knew that we were ready and that was our rock. We were intimidated, but there was never any question.

Chronological list of events

1950   Molly born in Pennsylvania.
1958   First ascent of The Nose.
1968   Arrived at Colorado College; joined Mountain Club.
1969   Led first 5·6 route.
1969–70   Led 5·7–5·8 new routes in Colorado Springs area.
1970   Fell off Snuggles and Stetner's Ledges.
1971–76   Taught for Colorado Outward Bound School.
1972–74   Climbed 5·2–5·6 routes in Colorado with female friends.
1974   First trip to Yosemite.
     Peak Lenin.
     Led 5·8 in Yosemite area; became full-time climber; teamed up with Barb Eastman.
1975   Led 5·9 South face of Washington.
     First women's team ascent of Diamond on Long's Peak.
     Met Larry Bruce.
1976   First women's team ascent of Steak Salathe on Sentinel, with Barb Eastman.
     First women's team ascent of N.W. Buttress of Half Dome, with Barb Eastman.
     North face of Tour Ronde, South face of Midi, Torre Trieste.
     Gold Wall.
1976–77   Ski mountaineering.
1977   First women's team ascent of The Nose of El Capitan, with Barb Eastman.
1978   Graduated from Colorado University School of Medicine.
     Canada: traverse of Mt Temple, North face of Athabasca, tandem solo of Skyladder on Andromeda.
     Winter climbs in the Rockies.
1979   D1 Long's Peak, Enclosure Couloir, East Face of Bugaboo Spire, East Face of Washington Column.
1980   Married Larry Bruce.
     Moved from Boulder to Aspen, to pursue ski racing in earnest.
1980–84   Cross-country ski racing.
1983   20 km (12½ miles) World Masters Champion, 11th in U.S. Birkebeiner.
     Mt McKinley.
1984   30+ Colorado State Champion.
     Peak 3, Nepal.

References

[1]Robert W. Craig, *Storm and Sorrow in the High Pamirs* (Gollancz, 1981), p. 188/[2]ibid., p. 198/[3]ibid., p. 202/[4]ibid., p. 206/[5]ibid., p. 208/[6]ibid., p. 209/[7]Interview Molly Higgins/Birkett (April, 1984)/[8]ibid./[9]ibid./[10]ibid./[11]ibid./[12]ibid./[13]Robert W. Craig, *Storm and Sorrow in the High Pamirs*, p. 100/[14]Interview Molly Higgins/Birkett (April, 1984)/[15]ibid./[16]ibid./[17]ibid./[18]ibid./[19]*Yosemite Climber* compiled by George Meyers (Diadem Books, 1979), p. 62/[20]Interview Molly Higgins/Birkett (April, 1984)/[21]*Yosemite Climber*, p. 63/[22]Interview Molly Higgins/Birkett (April, 1984)

10

Wanda Rutkiewicz – throwing away the crutches

A climbing philosophy

> I climb for three reasons: to be with nature and appreciate the mountain environment, because of the people – fellow climbers, and just for the climbing. Sometimes climbing is the most important, sometimes people and sometimes nature.[1]

So said Wanda Rutkiewicz, probably the greatest and most accomplished woman mountaineer of the present era, sitting by a Lakeland log fire answering my ceaseless stream of enthusiastic questions.

We had climbed together that winter's day on England's highest mountain. Conditions on Moss Ghyll (IV) were bad, and we had shared leads on melting/avalanching snow and wet rock, eventually retreating to the warmth and comfort of Bill Peascod's spacious farm house. It was easy for me to relax, and to question and to wonder how this climber from Poland had achieved incredible success in Europe and the high Himalayas: from the high Troll wall in Norway to the Eiger north pillar, the Matterhorn north face in winter, to Noshaq, Gasherbrum III and II, to the famous Mount Everest and beyond.

The emerging story was not one of achievement without effort, but rather a human glimpse into what can be attained by a strong individual with vision, determination and courage. She has earned her status, often against seemingly impossible odds. Also, I learned that for Wanda, climbing was more than a daring episode in life, more than a game to excel at: it was freedom, expression – it was life.

Wanda Rutkiewicz, April 1984. *(Bill Birkett)*

The adventures in Wanda's life have been many; she has seen success, and achieved more than most mountaineers could even dream of. Yet she has also seen failure and tragedy. By the end of my meeting with Wanda, the pre-conceived labels I attached to her such as 'first European woman to climb Everest' seemed irrelevant. It is her philosophy to life and climbing that stays with me, the doing rather than the achievement that impresses me most.

A short time prior to our meeting, Wanda had presented a paper entitled 'Women's Mountaineering in Himalayas and Karakorum (in the last 25 years)' at the 25th Jubilee of the Indian Mountaineering Foundation. Her philosophy is interesting. She said:

> The best women's team has been and will be worse than the best men's team. This is reflected in history and reality. Twenty-five years after the first ascent of an 8,000 m [26,350 ft] peak the first female conquered that physical barrier. It was already 10 years after men conquered them all. But now, as in many other sport disciplines, women achieve results that have previously been unattainable for men and even now not for every man. This development of achievements would not have been possible if among other things men had not shown the way, and had not proven that it is within the boundaries of human potential.
>
> Women learn fast, they profit from the experience of others and they improve their climbing style. The gap between the first ascent in 1975 of a two-men team, R. Messner and P. Habeler, of the eight thousand m [26,000 ft] peak Gasherbrum I and a similar ascent of two women, A. Czerwinska and K. Palmowka (note both Polish) this year of Broad Peak in Karakorum is only 8 years. They climbed the top in two days from the basecamp without oxygen, without any companions or high altitude porters.
>
> I think that nowadays men and women should not compete in mountaineering but compare – how far behind we are – and learn – talk less, climb more. Learn to be self-sufficient.[2]

Wanda has strong feelings that to derive full satisfaction from the challenge of big mountains, women should climb together, without the 'crutch' of male support. This has nothing to do with not enjoying climbs with males or a mixed group; it is just that the full challenge, the full responsibility and the full rewards of mountaineering, can for her only be appreciated by directly shouldering the problems.

> If men and women are members of the same expedition, a man either consciously or subconsciously will take over the leadership in the mountains, or a woman consciously or subconsciously will give the leadership to the better one and will concentrate only on the problem of 'whether *she* will climb to the top'.
>
> This is reasonable until she checks her independent abilities while in action.
>
> Therefore it is necessary to test one's abilities and to learn to be independent in the mountains, not only to learn how to climb. The best way is to do that with women's teams, when a woman asks herself 'whether *we* will climb to the top' or 'whether it is possible to climb this route' when new routes or ascents to unconquered peaks are contemplated.[3]

Wanda quietly explained to me her feelings:

> Mountaineering is many things, it is not only perfect climbing. I enjoy climbing more if I take the risk and carry the consequences of my decisions. You must consider your position on the mountain. Is it late? Should we descend or go up? Which route should we follow? Where can we put the pegs? Is it good or not? What will the weather be like? If you climb with a better partner you are free from many problems.[4]

Wanda was brave enough to make a very fundamental point here. In addition to the male/female aspects of her statement, important as they are, she also spoke openly about the role/status of the sherpa.

Countless expeditions (predominantly male) in the past have relied heavily on their sherpas for success, and Tensing Norgay was, of course, along with Edmund Hillary, the first person to climb to the highest point on earth. Yet, in most instances, their climbing ability goes totally uncredited. Such self-glorification at the expense of others is simply not acceptable to Wanda.

> Now an explanation of a definition of the term: 'a women's expedition'. I submit a proposition: all expeditions until 1981 to eight thousand metre [26,250 ft] peaks were not really women's expeditions, because sherpas participated in each of them.
>
> Let's say it openly – sherpas are also mountaineers. I do not see why it is necessary to make a distinction between the mixed men–women's expeditions and women's expeditions with sherpas. Previously I thought that if decisions are made by women then an expedition should be treated as a women's expedition, and sherpas should be treated the same, as in men's expeditions, as high altitude porters.
>
> Now I am of the opinion that sports expeditions to the high mountains should mainly rely on themselves, and if sherpas or other high altitude porters are included in the expedition they should be treated as *members* of the expedition and the name of the expedition should also bear the name of their country. I want to be perfectly clear that this refers only to sports expeditions. Their relation toward other expeditions must be as fair as their relation towards the mountains.
>
> It does not mean that women neither individually nor as a team should not participate in men's expeditions nor go without the help of sherpas. On the contrary, they should do that to learn mountaineering, to try their abilities to climb the highest mountains.
>
> But on the classifying list the women's ascents with men's expeditions should be listed *after* individual women's ascents.
>
> During mixed expedition the confrontations between women's and men's abilities as for how many kgs they may carry should be avoided. I myself have experienced this during the expedition to Mt Everest; 'If you want to become famous as a conqueror of a peak, you do not do that at everyone else's expense. Work as we do, carry the same loads as we do from the base.'* And so I did. But it is not a good solution. Such confrontation should be only among men or among women, but not between men and women. Men and women on the same expedition can and should complement each other.[5]
>
> *Said by her male companions on the Everest expedition.

Early climbs

Wanda Blaszkiewicz was born in Lithuania on the 4th February 1943. Four years later the family found itself in Wrockaw (Poland) where she went to school, eventually gaining a Master of Science degree in Computer Science. Paradoxically, she was born near the sea, far away from the mountains. Her family were definitely non-climbers, and there were no connections with the hills.

She was an accomplished athlete and skilful volleyball player. At school and polytechnic she excelled in the high jump, shot-put and javelin. She also played volleyball for the Polish national youth team, and was a member of the team preparing for the 1964 Olympic Games in Tokyo – although she did not finally make the Olympics. It was not until 1961, as an 18-year-old student, that she first visited the rocks.

Her very first climb she described as an 'explosion'.[6] From that moment she knew climbing was *the* thing in her life.

I asked her about these first moments, and if she found that climbing came easily right from the start. She answered:

> I think so; it was not beautiful and I had not good style, but it was my first visit to the rocks. They were up to 100 m [330 ft] high and granite. My friends climbed with me but only a little because I was only a beginner and they wanted to climb themselves, but I was a little 'hungry' so I climbed alone. That first day I climbed some chimney – I went up and up and up. My friends below became very afraid for me because I was alone. This first time I made it to the top. I was very fit of course because of athletics and volleyball, but it was my first time ever in the mountains. Ever since I have never been able to repeat this route without a rope and someone to accompany me!

The rocks are known as the Gory Sokole (Eagle mountains), and are situated in the south west of Poland. Although there are other rock climbing areas in Poland, notably the limestone pillars of the Jura near Czeslochowa, and the sandstones on the border with East Germany, it is only the High Tatra which are large enough to be classed as mountains (the highest being Rysy at approximately 2,500 m or 8,200 ft). Here there is both rock climbing, and snow and ice mountaineering in winter.

After that first trip Wanda climbed every weekend. Travelling three hours by train, then walking for an hour, she would reach the rocks late, to spend the night in the forests below. With no sleeping bag or warm equipment, she and her group slept in caves and made camp fires to keep warm. During the day, and sometimes the night, they would climb. These hard early years, combined with her great natural ability, gave her the toughness and skill required for the very difficult climbs that were to follow.

The Alps

Wanda first graduated to the west European mountains in 1964; for six long, precious weeks she attended a rescue course in the Austrian Alps (the Zillertaler Alps). She practised crevasse recovery on the glacier, and on the heights she improved her ice climbing and learned big-wall rescue techniques.

It was not until 1967 that she could again fund a trip to the western Alps. This time it was the Mont Blanc area, and there she experienced both success and failure. But she was climbing with other women, and this was significant. She traversed Mont Blanc itself, and amongst the Chamonix Aiguille she succeeded, with Halina Krüger Syrokomske, on the east face of the Grépon (Mer de Glace Face of the Grépon).

A notable failure was the famous and difficult Bonatti Pillar, then one of the hardest and most daring climbs in the Alps. It is difficult, with considerable objective danger, even to reach the start of the climb. The foot of this great tower of rock, with an unbroken vertical face of 600 m (1,970 ft), is guarded by the notorious Dru Couloir (Death Couloir). The couloir is an exceptionally steep runnel of ice. It collects stone fall from the west face of the Dru, channels it and hurtles it down in a murderous salvo. Any climber caught by stone fall in this couloir has little chance of survival. If one fails on the Bonatti Pillar it is necessary, once again, to expose oneself to this risk. Quick movement and technical ability are essential. Wanda, at 24 years old, was competent and brave enough to dare and to survive when bad weather forced her retreat.

Trollryggen

Norway's Trollryggen Wall is a vertical mile (1,600 m) high, and is one of Europe's most impressive faces of rock. It presents a dual challenge in terms of both technical rock climbing and size and position, for an ascent of such a large rock wall involves a number of days' climbing. All food and clothing must be carried, either on the climber's back or by hauling on the end of a rope up the vertical rocks. One must carefully choose a site to sleep; hard rock climbing demands good physical condition, so it is necessary to find a suitably pro-portioned rock ledge. If no ledge can be found, the night must be spent either suspended in hammocks or 'tied' to the rock from pitons driven into cracks in the wall.

In 1968 Wanda, again with Halina, climbed the Trollryggen East Pillar. She later described the climb to me in her halting English:

> We had no stove and drank only cold water with citric acid [lemon powder]. It was difficult to find the water on these very steep rocks. It was crazy wasn't it? But our biggest problem was finding the way – it is a very big wall and clouds and bad weather arrived on our second day on the climb – it made it very exciting. We arrived on the top on the third day and made two bivouacs. The climbing was beautiful, Norway is so soft in July, the days are long and the darkness lasts for only four hours.

Later during the same trip, on a much smaller cliff, she fell and broke her leg.

In the Alps again

The next Alpine season saw her once more in Chamonix. Routes were climbed, but the big lines eluded her. She had two attempts and two failures on the Grand Capucin, a huge flake of red granite 490 m (1,608 ft) high, bristling with rows of overhangs. Both times she was forced to retreat due to bad weather; the second time was particularly epic. In terrible conditions and in the middle of a lightning storm, she was forced to abseil into space from above the first overhangs. It was 'Really an adventure'; regaining the rock and descending safely required con-siderable skill and self-control. Ten years later she returned and climbed the Grand Capucin.

The big mountains

Wanda's first big mountain expedition came in 1970, a combined Polish-Russian expedition in the Russian High Pamirs. It was not a happy occasion for Wanda. With ill-feeling and problems colouring the small group of climbers, she swore that she would never go with an expedition again. Despite this, she was successful on Peak Lenin (7,134 m or 23,406 ft). Eventually she realised that the expedition, although bad at the time, had given her valuable experience. Not least, it had introduced her to the problems generated by all expeditions: those of living, working and climbing together as a group in a harsh and foreign environment.

This experience paid off in 1972, when with Alison Chadwick-Onyszkiewicz and Janusz Onyszkiewicz she climbed Noshaq (7,492 m or 24,580 ft), the second highest summit in the Hindu Kush. Wanda regards it as one of the best expeditions of her life. By expedition standards it was small, with only ten members. The advantage was that everyone knew each other, were friends, and consequently worked harmoniously. They organised and equipped the trip themselves from a very tight budget ($1,000 each). They drove a truck overland (because it was the cheapest form of transport) from Poland to Afghanistan, and this proved to be an adventure in itself. What a journey: from Poland, through Soviet Russia to Afghanistan via Termez on the Amu Darya river.

It was on this trip that Wanda became great friends with Alison Chadwick-Onyszkiewicz. (Alison married Janusz in the autumn of 1971 in Cornwall, and then moved to Poland. Later she was to become one of Britain's most accomplished mountaineers of the modern era, and her story is inexorably linked with Wanda's.)

Wanda commented on her meeting and resultant friendship with Alison:

> It was very exciting meeting; two different cultures, East and West. Her mentality, her remarkable relationship with other people was fantastic for me. She was never aggressive and if she didn't agree you could see her smiling underneath; that was enough. I think the British character is very nice; you accept any person – you permit people to be different and you accept it. In Poland, mostly, they will change the person – it is different.

The Eiger

The Eiger North Face is undoubtedly the most notorious, unforgiving and challenging face in the Western Alps. The vertical section of the mountain has a height of 1,500 m (4,920 ft) and soars from the pleasant Alpine meadows of Kleine Scheidegg in a great concave face of black and white. Nine climbers died before it was first ascended and many, many more have done so since. Its name is hallowed in mountaineering circles, and an ascent, even in this rapidly changing and technologically advanced modern climbing world, is still something to be proud of. Difficulties are objective rather than technical; this vast face has a weather pattern predominantly its own – usually bad – and is constantly raked by falling stone.

In 1973 Wanda and her companions, Danuta Wach and Stefania Egierszdorff, thought it time they climbed the Eiger. On arrival at the face, however, conditions were extremely bad, and Wanda chose to attempt the easier Eiger North Pillar which lies to the left of the main North face. Still a difficult route, this climb had not yet received a second ascent. However, Wanda felt confident; she was the most experienced member of the all-women party, and this meant she was going to be where she is always happiest – out in front.

They were on the climb for three epic days. During the day, temperatures were mild (above freezing) and waterfalls cascaded down the face drenching them to the skin. During the night, however, the temperature dropped to $-10°C$ (14°F). Their equipment was primitive and inadequate beyond belief: 'In Poland we had nothing – no karrimats, no many things'. With their down jackets soaked and no windproofs whatsoever, they sat out the long nights with their backs to the bare ice.

They survived to make the second ascent; Wanda knew they could, and she knows about toughness and how to win.

> I was badly frost-bitten, my boots were too small for me and this was my biggest problem. Descending the normal route was terrible. If I took my boots off I couldn't put them on again. My feet were black and swollen. But I have good circulation and after Innsbruck clinic there are no consequences.

She smiled. I shook my head, knowing too well that this stage of frost-bite, when the digits are black, often means amputation!

I suppose this ascent marked the watershed in Wanda's climbing life – not that it changed her or her thoughts, just that others were now able to see her capabilities.

The High Pamirs

This expedition, organised by the Soviet Mountaineering Federation, was an international climbing meet with 160 climbers from 12 nations, including Molly Higgins from America and Doug Scott from Britain. Its story is that of one of the worst tragedies in mountaineering history. At this time Wanda fell ill, suffering from oedema at 7,000 m (23,000 ft), and was helicoptered from Base Camp to hospital.

I think fate was, perhaps disguisedly, kind to Wanda – for up in the mountains, racked with storm and the earthquake, 15 mountaineers died.

There were of course logical reasons for Wanda's illness. She was considerably run-down and anaemic prior to the expedition. A number of problems weighed heavily on her mind. In 1972 her father had died in suspicious circumstances. Additionally, there were many emotional problems at home: Wanda was divorced in 1973 and was living alone; work was putting undue demands on her time, with insufficient financial rewards.

Karakorum

In 1975 Wanda led the Polish Women's Karakorum Expedition, and this became one of the most important and successful women's expeditions of all time. Its objectives were Gasherbrum II (8,035 m or 26,362 ft) and Gasherbrum III (7,952 m or 26,090 ft). The Karakorum offers probably the most spectacular mountain scenery in the world. It ranges 400 km (250 miles), forming the geographical and political frontier between the Indian sub-continent and central Asia. Its melt-waters flow either south to the Indus or north to the Yarkand, to disappear in the desert wastes of the Sinkiang. The name Gasherbrum means 'Shining Wall', and the four Gasherbrums are all distinctive peaks, GII appearing as a bold point of rock and GIII as a sharp-edged pyramid.

The entire expedition comprised seven men, led by Janusz Onyszkiewicz, and ten women led by Wanda. They ascended the summit of GII with separate ropes (eight people in all), the third party being an all-women team. Halina Krüger Syrokomska and Anna Okopinska were the first all-women rope to have made an 8,000 m (26,250 ft) peak, and they did it without oxygen.

GIII had never previously been climbed when Alison Chadwick-Onyszkiewicz, her husband Janusz, Wanda and Krzysztof Zdzitowiecki completed the east ridge to reach the summit of the highest unclimbed mountain in the world at 6 p.m. on 11th August 1975. For the record, Alison, first on top, made GIII the highest peak to be first climbed by a woman and the second highest summit (after Kangchenjunga) to be first ascended by a British climber. The descent was made safely and Wanda, as well as succeeding in that tremendous first ascent, had led and organised the expedition from its conception. All round it was a brilliant achievement.

It was not easy for Wanda to lead this large group, the members of which had proven abilities but had never come together to climb before. Added to this was

From left to right: Alison Chadwick-Onyszkiewicz, Wanda Rutkiewicz and Krzysztof Zdzitowiecki on the summit after the first ascent of Gasherbrum 111 (26,090ft/7952m) in 1975. *(Wanda Rutkiewicz collection)*

the further complication of there being both a men's team and a women's team. Although Wanda and Janusz worked extremely well together, it was impossible to satisfy the demands of both. The combination of weather, logistics, difficult climbing and 16 strong individuals to organise and lead was asking a lot of Wanda. Not only did she lead, but she was also one of the strongest climbers, as evidenced by her successful summit bid. And here was a further difficulty: she could not stand back from the crowd by virtue of her age or her ineligibility for the summit.

She said:

> All parties were against me and I was against all parties. But this didn't present a problem; the mountain had to be the problem. I decided to be hard. I have no other way out because it is no good having split ideas and split decisions. If people did not like me, it didn't matter; that presented no problems with the mountain. In the end they accepted my solutions and my decisions and this was good. I think my attitude came as a shock to Alison; you are democrats, I was formal, but after one year we are great friends again. Janusz was fantastic. He understood both problems, men and women, and we worked together. After Solidarity was declared illegal and Janusz was in jail I think of him on Gasherbrum, in a conflict situation, quiet, thinking, democratic. Thinking of some possibility which is good for both – a solution for many, not for one.

Wanda Rutkiewicz in Gasherbrum 11 and 111 Base Camp in 1975. (*Wanda Rutkiewicz collection*)

Back in the Himalayas

One year after the Gasherbrums, Wanda was again in the Himalayas as a member of an Austrian/German/Polish expedition to Nanga Parbat. It is a deceptively dangerous mountain at 8,125 m (26,657 ft), and rises a clear 7,000 m (23,000 ft) from the valleys below. Its name means 'King of the Mountains'. Wanda described it as different from many mountains in the Himalayas, with its lower walls and base being green.

> You can make a campfire and around you there are trees and a river, and the smell of the leaves and the flowers is fantastic. Above you can see the big walls but it all looks kindly and you can't understand why it is the killer of the climbers.

Unfortunately, an accident on the mountain forced retreat, and the expedition was abandoned.

The Matterhorn

In 1978, five years after the Eiger, Wanda tackled the other great classic North face, the Matterhorn.

There was a little more to this all-women attempt; it was in winter, making it the *first* women's winter ascent. Winter is the toughest time to make an Alpine climb. Although the snow and ice may be more stable than in summer, conditions are harsh, and the severity and duration of storms and bad weather are increased. It is necessary to climb with more survival equipment and consequently more weight. Hence the climbs take longer than in the summer, and the exposure to danger is lengthened. In point of fact, the odds are considerably shortened.

All this may seem to make an attempt incredible enough, but again there is even more beneath the surface. In 1977 Wanda was hit by a severe illness; at first she suspected malaria, contracted on her previous expedition, but it was far more serious than this. It was, in fact, meningitis (infection of the brain tissue), and death escaped her by a very small margin. Afterwards she remained weak and incapacitated; she had to learn everything again: how to talk, walk and climb.

Irena Kesa, her friend of many climbs, helped her back to strength and to climbing. From easier climbs on the Eagle Rocks and the High Tatra's, who would have thought, who could possibly have imagined, that in the early winter months of 1978 she was to lead up one of the hardest and toughest challenges in the Alps? Only Wanda, I suspect.

The team for the ascent consisted of Wanda, Anna Czerwinska, Krystyna Palmowska and Irena Kesa. With the exception of Wanda, they had made an ascent of the North face in summer, and knew what problems might be encountered. Conditions were not good, but with only one month's leave from Poland, an attempt had to be made before time ran out.

The first day gave sunshine, but always there was a biting, cold wind. After a deteriorating night, the second day saw an increase in the ferocity of the wind. Irena, the youngest member of the party, began to suffer from frost-bite; her body was unable to cope with the extreme cold. On the rocks Irena was brilliant, very light, very strong, very gymnastic; but her low-calorie diet which was necessary for high performance on rock acted strongly against her on this cold Alpine face.

Wanda said: 'She took to the wall only low-calorie food, but temperatures were around −10°C [12° F] and conditions were hard. I think in these situations you must eat and drink normally.'

On the third day they reached the exposed summit ridge, but the wind was so violent they had to retreat back down onto the North face to attempt to shelter. To survive they had to escape this wind, and on the iced face they struggled to dig a snow cave. They partially succeeded in doing this, enough to stay alive. On the fourth day they reached the top again, but Irena by now was in a critical condition. Behaving like a doll, her face was expressionless and her limbs were barely responsive; there could be no safe descent for her.

On the 'walkie-talkie' they carried, Wanda took a difficult decision (for her): to summon the rescue helicopter. In Zermatt all eyes were trained on the mountain; the ascent was big news and the helicopter added to the spectacle.

Irena and Krystyna were taken off first, to leave Anna and Wanda alone on the summit. Wanda desperately wanted to descend the mountain. She felt that they had not completed the route and suspected that others would disclaim their ascent! I tried to reassure her that no one could, with any validity, question their ascent. She answered,

> Yes, but it is better if we go down – it would take one day more of course but we are ready to do it. But you can't say 'No we stay here' and fight with the rescue men on top. It was going dark. If they come with rope then you should say only thank you.

The weather was rapidly deteriorating, with a large depression moving into the area. As night fell, to stay and argue with the rescue team would put everyone at risk. The helicopter had to lose height rapidly; the rescue crew were subjecting themselves to extreme danger, and if Wanda had remained with Anna to descend the iced Hörnli ridge in storm conditions their chances of survival after four nights on the mountain would, I think, have been very slim. At that time and in those circumstances, to take the helicopter was the only reasonable decision.

Such was the rescue crew's necessity to descend quickly that as Wanda was being winched in after Anna, the helicopter wheeled away from the mountain and began its controlled fly down. Wanda hung with ice axes still dangling by loops from her wrists (modern ice-climbers climb with short axes attached to a cord looped round the wrist: when tired on steep ice one hangs from this loop with the 'tool' lodged in the ice) and with the wind tearing at her body.

Suddenly she found that her arm was being pulled violently out of its socket. She screamed, but no one could hear. The winchman stopped the overloading winch and tried to pull her inside the steeply banking helicopter, but to no avail: her ice axe had caught under the landing ski of the helicopter. So she flew back to Zermatt in the teeth of an Alpine winter, hanging outside!

Everyone except Irena remained comparatively unscathed. Initially she was in hospital at Zermatt; later Wanda managed to get her to Innsbruck, where there are very good facilities for treating frost-bite. Irena was lucky: there were no amputations, and one year later she was again doing incredible rock climbs.

Mount Everest

Wanda's next ascent that year was almost as impressive. It was the first European women's ascent of Mount Everest.

In October 1978, after her Matterhorn success, she was invited to join Dr Karl Herrligkoffer's expedition to Mt Everest. (It was a massive affair, with an array of international climbers from France, West Germany, Austria, Switzerland and Poland.) She already had the reputation of being one of the world's leading female mountaineers. Officially, it was a Franco-German expedition.

Herrligkoffer led the German team and Pierre Mazeaud led the French one. All previous records for summit success were broken, and 15 climbers topped Everest. Simultaneously, Alison Chadwick-Onyszkiewicz was participating in a 13-member American women's expedition to climb Annapurna I – 8,078 m (26,503 ft).

There had been no personality clashes or unpleasantness on Nanga Parbat with Herrligkoffer and his team, but about Everest Wanda commented,

> After Nanga Parbat I couldn't have possibly expected the troubles I had on the Everest expedition. Perhaps in Germany they do not have many independent women climbers who are leading and deciding for themselves.

Apart from the simple fact that Wanda is a woman, there are probably three other reasons why she suffered ill-feeling from many of the male members of this large expedition. Firstly, Herrligkoffer wished to honour her in some way, and he made her second deputy leader. Unfortunately, this only built up resentment amongst other expedition members, all of whom were excellent climbers in their own right. Many could not take this and saw it as a direct stab at their own egos. Secondly, she had to make a film of the expedition, and this of course involved getting in the way (as only camera persons know how to) whilst filming the other expedition members. Thirdly, expedition relations are always under strain. In large multi-national expeditions with climbers who have not known each other previously, this strain is considerably increased. For instance, the 1971 International Everest expedition led by N. G. Dyhrenfurth broke up in chaos despite his soothing influence, leaving Dougal Haston and Don Whillans, supported by the hardy Japanese, to fight out the bad weather alone.

In the long, enforced weeks in Base Camp Wanda learned to be thick-skinned, but when open aggression burst forth at 6,500 m (21,325 ft) she felt unable to contain her emotions. Below she had recognised that she must be seen to be 'pulling her own weight' and not shirking any of the work.

> I became determined to show my independence, I carried always 15 kg [33 lb] the same as the others and additionally I carried my filming equipment. I always climb without rope both on the icefall and above.

Four expedition members and three sherpas set out for the summit, but at the equipment dump on the South Col prior to commencing the summit bid, Sigi Hupfauer changed plans slightly and instructed that an extra bottle of oxygen should be carried a further 100 m (330 ft) higher. Since Wanda had the extra filming equipment, she objected to the change in plan. Suddenly Sigi exploded in a fit of anger. Wanda was completely shocked and upset by this; her knees and hands were shaking. The others turned and strode out for the summit, leaving Wanda dazed with emotion, struggling to find her full bottles of oxygen in the snow. Panic-stricken and afraid, Wanda was alone; she cried out to the rapidly disappearing expedition members.

Sherpa Mingma called back: 'I have your bottles, memsahib'. During the fighting he had quietly resolved the problem by willingly carrying the bottles himself to the extra height. Wanda rapidly caught up, and maintained the same tempo. In the powder snow, everybody shared the leading (it is much more exhausting to make the initial tracks in fresh snow, so the lead is alternated for each individual to conserve strength as much as possible). Interestingly, Wanda was now considered an equal!

The section from South Summit to the Hillary Step was a hard crusted knife-edge of snow. With no rope, Wanda balanced along the top of its crest with thousands of metres of rock, snow and ice plunging sheerly away on both sides. She hung back to film the others on the Hillary Step; at over 8,000 m (26,250 ft) she was alone again.

Willi Klimek was on the top of the Hillary Step and she called for him to wait. He did wait, and they approached the summit together, slightly left of the ridge because of a huge cornice overhanging the Tibetan side. Fifty metres (165 ft) from the top she found she could not breathe; her oxygen mask had choked with ice. Pulling the mask from her face, she climbed to the top without it. She was 15 minutes behind the others. It was 2 p.m. on the 16th October 1978.

Of this serious situation she said,

> It was not further than 50 metres [165 ft] and I could see the others on the top. When you bring in your reserve forces you can do many things; I think nothing could stop me at this moment.

Wanda became the first Pole and the first European woman to climb Everest.

> The others had already taken summit pictures with burgees of their home countries. I felt pity they had not waited for me. Willi took a picture of myself with a small Polish flag and an emblem of the Polish Alpine Association. I took out a small piece of rock I brought with me from a training ground in Poland where I had taken the first steps as a climber and buried it in the snow.
> Sigi congratulated me, very nice and friendly. I say my oxygen mask had finished working. He cleared out the ice for me, the filter had become choked with ice due to the strong cold wind, and he said that on the top of Everest we must be friends. Looking round the mountains I thought I could see the globocity of the earth. All the people seemed brothers to me and I felt the value of things.

They left the summit at 2.15 p.m. and arrived safely at the South Col at 4.00 p.m. On the descent, Wanda found herself remembering the numerous climbing friends she had lost in the mountains, and made herself concentrate hard.

> On the descent you must be more careful than before the top. Many relax and forget about the dangers and this is a serious error. You are tired and crossing back over the knife-edge. I repeatedly tell myself that I must not make any mistake. I spoke to myself out loud – suffering from a kind of high altitude sickness.

Later on, at the South Col camp, Wanda found everyone in the tents ensconced in sleeping bags. She searched for a spare bag, but there were none. The French team which had reached the summit the previous day was also camped on the South Col. Kurt Diemberger, whose ascent the previous day marked, at 46 years of age, his fourth 8,000 m (26,250 ft) peak, showed the true mountaineering spirit. He remarked that he had rested for one day since the summit and he asked Wanda to take his bag. (Incidentally, the leader of this successful French assault, Pierre Mazeaud, was 49 when he reached the top of Everest on the 15th October – the oldest man until then to have climbed Everest.) Kurt Diemberger is internationally recognised as one of the world's great mountaineers, and his philosophy of life and climbing expressed through his films and lectures has touched the hearts of many.

Back in Base Camp Wanda found nothing had changed, and she was glad to leave the expedition early.

On reaching Kathmandu in Nepal, she received a message from Arlene Blum, leader of an American women's party on Annapurna I. The first assault team had been successful, but the second assault had ended in tragedy. Alison Chadwick-

Onyszkiewicz and Vera Watson had fallen to their deaths while attempting the unclimbed centre summit.

Rock climbing in the Alps

1979 was a great season for rock climbing in the Alps. Wanda and Irena Kesa, now recovered from the frost-bite she suffered on the Matterhorn and climbing superbly, managed some extremely technical climbs. These included the Grand Capucin and the American Direct on the West face of the Dru. But Wanda's luck again took a turn for the worse in 1981: while climbing an easy route in preparation for a trip to K2 (the second highest mountain in the world, at 8,611 m or 28,250 ft), her companion fell, pulling her off, and she fell 200 m (650 ft), badly breaking her leg. There followed a series of four operations.

The accident happened on Mount Elbruz in the Caucasus. It is an easy mountain to climb. The party was merely reconnoitring in winter.

> We decided to come back near the rock of Poogartroff with only one more steep section on the route, but it was hard ice which for me was no problem. I ran down facing outwards, but I forgot about my group and one of the skiers was not a good ice climber. He slipped and pulled me and we fell together about 200 m [650 ft]. It was very bad weather and I hit a stone sticking from the ice on my way down.

Under her many layers of winter clothing, neither Wanda nor the others realised that she was losing a lot of blood. The temperature was low and the wind was strong. When the rescue party arrived she was in a very weak state. They gave her alcohol. Because of the lack of blood and the fact that Wanda is not used to drink, she rapidly became very drunk!

K2, described by Wanda as 'much more beautiful and more difficult than Mount Everest'. *(Wanda Rutkiewicz collection)*

When she arrived at the ambulance, she vomited and behaved in a most irrational manner; this was instantly diagnosed as brain damage by the attendant Russians!

K2 for the first and second time

Despite the seriousness of her injury Wanda continued with the planning and organisation of an all-women's K2 expedition. By July 1982 the expedition became a reality but Wanda had a problem: she could only walk with the aid of crutches! However, she felt her organisational experience was necessary on the mountain, so she walked to Base Camp – a distance of 300 km (186 miles) of rough going.

> It was not easy because it is not a motorway.

We both laughed.

> I think I shouldn't have gone with the expedition at that time; it would have been better for me perhaps to stay at home, perhaps better for my leg, but I was very engaged with this expedition and it was for me a challenge. Not for climbing of course, because I had no chance, but to go to Base Camp and to lead the expedition.

The weather was terrible, as witnessed by a film they made on the expedition. Wanda showed this film to an invited audience at the 1984 British Mountaineering Conference in Buxton, and all who saw it were impressed and moved. It showed the fearful conditions, with the wind continually howling and battering the women. It revealed a group of mountaineers coping and working tremendously well together at altitude. It illustrated Himalayan climbing at its limits, without oxygen or sherpas. It showed the death of Halina Krüger-Syrokomska, the compassion of her friends, and the retreat from a savage mountain. More than these facts alone, it added up to a poignant and profound statement about mountaineers who happened to be women, and about mountaineering.

Remembering the death of a close friend (they had made the first women's ascent of Trollryggen East Pillar in 1969), Wanda recalled:

> At 1.30 p.m. Halina reported by radio to Base Camp. She was in normal spirits and gave a colourful and funny report of the climb. 'I have to ask God what kind of weather he intends for tomorrow,' she said when asked her opinion of the forecast. Anna and Halina were lying in their tent after eating and were talking lazily. Suddenly, without warning, in the middle of their conversation Halina became unconscious and died within a few minutes.
>
> Then I made my decision: we would bring Halina's body back to base camp and bury her there at the foot of K2 in a burial place that already has a history. Mario Puchoz was buried there in 1954 and there hangs a plaque commemorating Nick Estcourt who died in an avalanche in 1978.
>
> The weather was varying from August 10th to 13th, on the 14th and 15th of August we had our last sunny, windstill days. On the 16th a wind came up from the west and south west and continued blowing until the end of September. At altitudes over 7,000 m [22,970 ft] the wind was 40 to 50 knots and the temperature was 30° [Celsius] below zero. The weather created a death zone where no human being had a chance. At the end of August and beginning of September we sometimes had sun down in base camp from where we could see almost vertical snow clouds on the enormous pyramid of K2. Afterwards the mountain was mostly covered with clouds.

In the end the weather defeated them.

Women's Expedition to K2 in 1982. From left to right: Maria Stolarek, Danuta Wach, Anna Czerwinska, Krystyna Palmowska (behind), Jolanta Maciuch . . .

Ewa Panejko, Aniela Lukaszewska, Christine De Colombel, Anna Okopinska, Wanda
Rutkiewicz. *(Wanda Rutkiwicz collection)*

Wanda high up on K2 in 1984. *(Wanda Rutkiewicz collection)*

On K2 without oxygen

After our climbs in the English Lake District (in the spring of 1984), Wanda again returned to K2, accompanied only by four other Polish women climbers (no sherpas or oxygen). They reached a height of 7,350 m (24,115 ft) before atrocious weather conditions again beat them. But it was a personal victory for Wanda, in so much as she was again climbing well on her previously broken leg. She wrote from New Delhi on 5th August 1984:

> I became very good condition and acclimatisation, but I couldn't use it. I'm only happy that my leg is O.K. But I'm still without success on K2.

Inspired by her achievements and philosophy, two young Polish women, Anna Czerwinska and Krystyna Palmowska, climbed Broad Peak (8,047 m or 26,400 ft) in 1983. They did so alone, with no other team members to share the responsibility, no sherpas to distribute the workload, and no porters to carry their equipment. They did so without oxygen, in a single Alpine-type push up and down the mountain. It was a significant step in the history of mountaineering. (See Appendix.)

On K2 once more

Since my first meeting with Wanda in 1984, her achievements have been considerable, with successful ascents of three more of the world's highest mountains: Nanga Parbat, K2 (at last) and Xixabangma. These, together with her triumph on Aconcagua and combined with her many retreats, e.g. from Broad Peak, Makalu and Annapurna, make up an incredible story of adventure and determination.

K2 women's team in 1984. From left to right: Dobroslawa Miodowicz-Wolf, Anna Czerwinska, Krystyna Palmowska, Wanda Rutkiewicz. *(Wanda Rutkiewicz collection)*

Yet it is the story of her finally successful climb of K2 that is perhaps the most poignant – a success mixed inexorably with tragedy. In that fateful summer of 1986, 13 mountaineers lost their lives on this immense mountain, second only in height to Everest.

The deaths encompassed some of the finest mountaineers in the world: Julie Tullis and Alan Rouse from Britain, John Smolich from the U.S.A., Liliane and Maurice Barrard from France, Renato Casarotti from Italy, Tadeusz Piotrowski, Dobroslawa Wolf and Wojciech Wroz from Poland, Alfred Imitzer and Hanns Weiser from Austria, and Mohammed Ali from Pakistan.

Wanda was a member of a small French expedition consisting only of herself, Liliane and Maurice Barrard, and Michel Parentier. They reached Base Camp on the 22nd May, and were the first expedition there to tackle the Abruzzi Ridge. They did not have oxygen or high altitude porters, and did not intend to fix ropes; their objective was to make the ascent fundamentally in Alpine style, i.e. quickly and lightweight without the cumbersome logistics of a large expedition. However, the Alpine style also means that climbers are out on a limb, with no back-up or support should things start to go wrong. It is the purest way to tackle a mountain – but arguably also the most dangerous.

All went well and according to plan, with all four successfully reaching the summit. Wanda recorded:

> On June the 23rd – the sixth day of our climbing – the weather was beautiful. We started about seven thirty. After a while my French partners decided to rest on a small platform under the small triangular serac. I had the feeling – the summit is near and I had to go up. I chose a way to the right of the serac; there the climbing was easier than from the left.

From left to right: Danielle Sierro (sitting) and Wanda at camp 111 (approx. 23,000ft/7,000m) on the successful women's 1985 expedition, the first all women's ascent of Nanga Parbat, a notoriously dangerous 8,000m peak. *(Wanda Rutkiewicz collection)*

Wanda, with the mighty K2 (second highest mountain in the world) behind, after her successful first women's ascent in 1986. Both her partners died during the descent and thirteen mountaineers lost their lives on K2 during the fateful summer of 1986. *(Wanda Rutkiewicʒ collection)*

The lonely finish for me was very exciting. I was really happy to be close to the summit, to realising my dreams about the second summit on the world, much more beautiful and more difficult than Mount Everest.

I reached the summit about 10.15 a.m. I had a feeling – I am on the middle of a big mountain arena, every summit of this arena was lower; in the valleys were clouds and above me only sky.[7]

Eventually the others joined Wanda on the summit. All were very happy with their shared triumph, but then began the fateful descent.

About noon we began the descent and a few hours later we reached our bivouac at 8,300 m [27,230 ft]. We spent the night here and it was a big mistake. We should try to descend as low as possible. The next day about noon came the bad weather. Michel reached the tents at 7,700 m [25,260 ft] at the last moment before the snowfall. I arrived after a few minutes of bad weather. Before I arrived at the overhanging seracs above the tents, I turned back looking for Liliane and Maurice. They had climbed the biggest difficulties and were in the couloir. I saw them for the last time alive.

During the storm-weather Michel waited for the Barrards at 7,700 m [25,260 ft], I at 7,000 m [22,965 ft] – one day. But they didn't come. Nobody knows what happened. Three days I was completely alone on the mountain making the descent during very bad weather. I missed my gloves and got frostbitten. But I didn't take from the tent the gloves of the Barrards. I tried to believe – they will come back. On the 27th I reached the Advanced Base Camp of the South Korean Expedition and met also the Polish climbers looking for me. One hour after me came also Michel. I was happy to see the peoples.[8]

Triumph and tragedy: Wanda and Liliane were the first women on the summit of K2, but Liliane and her husband Maurice never returned.

On hearing the news of that fateful summer on K2 – the savage mountain – the full meaning of Wanda's words spoken to me some years previously became profoundly clear. Speaking softly, this great mountaineer simply said,

> I have some achievements in my life, but nothing is coming easily – it means I have many adventures, many downs and ups – no easy way.[9]

Chronological list of events

1943   Wanda Born.
1961   First climbs, in the Gory Sokole.
1962   High Tatras, Poland.
1964   Austrian Alps.
1967   East face of Grépon; traverse of Mont Blanc.
      17 m (56 ft) fall on Polish rocks.
1968   Trollryggen, East Pillar.
      Broke leg in Norway.
1969   Alps.
1970   Peak Lenin (High Pamirs).
      Married.
1971   Triglav (Julian Alps).
1972   Noshaq (Hindu Kush).
1973   North Pillar of Eiger, second ascent.
      Divorced.
1974   Failure in High Pamirs due to illness.
1975   Gasherbrum II and first ascent of Gasherbrum III.
1976   Failure on Nanga Parbat.
1977   Contracted meningitis.
1978   First all-women's winter ascent of North face of Matterhorn.
      First European woman and first Pole to climb Everest.
      Death of Alison Chadwick.
1979   East face of Grand Capucin, West face of Dru.
1980   Rally car licence.
1981   Accident on Elbruz (U.S.S.R.).
1982   Married Helmut Scharfetter.
      Failure on K2 (on crutches).
1984   Lake District (Britain).
      Failure on K2 due to poor weather.
      Reached altitude of 7,150 m (26,460 ft) in one day on Broad Peak, Karakorum.
      Divorced.
1985   South face of Aconcagua in Alpine style.
      First all-female ascent of Nanga Parbat, without oxygen or high altitude porters.
      Attempt on Broad Peak, reached 7,800 m (25,590 ft); met Liliane and Maurice Barrard.
1986   Success on K2.
      Reached 8,000 m (26,250 ft) on Makalu.
      Unsuccessful winter attempt on Annapurna North Face.

Julie Tullis (the British mountaineer who died descending K2) after making a successful ascent in the summer of 1986. *(Bill Birkett)*

1987   Xixabangma; Wanda's fourth summit over 8,000 m (26,250 ft).

1988   Unsuccessful attempt on Cerro Torre, Patagonia, due to bad weather.

References

[1]Interview Wanda Rutkiewicz/Birkett (April, 1984)/[2]Wanda Rutkiewicz, *Women's Mountaineering in Himalayas and Karakorum* (a paper delivered at the 25th jubilee of the Indian Mountaineering Federation)/[3]ibid./[4]Interview Wanda Rutkiewicz/Birkett (April, 1984)/[5]Wanda Rutkiewicz, *Women's Mountaineering in Himalayas and Karakorum*/[6]Interview Wanda Rutkiewicz/Birkett (April, 1984)/[7]Wanda Rutkiewicz, 'First Women's Ascent of K2' (private letter written in an aeroplane from Moscow to Buenos Aires on 13.11. 87) (Birkett collection)/[8]ibid./[9]Interview Wanda Rutkiewicz/Birkett (April, 1984)

11

Catherine Destivelle – a matter of style

Free rock climbing

Traditionally, climbing in Europe meant the Alps, the obvious challenge being to conquer a virgin snow-clad peak, or to be the first to traverse a challenging Alpine ridge or pass. Then in the early 1880s an extraordinary character called W. P. Haskett Smith started to record rock climbs in the English Lake District. He stated that his object was not to reach a specific peak or summit, but only to climb for its own sake – for the pure simple joy of its execution, nothing more. He decried the use of 'ropes or other artificial means'; the sport of free rock climbing was born, and Haskett Smith is now regarded as its founder.

Certainly the two aspects of the sport, Alpine climbing/mountaineering and *free* rock climbing, grew together and overlapped, but they remain today as distinctly separate activities. In the case of free rock-climbing – climbing without the use of artificial aids to make upward progress – Britain undoubtedly led the development of the standards of difficulty, and was the single most influential nation in the sport of free rock climbing until the 1960s. The reason for this was that with only relatively small faces of rock to climb on, from the gritstone edges (10 m or 33 ft high) to Scotland's granite (400 m or 1,310 ft high), the participants had no good reason to use artificial aids. They recognised that to climb harder routes it was necessary to develop ability and technique, rather than resort to artificial means. This spirit of free rock climbing, the competitive approach by many leading climbers, the strong ethical sense of tradition and easy access to the hills, all helped to maintain the healthy development of the sport.

In the 'sixties the vertical world of Yosemite in the U.S.A. began to set the pace. By the early and mid 1970s it had become the Mecca for free rock climbing. Its influence touched the world. Rock climbing ('sport climbing' or 'free climbing') took off in many countries. From Japan to Poland, free rock climbing is now capturing the attention of many who would have previously directed themselves towards mountaineering or Alpinism.

In France, unheeded by previous generations and away from the great Alpine peaks, rock climbers found tremendous and spectacular faces of limestone. Superbly technical climbing areas were seemingly blessed with unrelenting sunshine. Possibly the most difficult and, more importantly, some of the most beautiful, rock climbs in the world are now to be found in France.

In southern France, not too far from the crowded beaches of the Riviera, lies Le Grand Canyon du Verdon: the magnificent centre-piece of French rock climbing. Some 600 (2,000 ft) deep and 20 km (12·5 miles) long, it is set in rugged, unspoilt countryside; an awe-inspiring cleft cut deep into the surrounding fields of lavender. Both charming and impressive, it is arguably Europe's finest free climbing locality.

Looking into the spectacular vertical world of the 2000ft/600m deep Verdon Gorge in southern France, where Catherine Destivelle began a climbing career that has taken her to international stardom. *(Bill Birkett)*

Here on these precipitous white limestone walls, Catherine Destivelle has shown herself to be one of the most able women rock climbers. Indeed, she is one of the most naturally talented rock climbers of either sex in France.

Internationally, Catherine's talents were first recognised when participating in the British Mountaineering Council's French Ladies' meet in Britain in 1980, when she climbed a number of exceedingly difficult routes. She was only 19 years old, and the routes climbed were harder than anything ever led by a woman in Britain before. Perhaps of more significance was the way she apparently effortlessly floated up these desperate climbs. In Wales, Vulcan and Void with 1 pt aid (both E3 6a), Tyrannosaurus Rex (E3 6a) and Citadel (E4 with 1 pt of aid) were climbed with a grace and rapidity that caused a sensation. I think it fair to say that no one in the British climbing scene imagined that a woman of any age, and particularly one so young, could possibly lead routes of this standard. Its influence on British climbing was profound.

Having now met Catherine, climbed with her and learned something of her life, I realise and accept that these climbs, which appeared to me to be so extraordinarily difficult, would have seemed very ordinary for her! In fact, they were rather 'an easy day for a lady'!

Beginnings on the Bleau

Born in Oran, French Algeria, on 24th July 1960, Catherine is one of a talented family of four sisters and a brother. I gained the impression that her father thought that if she had to pursue a sporting activity seriously, he would have preferred her to have been a champion downhill skier. (She skis brilliantly, of course.)

However, in so much as he introduced her to the sport, her father is responsible for launching her into a climbing career. On family picnics in the forest of Fontainebleau, the very young Catherine scrambled on the sandstone boulders. She fell in love with the 'Bleau', with the movement on rock, with nature and with climbing.

Parisians often relax at Fontainebleau at the weekend, and it is a magical place to be. The mixture of old conifer and young deciduous trees, the dappling effects of sun and shade, the forest flowers, warm sand between the toes, the sharp smell of pine resin and freedom from commercial exploitation all contribute to this very French environment. Add to this the many hard, grey-red, sandstone boulders sculpted into fantastic, smooth, curved forms by the millennia of wind blown sand, and you begin to realise why the Bleau is recognised amongst climbers to be the best bouldering area in the world. Pierre Alain is reputed to have said to Raymond Leininger, after their ascent of the North Face of the Dru, 'It's been a long time since we've done any serious climbing, I suggest we get back to Bleau.'[1]

Bouldering is the sport of climbing on rocks that rarely exceed eight m (26 ft) in height. Extremely difficult climbs can be made in comparative safety, and bouldering is usually recognised as an important aspect of the rock climber's training programme. It develops fitness, stamina, strength and technique but, unlike other forms of training (lifting weights, for example), it is a delight to perform. In fact, some rock climbers, known as boulderers, treat it as an end in itself and do no other form of climbing.

If you fall from the Bleau boulders, you generally land in the soft sand below, with only your pride dented, and for this and all the above reasons, climbing here can be very much a family occasion.

Catherine Destivelle in action on Elephant Rocks, Fontainebleau. *(Bill Birkett)*

Further afield

An 'official' start to Catherine's climbing began when she was 14, with a group of boys and girls of her own age. On Saffres, a crag of excellent grey limestone near Dijon, she found there were not enough teachers to go round, so she soloed a very hard route. No longer on the friendly Bleau boulders with soft sand below, it was an extremely dangerous thing to do: 'I was unconscious – I didn't know what I was doing.'

By the time she was 15 years of age, climbing in a hard group, she had climbed on the great cliffs of Verdon (France), the Dolomites (Italy) and Freyr (Belgium). She either led these climbs or alternated leads with her (inevitably male) companion. I say inevitably, because for Catherine there were few, if any, female climbers at that time who were capable of climbing the hardest routes she was leading.

In actual fact there were not many male climbers capable of doing these routes either. She was deceptive, a young 'slip of nothing' speeding up the hardest, most difficult climbs, and making them look simple.

Many caught in this trap, having just observed Catherine, would attempt the route, thinking it easy. How could a mere youngster, a girl, do that route if it is really one of the hardest? Male egos were not all that fell, as enticed leaders stretched themselves to their limit and beyond. Out of control, unable to retreat, many screamed through the air grasping the reality that this girl was indeed a gifted climber.

She said:

> Yes, when I was 15/16 many climbers would try to do the same routes – it was very funny.[2]

Verdon

When only 15 she climbed many of Verdon's hard, now classic, rock climbs, Pilier des écureuils (ED–E2 5c), Triomphe d'eros (ED+–E3 6a), ULA (ED–E2 5b). It was the 'beginning of the Verdon', when the free climbing possibilities were just being realised in France. It was an exciting and stimulating period in the development of European rock climbing.

I first visited Verdon in 1980, and it was an experience I will never forget. After two weeks climbing in the Alps in very bad conditions, we had barely escaped with our lives. In the end my partner, Steve Hubbard, put his foot down and said it had to be the new limestone area of Verdon for our remaining week's holiday.

The weather, he said, was good and the climbing worthwhile. My previous experiences on French limestone at this time were not good; I had spent a few days being baked in the hot sun at Les Calanques on the Mediterranean, near Marseilles, and had been less than impressed. So, it was with great reluctance that I conceded our defeat in the high Alps, and drove to Verdon.

The weather was excellent; the climbing was not just worthwhile but superb and challenging, and the setting was idyllic. The contrast between the storm-lashed Alps and this great limestone gorge could not have been larger. I thought it to be the most perfect rock climbing ground on earth.

Aged 16, Catherine progressed on to even harder climbs in Verdon (she also climbed in the Italian Dolomites). She made what was probably the fifth ascent of La voie des enragés on the Falaise du Duc, a route which climbs one of the most impressive pieces of rock in the whole gorge. It is a stained, black and sombre cliff, and it towers almost 330 m (1,000 ft) above the car park area at the Point Sublime. Its vertical or overhanging mass is scalloped with huge caves, and it presents an almost human and decidedly evil face. It is an awe-inspiring sight. Its first ascent in 1968 took 20 hours, and employed 150 points of aid. Catherine climbed it in seven hours and employed only a minimum amount of aid, mainly on the final overhanging wall, which is climbed on bolts. (Expansion bolts are fixed into the rock by first drilling a hole, and then hammering in an expanding metal device.)

I asked Catherine if she was frightened, at 16, to start out on such a route:

> It was very black, very impressive, but the climbing was O.K. There are a lot of ledges and you traverse to find the easiest way; it's not difficult. At the top many 'hangers' were missing from the insitu bolts and I had to use the nylon line over the bolt heads. I was glad when I had done this for there have been many accidents on the route. But frightened – no.[3]

Many more rock climbs followed, and when she was 18 she enjoyed her first trip to the French Alps, completing a number of notable 'TD' (Très difficile) climbs. Later, she climbed the American Direct on the West face of the Dru 'ED' (Extrêment difficile) in a remarkable seven hours.

A full-time commitment

Initially, Catherine climbed to fixed pitons, climbing very rapidly in between and then using them for aid if necessary. This was how it was done in France. After visiting Britain in 1980 she realised that the ultimate ethic was to use no pitons or aid whatsoever, and this is the course she now follows.

In the early days she did not train for climbing. She ate what she wanted to and considered her climbing at the Bleau to be sufficient to keep her on form. Working as a physiotherapist for a women's hockey team, she felt that an individual should give something to society. Valuing her independence, she regarded full-time jobless climbing, living off the state, as a rather empty existence.

However, a venture into Alpinism whilst crossing an innocent-looking snow-covered glacier resulted in a fall into a hidden crevasse. The injuries she sustained meant that climbing recovery could only be achieved by extraordinary effort. Despite the pain, Catherine was determined to regain her climbing prowess, and embarked on a strict rehabilitation programme. Lifting weights, running and doing scientific training not only enabled Catherine to return to a high standard of climbing, but took her beyond her previous level of performance.

In 1986 Catherine became a full-time professional climber, and her record of success has been dramatic. Winning many international climbing competitions, and making a number of films, she has been transformed into an international media star. There is scarcely a magazine or climbing equipment shop in the world that does not have a photograph of Catherine Destivelle in action, advertising some piece of equipment that she uses. From a personal point of view she climbs better than ever and, in France, she has managed to break into the amazingly difficult world of grade 8 rock climbing – one of the few to do so.

Despite her natural ability and the obvious pure joy she derives from her climbing, she is still one of the most determined climbers I have met. If she decides to climb a pitch, she totally commits herself to it; there are no half measures, no self doubts.

When I see somebody doing a difficult route or new boulder problem I want to do it. I see him and I think may be I will do it. In Fontainebleau, for example, when I see the very hard boulder I say may be next year – but one day I will do it.[4]

Some women climbers I have met doubt that they will ever be able to climb at the same level as the top male climbers. But in climbing you don't have to be 'super strong' in an absolute sense; you merely have to be able to lift your own weight, and have a good power-to-weight ratio.

When I climb with the strongest in Fontainebleau they don't say there is a difference. All the time they try and try and they help me and it is just the same as if I were a man.

I asked Catherine if she thought it possible that a woman could be a better rock climber than a man; could this judgement, in fact, be based on personal performance rather than gender?

Maybe – why not! I know all the best now and I climb with them and they climb a lot more than me but after I was the same as them. So why not if I climb all the day – but I could not, I have not the head nor the motivation – but why not?

I put this same question to Don Whillans, one of Britain's greatest rock climbers and mountaineers of the 'fifties, 'sixties and 'seventies. His answer, short and to the point, yet humorous and fully illustrative, was not what I expected. He answered,

Never noticed a female monkey not climbing as well as a male – have you?[5]

Certainly for my part, having watched Catherine in action displaying tremendous power, grace and determination, I have no doubts.

I last met Catherine in Britain, at the 3rd Women's International Meet in June 1984, when she was cruising British E5 (6a) standard, and still enjoying her climbing tremendously. As I talked with her about climbing and about her future, I sensed an appetite for climbing and mountains that could not be satiated. Time alone will tell.

Chronological list of events

1960   Born in Algeria.
1974   Climbed at Saffres, near Dijon.
1975   La Pelle.
1975–76   Verdon: Pilier des écureuils; U.L.A.; Triomphe d'eros; La voie des enragés; La pairi rouge.
        Le Diedre livanus cima su Alto.
1977   Verdon: Pichnibule; Istemporanée.
1978   East face of Aiguille du Moine; South face of Aiguille Mummery.
        Demaison route of Les Grands Charmoz.
1979   Verdon: Diedre des rappels; Vinilimilé; Luna Bong; Solanut; Epui-color; Monguistine Scatophage; Dingomaniaque.
1980   French Ladies' Meet in Britain.
        Void and Vulcan; Tyrannosaurus Rex; Citadel.
1981   Est des Bans; East Pillar of Pic de Bule; L'olan couzy Demaison; North west face of Ailcforoide occidentale.
        American Direct of Petit Dru.

1982 Verdon: Frime et Chatiment; Surveiller et Punir; Manacre à la tronyon-
       neuse; Rêve de Fer; Nunandal.
1984 Third International Women's Meet, in Britain.
1986 Became full-time professional climber.
1988 *Danseuse de Roc* published in France.

References

[1]Bob French, 'Fontainebleau – A Commentary' (*Mountain*, number 89, January/February 1983), p. 26/[2]Interview Catherine Destivelle/Birkett (May 1984); *see also* Bill Birkett, 'Catherine Destivelle – Rock Star' (*Climber*, December 1986), p. 35/[3]ibid./[4]ibid./ [5]Conversation Don Whillans/Birkett (May, 1985)

12

Jill Lawrence and the British scene

It requires a unique combination of circumstances to inspire a generation, and the extraordinary talent of an individual or elitist group to motivate a trend and to set the pace. In Britain in the 1960s there was a considerable change in social attitude and in freedom of thought. The period was known as the 'Swinging Sixties', and the message was love and peace, communicated through the common language of art and music.

British free rock climbing also underwent a metamorphosis, with an explosion of extremely hard climbs. Personalities such as Joe Brown, Don Whillans, Dougal Haston and Chris Bonington (to name but a few) became household names through the media of television and the glossy magazines. But generally, with only a few notable exceptions, it was a barren period for British women climbers.

Brown and Whillans caused such an impact with their proliferation of hard climbs that to a certain extent, notably in Wales, they became legendary figures. The rapidly expanding mass of climbers, fed by increasingly efficient communications, genuinely feared their climbs. These often lay unrepeated for many years. Tales of falls and failures took on epic proportions.

Brown and Whillans were thought to be superhuman, and their climbs untouchable. They built up a 'hard man' image through their books *The Hard Years*[1] and *Portrait of a Mountaineer*,[2] and so perpetuated the legend. (In truth, they deservedly made one of the biggest impacts on rock climbing in Britain during its one-hundred-year history.)

Because of their great climbs and climbing ability, almost an entire generation believed that you had to be violent, hard-living and hard-drinking to be a climber. In 1974, Dave Cooke wrote:[3]

> If you had wanted to compose an identikit advertisement style prototype of your aspiring hardman in 1963, you would have to include the following. Firstly, the 'h' on 'hard' would have to be dropped, certain insignia would have been adopted, in the Alps it would have been compulsory to be very dirty, and in bars everywhere to drink loud and long.

And he went further:

> British climbers have always had a chauvinistic attitude towards their climbing. By definition the continentals were unable to free hard rock, while Americans only got up cliffs because of the power drills on their backs. The most essential ingredient was a sort of exaggerated workerism.[4]

It was hardly surprising that women did not, and were not encouraged to, develop their climbing skills.

Looking up to the steep cliffs of Dinas Cromlech in Wales. The extreme Right Wall rock climb takes the blank looking wall to the right of the distinct corner (Cenotaph Corner). Jill Lawrence made the significant first women's ascent in 1984. *(Bill Birkett)*

Right Wall

Jill Lawrence is currently recognised as Britain's leading woman rock climber. Over the last decade she has been a prominent figure in the small circle of élite British women climbers. She has climbed extensively in Europe and the U.S.A., and she has led many of Britain's greatest rock climbs. The story of Jill Lawrence, and the awakening of a new generation of women climbers to their true potential, is probably best epitomised by her involvement with one single route: the 'Right Wall' of Dinas Cromlech.

Right Wall is a plumb vertical, totally blank-looking sheet of rock (in point of fact the right-hand wall of Joe Brown's classic climb, Cenotaph Corner), situated precipitously above Llanberis Pass in the Snowdonia National Park in Wales. Graded E5 6a, its ascent by Pete Livesey in 1974 was hailed as one of the greatest breakthroughs in British climbing. It was thought impossible; the only previous attempt on this preposterous piece of rock had been by that famous Scot, Hamish McInnes. He failed, even using expansion bolts which he had drilled into the rock for aid.

Pete Livesey needed no such artificial aids, and in his own inimitable style led the route completely free. As was absolutely obvious, the climb involved many difficult moves a long way from safety. Failure on the route, a fall or an attempted retreat would have had the most serious consequences. A young woman who had been climbing barely a year carefully held Pete Livesey's ropes.

There was no shock when Jill Lawrence felt unable to follow, as second, Livesey's great achievement. Acclaimed as a breakthrough in standard, the widespread publicity did not mention the woman who had safeguarded the great man.

So who would have thought, at that time, that this inexperienced climber would return ten years later? I think no one, not even Jill herself. However, return she did, and in 1984 she led the climb. It was the first woman's ascent, the first woman's lead, and the first woman's free lead of an E5 climb in Britain. It was certainly the most significant step in British women's rock climbing, and also a great personal victory for Jill.

Early climbs in Britain

Born in Chester in January 1950, Jill came from a traditional working class family. At her girls' grammar school, she found it difficult to adjust, and clashed head on with the system. She has said:

> It became a challenge to see how far I could go.[5]

She considered herself a failure academically, but quite good at sports, which she entered into enthusiastically. In swimming she held the Chester and District Junior and Senior women's title for breast-stroke. Hockey was also an important sport for her, and she played for her school despite her problems elsewhere.

In 1966 her exam results were not devastating after all, so she attempted to make good by attending the local technical college. It did not last, and between 1967 and 1972 she took on numerous short-term jobs. In addition, she

> Had done some hill walking in Wales and had seen people climbing – fancied having a go but couldn't find anyone to do it with.[6]

In 1973 Jill became a student at Bingley College, where she became the first female president of the students' union in 1974, and from whence she gained a B.Sc. (Hons) and a Certificate of Education (with distinction) in 1977. But, perhaps more importantly, it was here that she started to rock climb.

Her first climb, on a local gritstone crag known as Almscliff, provided both excitement and, immediately, the feeling that this was to be the 'thing' in her life. The climb was a 'severe' called 'Bird's Nest Crack', and she described[7] the incident thus:

> John Stange took me there on his motorbike; the thing was held together with bits of string so the ride there was infinitely more scary than the climbing. I remember the feeling of elation on reaching the top, excitement caused by bubbling adrenalin made me bounce around with a giant grin on my face – basically I was hooked from the first climb.

Jill met Pete Livesey soon afterwards in early 1974 whilst climbing at Ilkley Quarry. He supplied her with a top rope on a couple of V.S.'s, and soon she was to discover that he worked at Bingley College. They began occasionally to climb or boulder together, and soon a steady climbing relationship developed. Jill described this situation as follows:

> Eventually we spent more time climbing together and I improved a great deal – quickly, but I also fell into the role of second. I still did some leading but a gap developed between what I could lead and what I could second. I liked the physical sensation of having muscles tensed and of the focused concentration that was required. I enjoy problem solving, then having figured out a sequence, the concentration required to test one's skills trying to blank out the 'risk factor'.
>
> I did lots of routes with Pete in 1974, many first ascents, also first trip to Yosemite where I was overawed by the size of the place. I was able to second Pete on lots of routes but there were times when I needed to rest on the rope or have some tension,

so my confidence on very hard routes wasn't high. I hadn't been climbing a year when Pete did Right Wall and I was still pretty much in awe of Peter's talent and Right Wall looked blank to me. Basically, it never entered my head to even consider following it and Peter wasn't expecting me to. I guess that affected my expectations. He'd inspected the route by abseil and cleaned it, so had a fair idea of its difficulty. He also knew it was going to be run out with poor protection. No 2½ friends then. [A 'friend' is a modern camming device used to protect climbs.] I always thought if I could ever lead anything as scary and difficult as Right Wall my climbing ambitions would be fulfilled.[8]

Despite the experience of climbing a great number of hard routes in Britain and the U.S.A., she did not feel fulfilled as a climber; something was missing. This became increasingly apparent to her whilst working in outdoor education:

I worked at Bewerley Park Centre for Outdoor Education from 1977 to 1979. My time off didn't coincide with Peter's. Started climbing with other people – formed a regular climbing partnership with Kit Stewart. 1979–81 really developed my leading ability, being the stronger partner and more experienced I did a lot of the leading, but more than that, now started making decisions about crags to go to, climbs to do. My decisions, my elation at success, my responsibility for failure. There was no longer a stronger partner to get me out of trouble, the bottom line was me. Actually this was quite a scary time; I'd thought of myself as independent and prepared to take risks, but now realised part of my boldness stemmed from having a buffer from the consequences, i.e. Peter.

The 1980 French Ladies' Meet

In 1980 several French females came to Britain. There were a number of good climbers, but Catherine Destivelle stood out from the rest for her boldness and ability to push to her physical limitations. Catherine and I climbed together. For me this was the first time I'd met a female who climbed as well as I did. In fact, Catherine was far bolder than I and jumped on routes I was still 'building up to'. Catherine made me think more about where my limits might be; physically our ability was comparable but psychologically she was well ahead. Realising it was mental barriers and confidence, the best solution seemed to be to climb as much as possible.[9]

This meeting with the French acted as an inspiration to Jill. The occasion was the French Ladies' Meet held in Britain during April 1980. Six top French women climbers were invited by the British Mountaineering Council to Britain on a ten-day visit.

The results were remarkable, and particularly impressive to me were the achievements of Catherine Destivelle. She led some extremely hard rock climbs,[10] certainly the hardest leads ever achieved by a woman in Great Britain at that time. In Wales Vulcan and Void, both E3 6a, on the rhyolite cliffs of Tremadog, were climbed in the company of Jill Lawrence. From here she went on to the intimidating quartzite sea cliffs of Gogarth on Anglesey, succeeding on routes such as 'Tyrannosaurus Rex', E3 6a (so named because it was the fiercest of the dinosaurs), and Citadel, E4.

The first woman to lead Right Wall

Jill's climbing took on a new urgency and vitality as she realised what she could achieve.

From 1979 to 1982 Jill worked at a school in Barnsley. Her job allowed time to train and boulder, and she had several trips to southern French limestone, Verdon and Buoux, etc., and also to the Alps – in all-female groups.

Jill said the following about the 1982 Women's International Climbing Meet in Britain:[11]

Two Americans, Rosie Andrews and Catherine Frier, really gave complacent British females a push into action. Rosie was an excellent face climber, poised and thoughtful, solving problems in a vertical world. Catherine was dynamic and powerful on cracks; more importantly, both pushed their limits. The attitudes and abilities of these two females influenced me – not to mention now being 33 – and wondering when physical deterioration would set in.

Jill Lawrence had made the decision: from now on she decided to commit herself fully to rock climbing:

Decided to go for broke, pack in my nice secure boring job, sell my car and go to the U.S., becoming a climbing bum. Spent one year in the U.S. 1982/83 Joshua Tree, Boulder, Yosemite, New Hampshire, Shawangunks. Climbed with Catherine Frier and Rosie Andrews over here. November 1983, returned to Britain for three weeks, got a sunny day in Wales and did Resurrection (no falls) – motivated to do this by tales of Geraldine Taylor's ascent with a number of falls. Yes, I am competitive – aren't all climbers?

1984 spent the spring in France. Climbed a lot, my confidence increased. Really wanted to be back in Britain for the planned female meet in May/June. I knew Catherine Destivelle would be there and another French female, Christine Lambert. I'd heard of Christine's prowess through Louise Shepherd. Rosie Andrews from the U.S. had climbed with me in France and we were both in good shape. As the meet progressed many good ascents were done. I was ready to tackle a number of routes I'd not previously considered doing: Cream, Pippikin, Zukator at Tremadog, increased my confidence. Of course Right Wall was at the back of my mind (everyone said 'Oh it's no harder than Resurrection' etc., etc.), but that wall still looked blank to me and I was incredibly intimidated by its reputation; tales of long falls made my legs feel watery. I sort of hoped no one else would try it, so wouldn't have to deal with my fear. Eventually it was obvious several of the other females had their eye on this route. Rosie for one and Catherine and Christine (French).

I'm standing at the bottom looking up, matching the features to the description. It had rained earlier in the week so Right Wall lost its tell-tale chalk line. Rosie and I flip a coin, I win the toss. My lead first (we planned to clean on abseil so each could lead the route). It felt as though I was trembling from head to foot, adrenalin was cruising round my body getting dangerously near to fear level. The wall contained 3 cruxes (so the guide said) and No 1 was right above my nose. Stopping, I would hold on tight and stare at the last moves of the sequence, freezing there; my mind refused to let my body function, climb down, try again, freeze!!! Mind over matter?? Flash, did it!! How, it's a blankness, totally concentration?? Maybe, but I was above the first crux. The subsequent cruxes presented a similar scenario, 'No, No, No. Can't do it, I'm scared, what am I doing here; breathe deeply, count to ten, calm'. Flash – done it.

The ascent took quite a while. I would regather my physical/mental resources after each crux at the excellent resting places. After what seemed like an age, yet no time at all; in fact I've really no idea how long it took. The feeling from people around was really positive. They wanted me to succeed, female voices sent calls of encouragement, smiles greeted me off other routes. There were females on Left Wall, Resurrection and the Corner.

A climber begins the difficult and committing moves on Right Wall. *(Bill Birkett)*

Success on Right Wall was a brilliant personal achievement and the fulfilment of an ambition. It was also a highly significant step in the history of British women's rock climbing.

Contemporary British climbers

There is now a strong new movement in women's climbing in Britain, and there are some extremely able and talented female climbers etching their personalities on the scene. They are not only gifted with natural ability, but have both psychologically and physiologically come to meet the challenge presented by high standard rock climbing. Although it is presently true to say in international performance terms that British female rock climbing is in an embryonic state, the signs are very healthy and the possibilities are exciting.

It is now apparent that, at last, British women are accepting the challenge with a frankness, openness and commitment not seen for a number of years. No longer do many women climbers demurely accept an inferior role in climbing. They are beginning to assess accurately their ability and seriously question the subservient role which is sometimes played to the male leader. This is a healthy situation, and does not mean that everyone should participate at the highest level, but that women have gained the confidence and resolution 'to do their own thing'.

Geraldine Taylor

I will quote again the words of Emily Kelly, founder of the exclusively female Pinnacle Club:[12]

As in other walks of life, women wanted to find their own feet: it was very splendid for some women to be always able to borrow crutches in the shape of a man's help, and a man's rope, but it is even better to find we have feet of our own and we can climb some things as well as a man climber. There need be no question now of who shall lead. When two climbers marry, they can take it in turns to lead.

There is nothing like personal experience to impress the facts upon one, and it was on the steep little sea cliffs of Pembroke that I witnessed for myself the outstanding ability of a top woman climber. The rock here is sea washed limestone and on the day in question, at Easter 1983, the waves were driving wildly against the rock shelf below the cliff.

April is early in the British rock climbing season, when the sun has just again begun to warm the rocks, but I tackled an extreme climb. One of the features of sea cliff climbing is that where the foot of the climb has been washed by the sea, it is usually eroded, and consequently undercuts the cliff above. This was the case here, and struggling over the overhang to gain the vertical rocks above I felt weak, stiff and inept. Eventually I succeeded and returned along the top of the cliff and down an easy scramble to the foot of the climb.

I was in time to witness Geraldine Taylor start up the climb. I turned to my companion, and with a wink said: 'If she climbs that, I'll eat my hat'. She climbed effortlessly over the vicious overhang, and pausing only to shout down to her male second that it really was perfectly straightforward, she proceeded to romp up the vertical wall above. It was good to watch – even if I did have to eat my rather shabby woolly hat afterwards.

The climb was graded extremely severe (E2-5b) and until that time – and I have been rock climbing for many years (I led my first extreme rock climb aged 16 in 1968) – I had not seen any woman lead a climb of that grade in such a competent manner.

Leading British women climbers are not satisfied with their inborn natural ability, but treat their bodies as would any top athlete. Geraldine, for example, eats only a carefully controlled diet. She actually weighs and records her food intake at each meal to ensure an optimum power-to-weight ratio – which is so important in rock climbing. (In climbing it is only necessary to lift your own weight; you do not have to be strong in the sense of a champion weight-lifter.) She trains very hard for rock climbing, both in the gymnasium and on specially-built climbing walls.

Alison Hargreaves

While talking with women climbers in Britain, one name repeatedly cropped up and was held in high esteem as belonging to a climber capable of great things, without sacrificing a warm smile and friendly disposition on the altar of performance. Alison Hargreaves is young and intelligent and, it seems, represents the new wave of thought and development in British women's climbing in the 1980s.

From an early age she had always enjoyed being in the hills on family outings. Climbing was just one stage on from this. She liked the movement on rocks and the appeal of something different and exciting. During conversation,[13] she described these first climbing experiences to me:

I teamed up with another girl of my own ability. We used to go to youth hostels and take a rope. Two girls in a youth hostel with a rope was highly novel, for all the other women were just walkers. That was nice.

Alison Hargreaves, a British team member of the first successful ascent of Kantega and the first British woman to climb the North Face of the Eiger. *(Bill Birkett)*

The next phase began when my friend lost interest. I was climbing harder than she wanted to, and I started climbing with blokes. Just following them up routes, and for a long time I became a second.

Leading climbs

Since that time Alison has represented Britain on a number of international climbing meets, establishing the fact that she prefers to lead climbs rather than play a secondary role.

I think leading is a much more satisfying experience. It isn't just the technical ability, there's a lot more to think about, i.e. the 'bottle' [nerve required for climbing] and 'putting the gear in' [placing runners for safety].

I put it to her, seeking a considered opinion, that during the last 20 years or so in Britain, women chose to take a secondary role in climbing, being prepared only to lead simple climbs or to follow behind a male leader on harder routes. She explained that there were possibly a number of reasons for this:

Women are different both physically and mentally. I have trouble getting myself in the right frame of mind to want to lead something; it's so easy to 'chicken out' and follow someone up a climb. Partly that, and partly it's been accepted that women couldn't climb, and consequently it was the guys who put the gear on and led the climb. Also, most of the clubs had mainly male members and the women were left at home at weekends. So it's a variety of things, the mental and physical differences and to some extent social attitudes.

For example, when I started climbing with this other lass, we were thirteen and fourteen at the time. The local climbing club used to meet Wednesday nights in the pub. As two young lasses we could hardly go into the pub to find out where they were going on the Sunday, and also older married blokes daredn't be seen with young females because their wives would kick them to death when they got home. So there were all sorts of difficulties just getting to the crag.

The mental approach to climbing

Alison is a very gifted and natural climber, with a string of hard rock climbs to her credit. Additionally, she climbs ice and snow routes in winter. She has climbed hard classic Alpine routes such as the North face of the Matterhorn and in 1986 she made the first British ascent of Kangtega in the Khumbu Nepal region of the Himalayas. She has earned the experience to be able to comment knowledgeably on the problems for women to start and participate in climbing.

I think my main problem is the mental approach. Also, there are some routes I can't do, not because I'm not strong enough, but because I'm not tall enough. I do have a good power-to-weight ratio, but I feel I lack stamina. When I was thirteen I was a lot neckier; all women go through a change and around fifteen my head actually changed. I became a lot less bold.

On a radio interview recently the guy said did I mind ripping my nails, but that sort of thing doesn't bother me. I don't mind scars on my hands. But it's swings and roundabouts – just being out in the fresh air everyday gives me a nicer skin. I think the mind must be very strong and really it's one of the overruling characteristics. But you can't build the same muscles, and women's fingers will never be as strong as men's. So you have to pick your routes and compensate with better footwork, etc. The most important asset is having the right mental attitude. If you think you can do a climb and really want to do it, you'll do it.

Alison outlined the necessary mental approach required to be a climber, and went on to highlight other essential qualities, those of toughness and independence:

I've had my share of accidents and injuries. The classic was when I was fifteen, climbing Black Slab at Stanage and a guy was soloing Whillan's Pendulum which comes round from the left. He fell off and grabbed my rope, pulling me to the ground. I had a compound fracture of my left leg and broke my right heel as well.

Some time after this I was due to go on a school trip to Norway on a Monday and the Sunday before, I needed to go out for a day's cragging because there was to be no climbing on the trip. My friend and I hitched up to Froggat and I was doing 'Sunset Slab' and got right to the top. There were lots of people watching – 'look mum, there's a young girl climbing' – and I suppose I just lost my bottle. I was there twenty minutes and just dared not move to the top. In the end I just slithered all the way down about thirty feet. I badly twisted my ankle.

I shouldn't have hitched up to Froggat anyway – two young girls alone – so I daredn't tell my parents about my ankle and hid it from them. That night I 'snuck' out of my room and bandaged it up. The following morning I managed to hobble onto the bus to Norway. The price I paid was not to reach the top of one of the highest peaks in Norway.

Alison and her contemporaries no longer feel it necessary to fit into artificial and outmoded social patterns at the expense of their own potential and performance. It seems that as society in Britain changes, modern women are free not only to compete on equal terms with men but, perhaps, also to offer an elegance and grace to climbing technique that cannot be achieved by their male counterparts.

When others could see the possibilities so ably demonstrated on the French ladies' visit in 1980, and later at the first international women's rock climbing meet held in 1982, the all-important physiological barrier was questioned. Bonny Masson, herself one of Britain's top women climbers, wrote,[14]

I don't believe that women will ever be as strong as men but most women can become strong enough to climb very hard climbs . . .

As far as the question of mental qualities is concerned, I feel that the relatively small number of women leading harder climbs in Britain still reflects social conditioning rather than the lack of any innate qualities. On the whole the British still find independence and aggression difficult to accept in a woman. Add to that the dangerous and ever irresponsible image many of the general public have of climbing and you can see why few women enter the activity. If there are few beginners, there are even fewer experts. Add to that the wastage of gifted women through commitment to a family and the small number of good women climbers in Britain is explained. The argument that social pressures are responsible for the number of women in climbing is borne out if we consider other countries. In Europe, especially France, there is a more generally accepted tradition of Alpinism and many more women are active in the mountains. The greater emphasis on feminism in the U.S.A. may likewise be responsible for the high activity and levels of achievement of women there.

Grace Penney studied seven women climbers in Britain and in 1983 produced a thesis (unpublished) entitled *A Psycho-Social Profile of Outstanding Female Rock Climbers*. She wrote:[15]

A climber as claimed by the women interviewed, needs a certain amount of physical strength and stamina, enthusiasm, self-motivation, aggression, single-mindedness and confidence. These may be considered unfeminine by many people, but they themselves see no reason why these attributes should in any way contribute to a decrease in femininity.

This, indeed, illustrates that there is now a strong feeling by women climbers that they are capable of achieving much in rock climbing without feeling that they are at odds with their sex.

Jill Lawrence's achievements

In the U.K. today there is a nucleus of top women climbers who are pushing down barriers that were seemingly built over the last two decades. In retrospect, hasn't that always been the case for women, especially in climbing? Indeed, this magnificent pastime requires a very fine balance of courage and commitment; it demands the qualities of both exceptional power and mental control. Yet during its long history, these barriers for women have often been the least to be contended with. When one looks again at these barriers it clearly puts women's achievement into perspective. None is perhaps greater than Jill Lawrence's in ascending 'Right Wall'.

> Post Right Wall: the type of climbing Right Wall presents poses the biggest barrier for me. Technically, the moves are hard but never desperate, but the sequences of hard moves are made going away from protection and one has to continue for a fair distance before security of new protection is gained. I guess this is why E5s are E5 and frankly they scare me. Without the pressure/knowledge that those other females were going to do Right Wall I'm unsure as to whether I'd have tried. Mentally I wasn't ready; maybe one never is for a hard route. Somehow that represented an ultimate goal so where to from here. In the last year, 1983–84, it seems female climbers have made huge jumps, perhaps because they are generally more visible, i.e. media magazine coverage certainly highlights individuals and provides incentive to pursue one's own limits. I'm sure '85 will see several more British females leading Right Wall (look out for Gill Price, particularly).
>
> I didn't climb for the summer in 1984; I was working outside Boston in the U.S. In the late summer and autumn I began to enjoy climbing again, although obviously not as fit after my lay-off. This winter I've again not climbed, partly the situation I'm in, partly motivation. In order to stay climbing 6a+ it requires a hell of a lot of time devoted to training and there are so many other things I want to do. Just had my 35th birthday and feel I must be at my physical peak anyway and wonder if stamina and confidence, which continue to improve, are enough to enable me to stay climbing hard? Or even if I want to!?[16]

No one knows for certain what will happen in the future, but I have a feeling that Jill will stick with climbing. It may be rock climbing of a different nature, such as the very big walls of Yosemite rather than the shorter more technical routes, or she may move into the very different world of big mountains. It does not matter, for she has made that important step from which others can spring. Of climbing with other women she says:

> Climbing with other females is definitely important to me. Initially I wasn't conscious of why and would even get frustrated by it. But having been involved in several female meets and climbed with many different females I'm clearer on the benefits. Firstly, there's the role model competitive side: seeing another female do a route provides an incentive – feelings of 'if she can, so can I'. If it was a male there could be doubts: 'he's stronger', etc. There's the satisfaction of dealing with everything, having to accept responsibility and consequences of one's own actions; generally it's a more equal sharing of responsibility – no one is definitely in charge. Concrete sense of achievement from successes – there is no 'stronger male' partner others can point to, attribute success to. Also at this point most of the guys I know who climb are in their mid-twenties, whilst many of the females I know are 30+, so

I feel I have more to share with them, more in common, so enjoy spending my time with them. Having climbed a lot with females and gained confidence about making decisions, it's easy for me to climb with anyone now, male or female, and continue to just be me. Unfortunately, I think many females lack confidence and in mixed climbing pairs allow the male to take charge of the situation even if both have equal ability.[17]

However, the single outstanding quality that strikes me most about Jill Lawrence has nothing to do with her ascent of Right Wall, or with her gender or obvious ability. It came to me a long time ago, before her incredibly hard ascents. It struck me on a little rock ledge on a Welsh cliff called Tremadog, where we once shared a belay. A rather thin and wiry specimen had just led a rope behind myself on a climb called Fandango (then E2 5c, now partly fallen down and called Technical Master) and we met as I waited on the ledge.

She had not found the lead hard, and nor had I, but she had not found it easy; neither had I. What struck me was her total joy and enthusiasm for the climb. Purely and simply it was her love for climbing. As they once said, albeit with a change of gender, about another well-known climber: she's got rock in her blood![18]

Chronological list of events

1959 Jill born in Chester.
1974 First female president of students' union.
      Met Pete Livesey; first trip to Yosemite.
      First ascent of Right Wall by Pete Livesey.
1980 Met Catherine Destivelle on French Ladies' Meet in Britain.
1982 Women's International Climbing Meet in Britain.
1982–83 Joshua Tree, Boulder, Yosemite, New Hampshire, Shawangunks.
1983 Resurrection (Wales).
1984 France.
      Women's Meet in Britain: Cream, Pippikin, Zukator.
      First female ascent and lead of Right Wall.
1985 All-female ascent of The Nose (Yosemite).
1986 Alison Hargreaves made first British ascent of Kantega in the Himalayas.
1988 Alison Hargreaves made first British women's ascent of the North Face of
      the Eiger.

References

[1]Joe Brown, *The Hard Years* (Gollancz, 1967)/[2]Don Whillans, *Portrait of a Mountaineer* (Heinemann, 1971)/[3]Dave Cook, 'The Mountaineer and Society' (*Mountain*, number 34, April 1974), p. 38/[4]ibid./[5]Personal correspondence Jill Lawrence/Birkett (23 February 1985)/[6]ibid./[7]ibid./[8]ibid./[9]ibid./[10]Jill Lawrence, 'French Climbers' Visit' (*Mountain*, number 74, August 1980), p. 46/[11]Personal correspondence Jill Lawrence/Birkett (23 February 1985)/[12]Emily Kelly, 'The Pinnacle Club' (*Fell and Rock Climbing Club Journal*, number 15, 1921), p. 324/[13]Interview Alison Hargreaves/Birkett (August 1983); *see also* Bill Birkett, 'Alison Hargreaves' (*Climber and Rambler*, April 1984), p. 46/[14]Bonny Masson, 'Ideas – Women and Climbing' (*Mountain*, number 85, June 1982), p. 44/[15]C. Grace Penney, *A Psycho-Social Profile of Outstanding Female Rock Climbers* (Ilkley College, May 1983), p. 69/[16]Personal correspondence Jill Lawrence/Birkett (23 February 1985)/[17]ibid./[18]Tony Greenbank, 'Rock In His Blood' (*Mountain Life*, number 21, August/September 1975), p. 12

13

Louise Shepherd – 'better than most'

Jim Birkett, one of Britain's greatest rock climbers and the first from a working class background to make his mark on what was then a 'gentleman's sport', once said during an interview:[1]

> There will always be real climbers . . . Every sport has its naturals – with application and dedication they become superstars.

He was making the point that whatever one's background, a strong and gifted individual can excel against the odds.

Australia, although a great outdoor nation and a country of competitors rather than spectators, has only recently seen any significant development and participation in free rock climbing.

Despite the fact that, in relative terms, only a handful of women actively rock climb in Australia, Louise Shepherd has played an integral part in this development. With the essential raw ingredient of talent, she has added dedication to become an internationally-known rock climber, and fits Jim Birkett's definition well of a real climber.

The Australian scene

The evolving story of women's involvement with Australian climbing, although short, is impressive. A potted history of Australian climbing with an emphasis on women's participation can be summarised as follows.

Mid 1930s: rock climbing began in Australia, centred around the Blue Mountains, near Sydney, with occasional minor forays to the Warrumbungles.

1950s: Bill Peascod, Lakes pioneer, arrived to make a number of important ascents in 'new' areas, e.g. Warrumbungles, Glass House Mountains, The Steamers and Bombo. Later Bryden Allen arrived in Australia from England and pushed standards to grade 18.

1960s: John Ewbank arrived in Australia, instigated the Australian grading system and pushed standards with his legendary ascent of Janicepts at Mount Victoria (Blue Mountains), graded 21 with 2 rests.

Mid 1960s: Ann Richardson emigrated to Australia from England, later to become Ann Pauligk after marrying Roland. She impressed the resident local climbers, for she had already climbed some large Alpine faces – the famous North Face of the Piz Badile, for example.

Late 1960s–'70s: Rick White began developing Frog Buttress in Queensland.

1970s: a new generation of schoolboys (Michael Law, Kim Carrigan, Greg Child, Chris Peisker, Giles Bradbury and others) rapidly raised climbing standards to those comparable with anything in the world. Climbing activity centred in the Blue Mountains and on the Arapiles, the latter being a superb and extensive cliff that now boasts over 1,300 high-quality climbs.

Mid 1970s: Coral Bowman arrived from the U.S.A. and started climbing in the Blue Mountains. Later she and Chris Peisker began climbing intensively at Arapiles. Her forte was bouldering, and she did some boulder problems which were unrepeated for several years. She led a new route at Arapiles (graded 23) and followed others.

1975: 'hot' Henry Barber (an American who visited the world's major rock climbing areas, climbing at the highest levels) visited Australia and accelerated the pace of freeing old aid routes, a process which Chris Peisker, Chris Dewhurst and Greg Child had already begun. Jill Kelman (who was to become one of Australia's foremost Alpinists before her disappearance from Grindelwald in 1981) began rock climbing.

August 1978: Louise Shepherd started climbing and, as Coral and Ann had done earlier, encouraged a growing number of women climbers.

1980s: free rock climbing standards were elevated by Kim Carrigan, Michael Law, Mark Moorehead, Jon Muir, Chris and Lincoln Shepherd (Louise's brothers). Evelyn Lees (another American) climbed extensively with Louise.

Climbing in Australia

How did Louise Shepherd, a woman from Adelaide, South Australia, ever get into the climbing game? She was born on the 24th April 1958, the eldest of three children (her brothers Lincoln and Chris also became significant climbers). Their father practised as a solicitor for several years, before turning his real interest as a marine ecologist into a career and starting work in the Department of Fisheries. The three went with him on many field trips to small islands off the coast of South Australia, climbing in the granite inlets, scuba-diving off the rocks, and camping in remote areas amongst the sand-dunes and ranges.

When she was 12 her parents divorced: Louise and her brothers were in the care of their mother, but still saw their father often, and continued the camping and island trips. In school her sporting activities were confined to the conventional team sports, and she competed in netball, with moderate enthusiasm but little aptitude.[2]

Early in her school life she had wanted to be a writer, but by the time schooling had finished her interest had strayed towards the biological sciences. At the University of Adelaide she embarked on a B.Sc. course, but withdrew early in her second year because of a lack of motivation.

After leaving university she obtained a job as a laboratory assistant in a high school. This coincided with her leaving home to live with her boyfriend, Kym Smith. For the first time in her life she had an income of her own and the freedom that went with it. With Kym she went scuba-diving and hang-gliding, flew a light aircraft and took up rock climbing, in quick succession.

> Hang-gliding was thrilling, but I reluctantly conceded defeat after my fourth crash. Flying a plane was fun, but expensive. I had clocked up 5 hours' solo time, when I abandoned it for the more rewarding joys of rock climbing.[3]

She came to climbing through a friend of Kym's who suggested they try it out. Immediately enthusiastic, she suspected intuitively that this was a pursuit at which she could excel. Weekend after weekend they top-roped on the local crags, despite the hazards of poor rock quality. After three months they made the five-hour trip for a long weekend to Mt Arapiles. Rob 'Cosmic' Thompson taught them how to lead.

> We started on a grade 3, the easiest climb on the cliff! Two months later, I went on my first 'long' climbing trip of 5 weeks during the school holidays and led my first grade 20. This trip had two significant consequences: my increasing absorption in rock climbing spelt the end of my relationship with Kym.[4]

Rapidly her brothers and father took up climbing. Louise introduced Chris to climbing after six months, and he in turn introduced Lincoln. The two brothers then took their father. Both Lincoln and Chris at different times have climbed full-time, and have made significant contributions to the development of the sport in Arapiles and Moonarie.

> Our father enjoys climbing on a recreational level, but our mother remains unconvinced.[5]

Climbing internationally

Louise has much respect for other women climbers. These include Jean Ruwitch, with whom in Colorado in 1980 she did many routes such as the Grand Traverse on the Diamond, Long's Peak (most probably the first all-female ascent of that route). In that year, also, she climbed in the Shawangunks (New York State) with Rosie Andrews, who, incidentally, led her first 5.11 with Louise. 1981 saw her in Wales with Australian Jill Kelman. Jill, Louise's great friend, was to become one of Australia's foremost Alpinists before her disappearance from Grindelwald (Swiss Alps) in 1981. Louise wrote Jill's obituary:[6]

> I recall the anecdote of two little old Welsh ladies who watched Jill haul stone building blocks outside her cottage and remarked to each other: 'They're doing a fine job on that house, those young people. And she's as good as any man!'

As good as any man? Jill was even better than most women.

However, the inclement British weather and the difficulties of job-finding caused her to return to California. Here she climbed with women from several countries, and was particularly impressed by the abilities of Catherine Freer and Maria Cranor. She continued to climb in the States until August of that year, and then returned to Australia.

Unemployed in Adelaide, she was joined by Evelyn Lees. The pair of them, sometimes with Kim Carrigan, climbed full-time. From Frenchman's Cap in Tasmania, up the east coast of Australia, into Southern Queensland, the two of them roamed, climbing on all the major crags in eastern Australia. They eked out an existence sustained by temporary jobs ranging from government departments to grape-picking.

Evelyn left Australia in mid-1982, leaving Louise to climb at weekends, train mid-week, and take on yoga and French lessons in the midst of her part-time work. By January of 1983 and being unemployed, she decided to leave for Europe, her intention being to meet Kim in London and to study French at the University of Avignon.

During this phase she met many of the best European and British climbers. After climbing full-time at Buoux, Buis-les-Baronies, Ste Victoire, Calanques and the Verdon (the cream of the French limestone cliffs) she drove to Paris to join the *Federation Française de la Montagne* climbing meet on which she had been invited. Catherine Destivelle's remarkable prowess on the Fontainebleau boulders particularly impressed her.

After the international meet, accompanied by Kim, she returned to Buoux, Verdon and to the Salève outside Geneva. In early July she was in West Germany, and climbed in the Pfalz and Frankenjura and 'dossed' in the basement of a German climbing friend. September and early October found her in East Germany, where she climbed with Herbert and Karen Rielter in the Elbsandsteinebirge. She was impressed with the quality and boldness of the climbing.

From East Germany Kim and Louise travelled to Czechoslovakia and climbed at Adrspach and Teplice. Louise related one experience on a classic sandstone tower which she climbed with the small son of her host:

> It was a bitterly cold blustery day, punctuated with frequent rain squalls. The three of us struggled up, utilising classical Czech 'free-climbing' techniques, such as shoulder stands, lassoing, ring bolts and then hand-over-handing up the rope! We rappelled off just as more rain set in: a fitting finale to our eastern bloc travels.'[7]

Escaping from the approaching winter weather, they returned straight to Buoux, Verdon, Toulon and Ste Victoire and the magnificent sunshine of the South of France. Homesick at last, they drove to England via Fontainebleau and Paris, spent a week in Wales at Tremadog, where Louise climbed with Jill Lawrence ('who impressed me as being probably Britain's leading woman climber'[8]), then left for home.

She found the female climbing scene was expanding rapidly, and in between jobs climbed with Natalie Green, Maureen Gallagher, Nyree Dodd, Cathy Blamey, Dale Arnott and Ann Pauligk.

Louise's views on climbing

The attraction of climbing

> The aspect of climbing which appeals to me most is its unique amalgamation of physical, mental and psychological stresses. These stresses are even more pronounced in alpine climbing, as survival and the stoicism to endure physical misery become an integral part. For those reasons alpine climbing repulses me; I prefer fun in the sun!
>
> Climbing also appeals to me because it is a natural activity – I mean this in a physiological rather than 'hip' sense. In hang-gliding and scuba-diving and other 'adventure sports', one is physically and completely dependent on sophisticated equipment. In free climbing, the dependence on ropes and assorted paraphernalia is often only psychological and not physical, as demonstrated by its so-called ultimate form – soloing.
>
> Climbing combines the physical bodily exertions of gymnastics with the mental aspect of problem-solving and body control, and with the psychological impetus to 'get to the top', whether it be the top of a pitch, a cliff or a mountain. Furthermore, the more unknown the route is to the climber, the more highly esteemed is his/her ascent. This adds an extra dimension of excitement which places climbing above the realm of mere gymnastic sequences. Because of its unique nature, rock climbing attracts a gamut of bizarre characters. It is easily the most colourful and stimulating scene in which I have ever participated. However, rock climbing is entering a shady area between a leisure activity and 'Olympic amateurism'. The brilliance of a naturally gifted but spasmodic climber is becoming paled by those perhaps less talented but more mentally geared towards professionalism. This could herald the evolution of a new scene.[9]

Training

Trying to establish Louise's actual frequency of climbing to give an insight into how she has reached her present level of performance was something that interested me as a committed, but working, climber. How did she manage to live, to work and to climb? The answer is all-revealing: climbing comes first and foremost.

From 1980 onwards she has remained a committed and dedicated climber with only occasional, short-lived ventures into employment, and these have been only when strictly necessary to prevent imminent starvation. Her climbing diary is amazing; she has hopped from one country to another. Travelling around the world, she has sought the best cliffs, the hardest climbs and the sunshine.

To maintain and improve one's climbing performance, it is generally thought that training is essential. However, because rock climbing involves such a complex and rapidly changing muscle combination, some climbers feel that the only worthwhile training for climbing is climbing itself. This is the case with Louise. Basically, she finds running tedious, and as for other exercise, strength training for example, she is normally too busy climbing.

However, she believes diet to be very important for her climbing performance:

> I have been a vegetarian for 5 years but was interested in vegetarianism long before I began rock climbing. I strongly believe in the value of the Pritikin diet (high carbohydrate, low fat, low protein) and I use his regimen as a guide-line to my own diet.[10]

Pioneering

Finding new routes and making first ascents is a very important form of expression for the gifted and committed climber. Louise commented:

> Pioneering new routes has always been a normal part of Australian rock climbing for climbers of all levels. Due to strong early influences, I find doing first ascents one of the most creative and satisfying aspects of climbing. Most of my early first ascents were lines pointed out to me by other climbers (principally Kim Carrigan), but later on, the process of discovering an unclimbed line and brushing and bolting it if necessary, made the ascent even more personally rewarding.[11]

Louise has made a significant impact, putting up (pioneering) new rock climbs, and has tackled 'extreme' rock where no other individual has ever been before. Very few climbers, internationally, reach the stage where they feel competent or qualified to make first ascents. Those that do put their neck on the line. Posterity judges the quality and difficulty of the route and, in rock climbing, the style of the original ascent. Was the route led clean – without aid? Was it led in continuous push, or did the climber have a number of attempts (known as yo-yoing), to make the climb?

In the world of modern free rock climbing, many considerations are taken into account by the hungry competitors before they decide on the style of the ascent. The pioneer, then, is subject to the comments and feelings of a very critical pack, always prepared to feed on the weak. In 'Rock and Role'[12] Louise says:

> they [women] can flash and hence will often climb in better style. I believe that this is not because they have better ethics than men (for even the most ardent male yo-yoer appreciates the difference between a faultless ascent and a multi-day siege) but because they lack the psychological confidence in their ability to succeed on

Louise Shepherd in action on Pilot Error (21), Mt Arapiles, Australia. *(Louise Shepherd collection)*

their next try. A woman is more likely to complete a route with a rest and concede defeat if she falls off, than to lower off and try again. This tendency to give up means that women are inhibited from sieging in situations where it is appropriate or, at least more acceptable; for instance, putting up new routes, or pushing one's grades incrementally.

The result is that few new routes are put up by women, and even fewer by women in situations where a male partner has not provided the initiative. Every aspect of opening a new route requires commitment, confidence, even audacity: believing that the line is climbable at all, venturing into completely unknown territory, or on the other hand, being willing to expend time and effort to clean a line and perhaps place bolts or other fixed protection. It is the psychological hurdles which deter women from making commitments of this nature. Fear of failure, fear of trying one's belayer's patience (particularly if he/she is a better climber) are common intimidations.

'Pioneering' is a term which Louise defines broadly. She sees herself as a pioneer of hard free climbing for women, and is very conscious of the style in which her many new climbs are made. Normally she aspires to lead a route without falling, and avoids those on which a prolonged siege is thought necessary. Her reasons for this are partly due to personal ethics, and partly because she finds psychological aspects of sieging daunting. At any rate she feels the result is good: other climbers can see that women can not only climb hard but in very good style.

Pioneering in this sense – influencing other climbers, particularly women, in positive ways – is her greatest source of satisfaction, and gives her a very rewarding sense of purpose. Another pioneering venture was the establishment, in 1982, of a climbing school for women called Sheer Height. With her colleague, Maureen Gallagher, she introduces groups of female students to the basics of climbing, and many continue to climb after the course has been completed.

The table opposite is an assessment of the routes pioneered by Louise.

Women and climbing

In spite of all the rewards, Louise still feels a sense of ambiguity about her pioneering role. This she feels is largely due to the lack of healthy competition from other women.

> I have very rarely had the psychological spur of aspiring to a superior standard set by a woman, and even more rarely, witnessed it myself. Another drawback is the sheer lack of women in the climbing scene at all (I mean, women leaders, not mere hangers-on). It is frustrating to be constantly forced into the company of just males, many of whom I have nothing in common with but climbing. This situation has practically disappeared on weekends but is still a common irritation within the full-time climbing scene. This was a major incentive to found Sheer Height.[13]

Louise has firm opinions about the quality of the climbing and the abilities of female climbers to be found in Australia.

In terms of women rock climbers, the U.S.A. has easily the greatest number in the world, but when taken as a ratio to the number of male climbers, Australia probably ranks more closely with the U.S.A. than do Britain and the Continent. Louise commented:

> Britain has many fine women climbers, but they are vastly out-numbered by the male climbers. (By 'climber' I mean one who leads. The perpetual seconders-cum-portable-belayers that one sees especially in Europe, I do not count as climbers.)

Name and quality	Grade	Date	Location	Length
Femrock	17	27/1/79	AUST. Arapiles	20 m (65 ft)
Hurts	18	16/6/79	AUST. Arapiles	18 m (60 ft)
Frontispiece	19	17/11/79	AUST. Arapiles	30 m (68 ft)
Crooked Mile	18	13/12/79	AUST. Arapiles	30 m (68 ft)
Providence	20	6/3/80	AUST. Moonarie	90 m (295 ft)
Curtain Call	23	8/10/81	AUST. Arapiles	35 m (115 ft)
A B Ciege	24	2/12/81	AUST. Arapiles	20 m (65 ft)
Evelyn	21	15/11/81	AUST. Arapiles	12 m (39 ft)
Female Frenzy	23	5/82	AUST. Gara Gorge	60 m (197 ft)
Consenting Adults	22	11/9/82	AUST. Arapiles	40 m (131 ft)
School for Scandal	22	14/11/82	AUST. Arapiles	25 m (82 ft)
Hello Hollywood	23	3/83	AUST. Arapiles	50 m (164 ft)
Fall Out	23	3/83	AUST. Arapiles	100 m (328 ft)
Jeanie Vicious	21	3/83	AUST. Arapiles	13 m (43 ft)
Celine and Julie Go Bolting	25	25/3/84	AUST. Arapiles	13 m (43 ft)
In Serious Lather	24	4/84	Moonarie	30 m (68 ft)
Phallic Cymbal	22	4/84	Moonarie	20 m (65 ft)
Choral Bowman	21			20 m (65 ft)
Tales of Paua Fritters	24	8/84	Western Wall	30 m (68 ft)
Prickly Au Pair	22	8/84	Western Wall	30 m (68 ft)
The Lash	23	11/84	Eagles Head, Grampians	30 m (68 ft)
Diazapam	25	1/85	Mt. Stapylton Grampians	25 m (82 ft)
Warts and All	22	2/85	Mt. Arapiles	15 m (49 ft)
Venus Aphrodites	25	3/85	Grampians	30 m (68 ft)
Fritz and Cyclops	24	3/85	Grampians	15 m (49 ft)

Routes pioneered by Louise Shepherd

The ratio of female to male climbers in a country is a fair reflection on the cultural differences. In the USA, women are expected to be independent, confident and emancipated, hence it is commonplace to see women leading, often with other women partners. However, in the last few years dramatic changes have occurred in Europe. In France several women are leading grade 7 climbs although in West Germany, the women, who are relatively emancipated academically, have much to learn from their American sisters about rock climbing. In the eastern bloc countries I visited, it was interesting that it is not only commonplace, but also traditional for women, indeed the entire family, to climb. Women, however, did little leading, because the ethics of the areas and lack of equipment often make leading a very serious proposition, unlike Western Europe where the rock is ubiquitously and abundantly bolted.

Whilst she admits that her observations of the British climbing scene may be somewhat limited, she is firmly of the opinion that it fairs only marginally better than the Continent with respect to women climbers.

> Having experienced the onanistic pub scenes, the glorification of sleaze tips such as Stoney and the tasteless lascivious sensationalism in the national climbing maga-zine 'High', I salute those few top British women climbers for their remarkable persistence.
>
> Compared with women climbers in Britain and the Continent, those in Australia and the USA are more likely to aspire to lead and less likely to be in the stereotypic second-cum-belayer role. Women or girlfriends in Australia and the US are not as often regarded as liabilities; on the contrary, it is not unusual to see women climbing better than their male partners. Climbing partnerships are often more casual and intermingled; a woman is equally as likely to climb with another woman, another male or her boyfriend, if she has one. By far, the largest problem in the Australian climbing scene then, is the lack of women, rather than the status of the existing ones. And, overseas travel being in-built in the Australian character, those same few women climbers are as likely to be outside Australia as in it!

Since Louise first made these comments there has been somewhat of a rock climbing revolution in Europe, and her opinion has changed accordingly. In her article 'Rock and Role'[14] Louise presents a determined and reasoned examination of the subject of the equality of women in climbing:

> Having both borne and witnessed the frustrations of radically unbalanced climbing scenes, I am convinced that authentic equality can only improve the scene and the quality of every climber's experiences.

Climbing with men and women

In no way has Louise restricted her activities to all-female climbing parties. She particularly values the climbing experiences she has shared with Rob Thompson, Eddie Ozols, Neil Smith and Kim Carrigan, who in the early stages of her climbing career,

> taught me to lead and patiently belayed me on routes they had done before.[15]

Later, as she rapidly improved, she found that some of the enjoyment of climbing with men was marred by personal or social 'hang ups':

> Some males have psychological difficulty climbing with a woman whose abilities equal or excel their own (this occurs less in Australia where I am well known). Such men cannot always be blithely dismissed as sexist pigs; they may be victims of the conventional expectations imposed on them by their peers, the climbing scene and society at large. I can empathise with this loss of self-esteem, having suffered myself whilst climbing and travelling for significant lengths of time with a small group of males, all of whom climbed consistently better than me.

During these hard climbing days Louise has climbed with many partners, both male and female, but the name Evelyn Lees appears to have greater significance than the rest:

Climbing with other women *is* different from climbing with men. Often it is more carefree, often there is a greater sense of achievement, but this is not always true; it is difficult to point to any one specific quality to distinguish the differences. It is more often the person with whom I climb that makes the difference, rather than their gender. Notwithstanding my most satisfying climbing experiences were during the eight months I travelled with American Evelyn Lees. We both climbed better than we'd ever done before, and our abilities were happily complementary. I was better technically than Ev, and she, being an alpinist at heart, surpassed me in speed, boldness and efficiency on horrors such as offwidths and loose rock. The satisfaction of our partnership transcended mere climbing. Our friendship, wonderfully free of the sex-related complications of male/female relationships, and the support of each other's company in our male-dominated society (i.e. the climbing scene) were at least as valuable as our climbing experiences: the confidence to swing leads on long routes and a feeling of mutual responsibility for our success on climbs. Yet, our partnership was also relaxed. We felt no compulsion to always climb together, and during our travels we arranged separate climbing trips to areas in which the other was uninterested. There was none of the possessiveness or petty huffiness that frequently surfaces from changes of plan or differences of opinion in male/female partnerships.

The future

I was interested to know if Louise thought she had reached her peak performance as a rock climber:

No. I believe my potential is much higher than present, and that I am capable of extending both my physical and mental limits. The present climbing standards, the phenomenal achievements of modern female athletes and the technical brilliance of today's female boulderers, are tangible physical goals to which I can aspire. Mental limits are partly influenced by physical prowess and experience, both of which can develop over time.

Overall, my enthusiasm for climbing is increasing, albeit with substantial fluctuations! Fluctuations are determined by many factors: my company, partners, performance, physical health, self-esteem, the cliff at which I am climbing, the hang-out, the weather, etc. My overall enthusiasm stems from my beliefs that climbing is worthwhile, and that I can climb harder and better; that it is a matter of personal commitment and perseverance. This kind of attitude embodies the ingredients of professionalism, a state which I regard with ambivalence. Professional dedication has unfortunate whiffs of Barber's Breach Wall and Messner's 'honest harlotry'. I'd rather go grape-picking than be an honest harlot.

An individual with vision must have ambition, the harnessing of one's imagination being a necessary ingredient to carry one along one's chosen route.

Louise wants to climb the hardest routes in good style and to continue leading new climbs; also, as we have seen, she feels deeply about women in climbing. She is a talented and amusing writer, with the necessary personal experience to fuel her talent. This and her colourful Australian character is highlighted by the following story:

I have, however, remembered an experience I had in Chamonix in June 1983, which was amusing in retrospect, but a nightmare at the time. The route in question was The Contamine, on the Aiguille du Midi. It was the first brilliantly sunny day for several days, a Sunday to boot, and the Midi was swarming with French – five hundred would be a conservative estimate. My partner was Steve Webster, a British gritstone specialist. Anything higher than Stanage and without a boulder problem of it, he regarded as contemptible. Steve had already done all of the real climbing in

Louise Shepherd bouldering on Mt Arapiles, Australia. *(Louise Shepherd collection)*

Chamonix (Schnell's boulder), so everything else was just filler-in. The Midi was our first alpine route, so we prepared ourselves thoroughly. The previous evening we'd practised putting on crampons the right way round and in the morning, caught the first téléphérique to the top of the Midi. At the tunnel exit, we put on our EBs, plastic bags and crampons, and clumped, tripped and slid down to the bottom of the Aiguille. We relegated those medievalish steel prickles to the bottom of our day-pack.

I led off. We prematurely congratulated ourselves on our choice of the Contamine, for the classic Rebuffat was already encumbered with several parties of bovver-booted French. By the second pitch, we, too, had two parties sniffing our soles and by the fourth, we were like specks of hundreds and thousands sprinkled on fairy bread. It was at the apex of swarming masses that I fervently wished I hadn't had a second cup of tea for breakfast! Even a male would've had trouble pissing discretely in those circumstances, but for a woman it was nothing short of une grande spectacle pour tout! The two Frenchmen immediately below me didn't comprehend my French, but came to a rapid understanding shortly thereafter, and for some minutes, gazed at the view with fresh fascination. They kept a respectable distance after that, unlike other parties who seemed to barely touch rock for their human leap-frogging.

The climbing was enjoyable until I began to suffer the classic symptoms of altitude sickness at the top of the sixth pitch: nausea, spinning head and more irrational than normal. Steve had to tie me to the belay and put himself on belay, while I slumped inertly on the ledge and clutched my churning intestines. It was surely the ultimate ignominy: being hauled to the summit by a British gritstone specialist!

Louise has no inhibitions regarding freedom of expression, or for that matter freedom of thought or action. She has proved her abilities and convictions beyond any shadow of doubt, and despite her earlier reservations has now found her way to the high mountains to good effect. As a finale to this brief story of women in climbing, her contribution could not be more appropriate.

Chronological list of events

1958   Louise born in Adelaide, Australia.
1978   Began climbing.
1980   Yosemite; met Evelyn Lees.
        U.S.A.: Eldorado Springs, Long's Peak, Devil's Tower, Needles, Black Canyon, Turkey Tail Rock, Shawangunks.
1980–81   Britain: Tremadoc.
1981   U.S.A.: Joshua Tree, California, Yosemite, Tahquity, Suicide Rocks, Lover's Leap, Lake Tahoe, Donner Summit, Tuolumne, Colorado.
1981   Australia: Arapiles, Grampians, Moonarie, Mt Buffalo.
1982   Tasmania.
        Australian East coast: Booroomba, Sydney Sea Cliffs, Blue Mountains Frog Buttress, Gara George.
        Worked in Melbourne.
        Established climbing school for women.
1983   New routes at Arapiles.
        France: Boux, Buis-les-Baronies, Sainte Victorie, Calanques, Verdon.
        International Climbing Meet near Paris: Fontainebleau, Verdon, Saussois.
        Germany: Pfalz, Frankenjura, Elbsandsteinebirge.
        Czechoslovakia: Teplice.
1984   Australia: Natimuk, Moonarie, Adelaide, Frog Buttress, Western Wall
1985   U.S.A., Canada, Britain and Europe.
1986   Mount Cook, New Zealand.
1987   Australian Meru Expedition to the Himalayas.

References

[1]Bill Birkett, *Lakeland's Greatest Pioneers* (Robert Hale, 1983), p. 122/[2]Personal correspondence Louise Shepherd/Birkett (1985)/[3]ibid./[4]ibid./[5]ibid./[6]Louise Shepherd, 'Jill Kelman' (*Wild*, Jan/Feb/Mar 1983), p. 33/[7]Personal correspondence Louise Shepherd/Birkett (1985)/[8]ibid./[9]ibid./[10]ibid./[11]ibid./[12]Louise Shepherd, 'Rock and Role' (unpublished essay, 1984), p. 2/[13]Personal correspondence Louise Shepherd/Birkett (1985)/[14]Louise Shepherd, 'Rock and Role', p. 5/[15]Personal correspondence Louise Shepherd/Birkett (1985)

Conclusion

From the beginning in 1808, when Marie Paradis climbed Mont Blanc almost with a sense of guilt, through the stages of development when women were first suppressed, then ignored, then gradually accepted with reluctance, but only as something less than serious, we have now entered an era where no one can honestly doubt their achievements, abilities and potential.

It has not come easily and it has taken huge individual accomplishments to bring it to fruition.

Miriam O'Brien confounded the establishment of the day by climbing the hardest route in the Alps (and invoked once again the words of Mummery that reduced all Alpine climbs to an 'easy day for a lady').

Nea Morin announced that despite all, she would climb – *en cordée féminine*.

Junko Tabei took on the challenge of the highest mountain in the world and won.

Claude Kogan gave her life, but her indomitable spirit will always be felt above the howling icy winds of Cho Oyu. All the others in this book had very individual but far reaching actions; Louise Shepherd states emphatically that not only will women one day climb equally as hard as men but that they will, one day, climb harder.

This story, the story of women in climbing, is more than a history, more than a tale of individual daring or achievement; it is in a very real sense the ascent of women.

As Louise said about her friend Jill Kellman, 'As good as any man? Jill was even better than most women'.[4] It is patently obvious that the same profound words apply not only to Jill, but also to Louise and to all the other remarkable individuals in this book.

There have, indeed, been some very hard 'easy days for ladies'.[2]

References

[1]Louise Shepherd, 'Jill Kelman' (*Wild* Jan/Feb/Mar 1983), p. 33/[2]A. F. Mummery, *My Climbs in the Alps and Caucasus* (T. Fisher Unwin, 1895), p. 160: 'It has frequently been noticed that all mountains appear doomed to pass through three stages: An inaccessible peak – The most difficult ascent in the alps – An easy day for a lady.'

Appendix

Compiled by Xavier Eguskitza

(All figures correct to the end of 1984.)

General order of altitudes reached by women

No.	Climber	Feet	Nationality	Metres	Mountain	Date
1	Junko Tabei	29,029	Japanese	8,848	Everest	16 5 75
2	Phantog	29,029	Tibetan	8,848	Everest	27 5 75
3	Wanda Rutkiewicz	29,029	Polish	8,848	Everest	16 10 78
4	Hannelore Schmatz*	29,029	West German	8,848	Everest	2 10 79
5	Bachendri Pal	29,029	Indian	8,848	Everest	23 5 84
6	Rita Gombu	28,740	Indian Sherpani	8,760	on Everest, SE Ridge	9 5 84
7	Chamco	28,478	Tibetan	8,680	on Everest, NE Ridge	25 5 75
8	Gunsang	28,478	Tibetan	8,680	on Everest, NE Ridge	25 5 75
9	Zhasang	28,215	Tibetan	8,600	on Everest, NE Ridge	25 5 75
10	Chandraprabha Aitwal	28,018	Indian	8,540	on Everest, SE Ridge	9 5 84
11	Annie Whitehouse	28,002	American	8,535	on Everest, West Ridge	15 10 83
12	Laurence de la Ferrière	27,904	French	8,505	Yalung Kang	20 10 84
13	Yuriko Watanabe	27,887	Japanese	8,500	on Everest, SE Ridge	15 5 75
14	Mariska Mourik	27,550	Dutch	8,400	on Everest, SE Ridge	8 10 84
15	Shari Kearney	27,198	American	8,290	on Everest, West Ridge	14 10 83
16	Ruth Steinmann	27,067	Swiss	8,250	on Lhotse, NW Face	9 5 79
17	Sue Giller	27,001	American	8,230	on Everest, West Ridge	14 10 83
18	Vera Komarkova	26,906	Czech-American	8,201	Cho Oyu	13 5 84
19	Dina Sterbova	26,906	Czechoslovak	8,201	Cho Oyu	13 5 84
20	Cering Balzhon	26,903	Tibetan	8,200	on Everest, NE Ridge	5 5 75
21	Wangmo	26,903	Tibetan	8,200	on Everest, NE Ridge	5 5 75
22	Gaylo	26,903	Tibetan	8,200	on Everest, NE Ridge	5 5 75
23	Lutgaarde Vivijs	26,795	Belgian	8,167	Dhaulagiri	6 5 82
24	Masako Uchida	26,782	Japanese	8,163	Manaslu	4 5 74
25	Mieko Mori	26,782	Japanese	8,163	Manaslu	4 5 74
26	Naoko Nakaseko	26,782	Japanese	8,163	Manaslu	4 5 74
27	Liliane Barrard	26,657	French	8,125	Nanga Parbat	27 6 84
28	Irene Miller	26,545	American	8,091	Annapurna	15 10 78
29	Kim Young-Ja	26,545	South Korean	8,091	Annapurna	7 12 84
30	Marie-José Valençot	26,470	French	8,068	Hidden Peak	27 7 82
31	Krystyna Palmowska	26,401	Polish	8,047	Broad Peak	30 6 83
32	Julie Tullis	26,401	British	8,047	Broad Peak	18 7 84
33	Martine Rolland	26,401	French	8,047	Broad Peak	5 8 84
34	Halina Krüger-Syrokomska*	26,362	Polish	8,035	Gasherbrum II	12 8 75
35	Anna Okopinska	26,362	Polish	8,035	Gasherbrum II	12 8 75

General order of altitudes reached by women continued

36	Christine Janin	26,362	French	8,035	Gasherbrum II	6	8	81
37	Anna Czerwinska	26,346	Polish	8,030	Broad Peak Foresummit	30	6	83
38	Setuko Watanabe	26,312	Japanese	8,020	on Everest, over S. Col	17	5	70
39	Marianne Walter	26,286	West German	8,012	Xixabangma	29	4	83
40	Rekha Sharma	26,247	Indian	8,000	on Everest, near S. Col	16	5	84
41	Marty Hoey*	26,099	American	7,955	on Everest, North Face	15	5	82
42	Alison Chadwick*	26,008	British	7,952	Gasherbrum III	11	8	75
43	Cherie Bremerkamp	26,001	Australian	7,925	on Yalung Kang, N. Face	19	5	81

Women who have died on high Asian mountains

Exp.	Climber	Nationality	Mountain	
FEX	Claude Kogan	French	Cho Oyu	(8,201 m, 26,906 ft)
FEX	Claudine Van der Stratten	Belgian	Cho Oyu	(8,201 m, 26,906 ft)
?	Kei Ohara	Japanese	Bharanzar	(6,575 m, 21,572 ft)
FEX	Sujaya Guha*	Indian	Lalana	(6,136 m, 20,131 ft)
FEX	Kamala Saha*	Indian	Lalana	(6,136 m, 20,131 ft)
MME	Elena de Pablo	Spanish	Ghul-Lasht-Zom South	(6,400 m, 20,997 ft)
FEX	Teiko Suzuki	Japanese	Manaslu	(8,163 m, 26,782 ft)
FEX	Sreela Kundu	Indian	Hardeol	(7,151 m, 23,461 ft)
FEX	Vidya Ramachandran	Indian	Hardeol	(7,151 m, 23,461 ft)
FEX	Jill Tremain	New Zealand	Hardeol	(7,151 m, 23,461 ft)
FEX	Vicki Thompson	New Zealand	Hardeol	(7,151 m, 23,461 ft)
FEX	Eva Eissenschmidt	Swiss	Pik Lenina	(7,134 m, 23,406 ft)
FEX	Elvira Shatayeva*	Soviet	Pik Lenina	(7,134 m, 23,406 ft)
FEX	Nina Vasileva*	Soviet	Pik Lenina	(7,134 m, 23,406 ft)
FEX	Valentina Fateyeva*	Soviet	Pik Lenina	(7,134 m, 23,406 ft)
FEX	Ilsiyar Mukhamedova*	Soviet	Pik Lenina	(7,134 m, 23,406 ft)
FEX	Tatiana Bardashova*	Soviet	Pik Lenina	(7,134 m, 23,406 ft)
FEX	Irina Lubimceva*	Soviet	Pik Lenina	(7,134 m, 23,406 ft)
FEX	Galina Perekhodiuk*	Soviet	Pik Lenina	(7,134 m, 23,406 ft)
FEX	Ludmila Manzharova*	Soviet	Pik Lenina	(7,134 m, 23,406 ft)
?	Ewa Czarniecka-Marczak	Polish	Pik Kommunizma	(7,495 m, 24,590 ft)
MME	Christine Ertlen*	French	Gurja Himal	(7,193 m, 23,599 ft)
MME	Nanda Devi Unsoeld	American	Nanda Devi	(7,816 m, 25,643 ft)
FEX	Vera Watson	American	Annapurna	(8,091 m, 26,545 ft)
FEX	Alison Chadwick	British	Annapurna	(8,091 m, 26,545 ft)
MME	Hannelore Schmatz*	West German	Everest	(8,848 m, 29,029 ft)
FEX	Hiroko Fujii	Japanese	Patal Hiunchuli	(6,441 m, 21,132 ft)
FEX	Noriko Yamazaki	Japanese	Patal Hiunchuli	(6,441 m, 21,132 ft)
FEX	Lyn Griffith	Australian	Dhaulagiri	(8,167 m, 26,795 ft)
MME	Mitsuko Shiramizu	Japanese	Bogda	(5,445 m, 17,864 ft)
MME	Naoko Kanazawa	Japanese	Kun	(7,077 m, 23,218 ft)
FEX	Yoko Kominami	Japanese	Jaonli	(6,632 m, 21,759 ft)
FEX	Yoko Tajima	Japanese	Jaonli	(6,632 m, 21,759 ft)
FEX	Reiko Kato	Japanese	Jaonli	(6,632 m, 21,759 ft)
MME	Marty Hoey	American	Everest	(8,848 m, 29,029 ft)
FEX	Halina Krüger-Syrokomska	Polish	K2	(8,611 m, 28,251 ft)
M/F	Amalesh Sen-Gupta	Indian	Nanda Devi	(7,816 m, 25,643 ft)
M/F	Badal Dutta-Gupta	Indian	Nanda Devi	(7,816 m, 25,643 ft)
MME	Maya Senn	Swiss	Ama Dablam	(6,812 m, 22,349 ft)
MME	Brigitte Aucher*	French	Chogolisa	(7,665 m, 25,148 ft)

Number of women who have climbed above 7,925 m (26,000 ft) (to end of 1984), by nationality:

Tibetans (China)	7	British	2
Japanese	6	Dutch	1
Americans	6	Swiss	1
Polish	5	Czechoslovaks	1
French	5	Belgians	1
Indians	4	South Koreans	1
West Germans	2	Australians	1
		TOTAL	43

Date	Cause	Reference
2 10 59	avalanche	AAJ 1960, p. 156
2 10 59	avalanche	AAJ, 1960, p. 156
24 6 70	?	AJ 1971, p. 186
26 8 70	drowned	AAJ 1971, p. 446
26 8 70	drowned	AAJ 1971, p. 446
16 8 71	sickness	ALP ESP EEM p. 110
5 5 74	fall?	AAJ 1975, p. 201
30 5 74	avalanche	AAJ 1975, p. 205
30 5 74	avalanche	AAJ 1975 p. 205
30 5 74	avalanche	AAJ 1975, p. 205
30 5 74	avalanche	AAJ 1975, p. 205
6 8 74	exposure	AAJ 1975, p. 79
7 8 74	exposure	J. Nyka
7 8 74	exposure	J. Nyka
7 8 74	exposure	J. Nyka
7 8 74	exposure	J. Nyka
7 8 74	exposure	J. Nyka
7 8 74	exposure	J. Nyka
7 8 74	exposure	J. Nyka
7 8 74	exposure	J. Nyka
? 8 74	fall	J. Nyka
7 5 76	fall	AAJ 1977, p. 241
8 9 76	sickness	AAJ 1977, p. 21
17 10 78	fall	AAJ 1979, p. 57
17 10 78	fall	AAJ 1979, p.157
3 10 79	exposure	AAJ 1980, p. 607
9 10 79	avalanche	AAJ 1980, p. 627
9 10 79	avalanche	AAJ 1980, p. 627
7 10 80	avalanche	AAJ 1981, p. 269
10 6 81	fall	ITY 84, p. 106
8 8 81	sickness	ITY 86, p. 106
23 9 81	avalanche	ITY 86, p. 106
23 9 81	avalanche	ITY 86, p. 106
23 9 81	avalanche	ITY 86, p. 106
15 5 82	fall	AAJ 1983, p. 13
30 7 82	sickness	AAJ 1983, p. 273
13 9 82	fall	ITY 95, p. 201
17 9 82	fall	ITY 95, p. 201
27 10 83	fall	AAJ 1984, p. 237
26 7 84	fall	M&A 1984–4, p. 546

Abbreviations

EXP	:	Expedition
FEX	:	Female expedition
MME	:	Mostly male expedition
M/F	:	Mixed expedition
*	:	Died after having reached the summit
AJ	:	*Alpine Journal*
AAJ	:	*American Alpine Journal*
ITY	:	*The Iwa to Yuki*
M&A	:	*La Montagne et Alpinisme*
ALP ESP EEM	:	*Alpinismo Español en el Mundo*, by J. M. Azpiazu

Nationalities of victims

Japanese	9
Soviet	8
Indian	6
French	3
American	3
New Zealand	2
Swiss	2
Polish	2
Belgian	1
Spanish	1
British	1
West German	1
Australian	1
TOTAL	40

Progressive altitude records reached by women

altitude	mountain	climber	nationality	date		
6,952 m (22,808 ft)	Pinnacle Peak	Fanny Bullock Workman	American	29	7	1906
7,315 m (24,000 ft)	Sia Kangri West	Hettie Dyhrenfurth	Swiss	3	8	1934
7,600 m (24,935 ft)	on Cho Oyu	Claude Kogan	French	28	10	1954
8,020 m (26,312 ft)	on Everest	Setsuko Watanabe	Japanese	17	5	1970
8,163 m (26,780 ft)	Manaslu	Masako Uchida	Japanese			
		Mieko Mori	Japanese	4	5	1974
		Naoko Nakaseko	Japanese			
8,500 m (27,890 ft)	on Everest	Phantog	Tibetan			
		Chamco	Tibetan			
		Gunsang	Tibetan			
		Zhasang	Tibetan	5	5	1975
		Cering Balzhon	Tibetan			
		Wangmo	Tibetan			
		Gaylo	Tibetan			
8,500 m (29,029 ft)	Everest	Junko Tabei	Japanese	16	5	1975

Progressive list of the highest summits climbed by women

mountain	altitude	climber	nationality	date		
Pinnacle Peak	6,952 m (22,810 ft)	Fanny Bullock Workman	American	29	7	1906
Sia Kangri West	7,315 m (24,000 ft)	Hettie Dyhrenfurth	Swiss	3	8	1934
Ganesh Himal I	7,429 m (24,375 ft)	Claude Kogan	French	24	10	1955
Muztagh Ata	7,546 m (24,757 ft)	Phantog	Tibetan			
		Sheirab	Tibetan			
		Rabjor (Chamjin)	Tibetan			
		Chimmed	Tibetan	7	7	1959
		Wang Yi-chin	Chinese			
		Tsung Chen	Chinese			
		Chou Yu-ying	Chinese			
		Wang Kuei-hua	Chinese			
Kongur Tiubie	7,595 m (24,918 ft)	Phantog	Tibetan	17	6	1961
		Sheirab	Tibetan			
Manaslu	8,163 m (26,780 ft)	Masako Uchida	Japanese			
		Mieko Mori	Japanese	4	5	1974
		Naoko Nakaseko	Japanese			
Everest	8,848 m (29,029 ft)	Junko Tabei	Japanese	16	5	1975

Highest climbs, by nationality

notes	country	climber	metres	feet	mountain	date		
	Japan	Junko Tabei	8,848	29,029	Everest	16	5	75
	China	Phantog	8,848	29,029	Everest	27	5	75
	Poland	Wanda Rutkiewicz	8,848	29,029	Everest	16	10	78
	West Germany	Hannelore Schmatz*	8,848	29,029	Everest	2	10	79
	India	Bachendri Pal	8,848	29,029	Everest	23	5	84
(1)	U.S.A.	Annie Whitehouse	8,540	28,018	on Everest, West Ridge	15	10	83
	France	Laurence de la Ferrière	8,505	27,904	Yalung Kang	20	10	84
(2)	Netherlands	Mariska Mourik	8,400	27,550	on Everest, SE Ridge	8	10	84
(3)	Switzerland	Ruth Steinmann	8,250	27,067	on Lhotse, NW Face	9	5	79

Highest climbs, by nationality continued

		Name					
	Czechoslovakia	Dina Sterbova	8,201	26,906	Cho Oyu	13	5 84
	Belgium	Lutgaarde Vivijs	8,167	26,795	Dhaulagiri	6	5 82
	South Korea	Kim Young-Ja	8,091	26,545	Annapurna	7	12 84
	United Kingdom	Julie Tullis	8,047	26,401	Broad Peak	18	7 84
(4)	Australia	Cherie Bremerkamp	7,925	26,001	on Yalung Kang, N. Face	19	5 81
	Nepal	Nimi Lhakpa	7,745	25,412	Nuptse NW	?	10 84
(5)	Canada	Dianne Roberts	7,680	25,199	on K2, NE Ridge	2	9 78
	Italy	Marguerita Folari / Maria Teresa Bonetti	7,546	24,757	Muztagh Ata	19	8 84
	U.S.S.R.	Ludmila Agranovskaya	7,495	24,590	Pik Kommunizma	?	7 68
(6)	Austria	Renata Mosbacher / Santa Walter	7,495	24,590	Pik Kommunizma	Late '70s	
	Yugoslavia	Mariya Frantar	7,495	24,590	Pik Kommunizma	?	8 82
(7)	Spain	Mercè Maciá	7,350	24,114	on Lhotse Shar, SE Ridge	20	5 84
	Rumania		7,134	23,406	Pik Lenina	1960s	

Notes:

(1) Highest summit: Cho Oyu (8,201 m or 26,906 ft), by Vera Komarkova, 13 5 1984.

(2) Highest summit: Spantik (7,027 m or 23,054 ft), by Antoinette Brïet and Sabine Deneer, 22 7 84.

(3) Highest summit: Tirich Mir (7,708 m or 25,289 ft), by Hanna Müller, 3 8 1975.

(4) No complete ascent of a 7,000 m (22,966 ft) peak is recorded for Australian women.

(5) No complete ascent of a 7,000 m (22,966 ft) peak is recorded for Canadian women.

(6) The altitude of Pik Kommunizma is also given as 7,483 m (24,551 ft). If so, the Austrian female record would belong to Cilly Hayder who climbed Noshaq (7,492 m or 24,580 ft), 11 7 1971.

(7) Highest summit: Noshaq West (7,250 m or 23,786 ft), by Montserrat Jou, 22 8 1975.
Highest main summit : Shakhaur (7,116 m or 23,346 ft), by Trinidad Cornellana, 28 7 1976.

Abbreviations *see table overleaf*

AAJ	: *American Alpine Journal*		**TIB HIM**	: Tibet Himalaya
HJ	: *Himalayan Journal*		**NEP HIM**	: Nepal Himalaya
MW	: *Mountain World*		**GAR HIM**	: Garhwal Himalaya
LA	: *Les Alpes*		**PUN HIM**	: Punjab Himalaya
DA	: *Die Alpen*		**PAK HIM**	: Pakistan Himalaya
A&R	: *Alpirando*		**KARA BM**	: Karakoram, Baltoro Mustagh
M&A	: *La Montagne et Alpinisme*		**KARA MR**	: Karakoram, Masherbrum Range
RN	: *The Rising Nepal (Daily)*		**KARA RR**	: Karakoram, Rakaposhi Range
TWA	: Total woman ascents		**H. KUSH**	: Hindu Kush
FFA	: First female ascent		**T. SHAN**	: Tien Shan
*	: First absolute ascent		**SOV PAM**	: Soviet Pamir
c.	: circa (about)		**SIN PAM**	: Sinkiang Pamir

First female ascents to mountains above 7,000 metres (23,000 ft)

no.	mountain	metres	feet	area	FFA date	climbers	nationality	reference	TWA
1	Everest	8,848	29,029	NEP HIM	16 5 75	Junko Tabei	Japanese	AAJ 1976, p. 515	5
2	Yalung Kang	8,505	27,904	NEP HIM	20 10 84	Laurence de la Ferrière	French	A&R Dec 84, p. 6	1
3	Cho Oyu	8,201	26,906	NEP HIM	13 5 84	Vera Komarkova / Dina Sterbova	American / Czechoslovak	*Mountain* 99, p. 8	2
4	Dhaulagiri	8,167	26,795	NEP HIM	6 5 82	Lutgaarde Vivijs / Masako Uchida	Belgian / Japanese	AAJ 1983, p. 246	1
5	Manaslu	8,163	26,780	NEP HIM	4 5 74	Mieko Mori / Naoko Nakaseko	Japanese / Japanese	AAJ 1975, p. 201	3
6	Nanga Parbat	8,125	26,657	PAK HIM	27 6 84	Liliane Barrard	French	*Mountain* 99, p. 10	1
7	Annapurna	8,091	26,545	NEP HIM	15 10 78	Vera Komarkova / Irene Miller	American / American	AAJ 1979, p. 58	3
8	Hidden Peak	8,068	26,470	KARA BM	27 7 82	Marie-José Valençot	French	AAJ 1983, p. 268	1
9	Broad Peak	8,047	26,401	KARA BM	30 6 83	Krystyna Palmowska	Polish	AAJ 1984, p. 293	3
10	Gasherbrum II	8,035	26,362	KARA BM	12 8 75	Halina Krüger-Syrokomska / Anna Okopinska	Polish	AAJ 1976, p. 541	4
11	Xixabangma	8,012	26,286	TIB HIM	30 4 81	Junko Tabei	Japanese	AAJ 1982, p. 287	2
12	Gasherbrum III*	7,952	26,008	KARA BM	11 8 75	Alison Chadwick / Wanda Rutkiewicz	British / Polish	AAJ 1976, p. 541	2
13	Nanda Devi	7,816	25,643	GAR HIM	19 9 81	Rekha Sharma / Harsha Bisht / Chandraprabha Airwal	Indian / Indian / Indian	AAJ 1982, p. 242	3
14	Rakaposhi	7,788	25,551	KARA RR	5 7 79	Krystyna Palmowska / Anna Czerwinska	Polish / Polish	AAJ 1980, p. 651	2
15	Kamet	7,756	25,446	GAR HIM	14 6 77	Thrity Birdy / Chandraprabha Airwal / Bharati Banerjee	Indian / Indian / Indian	AAJ 1978, p. 605	3
16	Nuptse NW	7,745	25,412	NEP HIM	? 10 84	Nimi Lhakpa (Norbu)	Sherpani	P. Béghin	1
17	Tirich Mir	7,708	25,289	H. KUSH	3 8 75	Hannelore Schmatz / Hanna Müller	West German / Swiss	AAJ 1976, p. 550	2
18	Kangchungtse	7,678	25,190	NEP HIM	28 9 83	Monique Faure / Christine Janin	French / French	AAJ 1984, p. 231	2
19	Chogolisa	7,665	25,148	KARA MR	26 7 84	Brigitte Aucher*	French	M&A 1984–4, p. 546	1
20	Kongur Tiubie	7,595	24,918	SIN PAM	17 6 61	Phantog / Sheirab	Tibetan / Tibetan	*Mountaineering in China*, p. 60	2
21	Annapurna III	7,555	24,787	NEP HIM	19 5 70	Junko Tabei / Hiroko Hirawaka	Japanese / Japanese	AAJ 1971, p. 435	3

No.	Peak	m	ft	Range	Date	Person	Nationality	Reference	No.
22	Muztagh Ata	7,546	24,757	SIN PAM	7 7 59	Phantog, Sheirab, Rabjor (Chamjin), Chimmed, Wang Yi-chin, Wang Kuei-hua	Tibetan, Tibetan, Tibetan, Tibetan, Chinese, Chinese	*Mountaineering in China*, p. 22	14
23	Pik Kommunizma	7,495	24,590	SOV PAM	? 7 68	Ludmila Agranovskaya	Soviet	J. Nyka	c. 100
24	Noshaq	7,492	24,580	H. KUSH	13 8 69	Alice Liska	American	AAJ 1970, p. 30	12
25	Pik Pobiedy	7,439	24,406	T. SHAN	? 8 70	Ludmila Agranovskaya	Soviet	J. Nyka	c. 25
26	Ganesh Himal I*	7,429	24,375	NEP HIM	24 10 55	Claude Kogan	French	LA 1956, p. 102	1
27	Noshaq Central	7,400	24,278	H. KUSH	1 9 66	Isabelle Agresti	French	HJ 27, p. 185	13
28	Abi Gamin	7,355	24,131	GAR HIM	18 6 76	Thrity Birdy, Chandraprabha Aitwal, Fumie Nasu	Indian, Indian, Japanese	AAJ 1977, p. 257	3
29	Tirich Mir West III	7,350	24,114	H. KUSH	1 8 74	Marie-Françoise Amy	French	AAJ 1975, p. 218	1
30	Sia Kangri West*	7,315	24,000	KARA BM	3 8 34	Hettie Dyhrenfurth	Swiss	DA 1935, p. 81	2
31	Urdok I*	7,300	23,950	KARA BM	4 8 75	Lieselotte Schell	Austrian	AAJ 1976, p. 542	1
32	Istor-O-Nal West	7,300	23,950	H. KUSH	? ? 68	Kyoko Sato, Setsuko Watanabe, Hiroko Izumi, Yoko Ashiya	Japanese, Japanese, Japanese, Japanese	AAJ 1969, p. 465	4
33	Shingeik Zom I*	7,291	23,921	H. KUSH	13 7 66	Irish Trübsswetter	West German	AAJ 1967, p. 413	1
34	Diran (Minapin)	7,273	23,862	KARA RR	30 6 83	Ruth Steinmann	Swiss	AAJ 1984, p. 302	1
35	Noshaq West	7,250	23,786	H. KUSH	1 9 66	Isabelle Agresti	French	HJ 27, p. 185	15
36	Putha Hiunchuli	7,246	23,773	NEP HIM	19 10 78	Angelika Zintl	West German	AAJ 1980, p. 631	2
37	Gurja Himal	7,193	23,599	NEP HIM	22 10 72	Yvette Buttin	French	AAJ 1973, p. 483	2
38	Glacier Dome	7,193	23,599	NEP HIM	22 10 84	Herta Kantner	Austrian	RN 31-10-84	1
39	Pumori	7,161	23,494	NEP HIM	30 4 75	Claudine Lescure	French	AAJ 1976, p. 517	2
40	Nun*	7,135	23,409	PUN HIM	28 8 53	Claude Kogan	French	MW 1954, p. 82	2
41	Pik Lenina	7,134	23,406	SOV PAM	? 8 58	Ekaterina Mamleeva	Soviet	J. Nyka	c. 25
42	Trisul	7,120	23,360	GAR HIM	23 6 68	Nandini Patel	Indian	AAJ 1969, p. 451	c. 200
43	Shakhaur	7,116	23,346	H. KUSH	28 7 76	Trini Cornellana	Spanish	AAJ 1977, p. 278	c. 50
44	Pik Korzhenevskaya	7,105	23,310	SOV PAM	? ? 66	Tamara N. Postnikova	Soviet	J. Nyka	1
45	Kun	7,077	23,218	PUN HIM	20 7 77	Lieselotte Schell	Austrian	AAJ 1978, p. 611	c. 50
46	Ganesh IV (Pabil)	7,052	23,136	NEP HIM	22 10 78	Emiko Okutani	Japanese	AAJ 1979, p. 270	c. 25
47	Spantik	7,027	23,054	KARA RR	22 7 84	Antoinette Briet, Sabine Deneer	Dutch, Dutch	J. Bongenaar	1
48	Koh-I-Tez	7,016	23,018	H. KUSH	28 8 72	Alicja Bednarz	Polish	AAJ 1973, p. 497	3

Index